HOPEFUL PLACES

HOPEFUL PLACES

Migration and belonging in an unpredictable era

Edited by Chris McConville

The chapters in this collection were originally presented at the Place and Displacement Conference sponsored by the Community Identity Displacement Research Network, Victoria University, Melbourne, Australia

Connor Court Publishing

Connor Court Publishing Pty Ltd

Copyright © Chris McConville 2015

PO Box 224W
Ballarat VIC 3350
sales@connorcourt.com
www.connorcourt.com

ISBN: 9781925138573 (pbk.)

Cover design by Ian James

Cover illustration: Polish Immigrants in Rural Australia, December 1950, Bonegilla State Library of Victoria Collection

Reproduced with permission from the State Library of Victoria

Photograph donated to the Library by Mr. Wojciech and Mrs. Wanda Galaska, 2001

Printed in Australia

Contents

Figures

Contributors

Dvir Abramovich

Dr Dvir Abramovich holds the Israel Kipen Lectureship in Hebrew Studies and is Director of the Program for Jewish Culture and Society at The University of Melbourne. His most recent publication is *Hebrew Classics: A Journey Through Israel's Timeless Fiction and Poetry*. He was president of the Australian Association of Jewish Studies and served as editor of the Australian Journal of Jewish Studies for eight years. He is currently working on two books.

Paula Fernandez Arias

Since completing her M.A. in Gender Studies and Development Studies at Melbourne University Paula Fernandez Arias has worked in the NGO sector with refugees and migrants. She is currently an international Ph.D. candidate at Monash University looking at the interplay between official government narrative on migration and the resettlement experiences of African Humanitarian entrants in Melbourne, Australia.

Marsha Berry

Dr Marsha Berry is an artist and digital ethnographer. She teaches creative writing, new media and supervises Ph.D. and Masters students at RMIT University. Her creative practice includes poetry, video and participatory media. She has numerous publications in prestigious journals including *New Media and Society* and her creative works have been exhibited internationally.

Karen Berger

In 2013, Karen Berger was the recipient of Victoria University's College of Arts 'Most Outstanding Postgraduate Student by Research Award' for her M.A. entitled *Performing Belonging: Meetings On and In the Earth*. Besides writing, she works as a performer and director, most recently directing plays about Fyodor Dostoyevsky and Ron Barassi.

Irene Bouzo

Irene Bouzo is the Senior Policy Officer at Ethnic Communities' Council of Victoria and an elder of the Temple Society Australia. Her early career as an ESL teacher and Manager of Policy and Planning at the Victorian Adult Migrant Education Services developed her interest in multilingualism. Her doctoral research at the University of New England examined the displaced Templer community in Melbourne.

Gemma Tulud Cruz

Dr Gemma Tulud Cruz taught in the United States for several years before moving to Australian Catholic University where she currently serves as Senior Lecturer in Theology in its Melbourne campus. Gemma is the author of *An Intercultural Theology of Migration* (Brill, 2010), *Toward a Theology of Migration: Social Justice and Religious Experience* (Palgrave Macmillan, 2014) and several essays on her other research interests which include women and gender issues, liberation theologies, global Christianity, and mission studies.

Mike Dee

Mike was a youth worker in Kings Cross and Earls Court, London. He has taught previously in community education and social policy and human services at Edith Cowan University Western Australia,

De Montfort and The Open University UK and Griffith University, Brisbane. At Queensland University of Technology Brisbane, he completed his PhD on the topic of Young People, Public Space and Citizenship (2008). He is teaching at QUT.

Michael Deery

Michael Deery is a graduate of La Trobe University, where he studied history, philosophy and linguistics. He has arranged musical compositions, made short digital films, and exhibited photographs depicting daily life in Laos and Cambodia. He is a research associate at Victoria University, Melbourne.

Vivian Gerrand

Vivian Gerrand completed her Ph.D. at the Australian Centre, University of Melbourne. With interests in art, literature, migration, multiculturalism and post-colonialism, her dissertation explored representations of Somali belonging in Australia and Italy. She has taught at the University of Melbourne and at the University of Bologna. She has published on imagining Somali identities in the diaspora, representations of Somali settlement in Italy and on Italian influences in Somalia.

Catherine Gomes

Dr Catherine Gomes is an Australian Research Council DECRA Research Fellow based at RMIT University. Her current work looks at the evolving cultural and social identities of transient migrants in Australia and Singapore. Catherine has published widely in the areas of identity, ethnicity and gender in the media.

Brigitte Lewis

Brigitte teaches (and performs) in Anthropology at the University of Melbourne and also through Open Universities Australia. Her main areas of interest are performativity theory and practice, embodiment, feminism, masculinism, rationality, poetry, auto-ethnography and identity creation.

Chris McConville

Chris McConville is Senior Research Fellow, CRIC, Federation University Australia. He has previously worked at the University of the Sunshine Coast and Victoria University, Melbourne, Australia.

Yusuf Sheikh Omar

Yusuf Sheikh Omar, Ph.D. La Trobe University (2011). He specialised in Somali youth in Australia and USA. Currently he works as a researcher at Victorian Transcultural Mental Health, St Vincent's Hospital. Yusuf published widely in national and international academic journals as well as in the leading Australian newspapers. Yusuf was awarded with Ambassador for Peace by The Universal Peace Federation. He was a member of African Ministerial Consultative Committee for the Australia Federal Government.

Robert Pascoe

Robert Pascoe is the Dean Laureate and a Professor of History at Victoria University, Melbourne. Among his three dozen books in social history are *Buongiorno Australia: Our Italian Heritage* (1987), *The Winter Game* (1995), and *World History* (2 vols, 2013). He teaches subjects in World History, The Making of the Modern Middle East, and History and Memory.

Johannes Pieters

Johannes is a lecturer in regional and urban planning at the University of South Australia. His Ph.D. examined the role of housing in adjustment to retrenchment and this, combined with his experience of growing up in the high bushfire risk area of Warrandyte, Victoria in the 1960s, led to his interest in the role of rebuilding in recovery processes following bushfire related housing loss.

Christopher Sommer

Christopher Sommer completed a BA in History in Mannheim (DE) followed by a MA in Museum Studies in Oldenburg (DE). Since 2010 he has been a doctoral candidate at the University of Auckland (NZ). His research interests are the representation of immigration in New Zealand museums and the representation of pre-modern military history.

Introduction

Chris McConville

Place, belonging, hope

"Probably because they are made by fallible humans, most immigration policies are characterized by a Janus complex. One part of them looks to the future and tries to respond to new problems and new needs. Another part looks to the past, reflecting old shibboleths and prejudices. Australia's policy is no exception". "The Janus Complex in Australia's immigration policy", *International Migration Digest*, 1964, 1(1) Spring: 67-8.

Migration, as both displacement and discovery, colours the story of contemporary Australia, as it does of all the continents. And emigrants, just as much as migration regulators, share this Janus Complex, as they respond to new desires in strange places, whilst "reflecting old shibboleths and prejudices". Emigrants have lived out this dilemma in the United States and Argentina in the 19th and early 20th centuries, Australia and Canada in the later 20th century, and, in the post-2000 world, across the European Union and in the burgeoning cities of the Asian-Pacific Rim. Even if they have not crossed a national boundary, the rural displaced flock to the megalopolis: to Istanbul, Mexico City, Lagos or Shanghai. Mobility shapes the human condition and with this mobility comes both hope and loss.

Cosmopolitan urbanism, the product of this mobility, can bring a sense of belonging to the immigrant. It can also impose both conflict and confusion. Having chosen mobility, or having been displaced and made emigrant, the diverse citizens of a cosmopolitan world struggle with their twin desires. The emigrant inhabits a new place, with ambitions for security and belonging, obtained whilst renewing a cultural inheritance. The opportunities and obstacles, indeed impossibilities of such a contradictory pursuit are explored in this book. And although those recently displaced might feel this struggle to be uniquely theirs, sociologists have been exploring the quandaries of the emigrant for over a century. What is more, the challenges to internal migrants seeking an identity in the remote Australian Pilbara or peri-urban residents burnt out in summer bushfires around Melbourne, considered by Marsha Berry, Catherine Gomes and Johannes Pieters in chapters that follow, are sometimes no less than those of the transnational migrant. Neither dislocation nor discovery confront today's immigrants alone and newcomers to mid-20th century Australia were similarly caught between pasts and futures. Developing a sense of belonging to place is never easy. As the experiences of the Templers discussed by Irene Bouzo tell us, migration in the post-war decade, seemingly so benign in retrospect, could be harsh. The loss of ancestors to the Holocaust, and a recognition of aboriginal claims on place, as documented by Karen Berger below, can engender alienation from an Australian suburbia. And the discussion by Dvir Abramovich of Holocaust survivors in Israel, points to the fact that an ideology of the nation can exclude those whose life trauma ought to have made them its core citizens.

At the same time, immigration debates have moved some way towards a concentration on a symbolic ethnicity. As is clear in several of the chapters below, that discussion is now turning to an individuated subjectivity rather than to the group and class relations of the emigrant or of ethnic minorities. It is as if concerns for familial economic advancement, for stable social networks and maintenance of group hierarchies have become subordinated to the pursuit of individual cultural identity, the one unassailable core measure in assessing the success of any migration program. How well this might serve future immigrants and the displaced is uncertain. What it may mean for host nations is equally unclear.

Nation-state

Critics of Australia's migration processes and of multicultural policies generally, are apt to fall back on the notion of a white monolithic state in which, as in Gellner's original formulation of nationalism, political structures and cultural practice are congruent.[1] This whiteness is directly attached to Britishness and it is against such a distinctive historical inheritance that contemporary marginalisations of the immigrant are seen to take place. But such a dominant Britishness fits awkwardly with the influence of an Irish Catholic, often anti-British, but convincedly "white" strand in Australian society before 1945. Even the great architect of post-war migration, Arthur Calwell, despite what might be gleaned from his public pronouncements, remained in reality passionately unBritish, a devotee of Irish-language retention, member of the Gaelic League and supporter of a succession of anti-British Irish nationalists.[2] Despite his routine insistence on immigrant whiteness, the Catholicised Southern European migration waves of mid-century would no doubt have been pleasing to Calwell in their diminution of British Australia.

---

1 Gellner, 1997.
2 Calwell, 2012.

In other ways too, Britishness has a vexed and partly detached relation to whiteness. The notion of a "British subject" was applied to all persons in the British Empire such as it was until 1949, and then partially up to the 1981 British Nationality Act. Non-white subjects of the Crown in India could have found themselves in a position of relative legal if not cultural privilege in 19th century Australia, when compared to say a white citizen of Czarist Russia or Republican France. Because of such multiple identities, framers of the White Australia Policy struggled with the irrationality inherent in their racial hierarchies, an enduring challenge for them throughout the half century in which the policy was applied. How to fit Southern Europeans into an umbrella of whiteness was problematic enough. But Maltese immigrants were both Southern European and at the same time British subjects. Moreover a recent diversity in country of origin figures obscures the fact that a reduction in UK arrivals has not necessarily meant a fading of "Britishness". Of the principal sources of settlers in the 21st century, Indians, South Africans and New Zealanders all shared at least some experience of British business methods and legal systems, and typically arrive with English-language skills (as do emigrants from the Philippines or Germany). The exclusionary strategies of White Australia from 1901-56 onwards did work against the settlement of British subjects from India as they did against both British subjects from Hong Kong or non-British subjects from mainland China. Yet even in this period the coherent mass white nation hardly existed. It could further be noted, as Gemma Tulud Cruz's chapter on Filipina house-servants in post-colonial Hong Kong makes plain, discrimination against immigrants did not always depend on an ongoing Britishness.

Nationalism as Eric Hobsbawm insisted, preceded the nation, and in Australia as elsewhere the translation of this ideology into a territorial and legally acknowledged nation-state was driven by elites for whom the nation served both political and economic purposes. Trade interests, the romanticism of a small literary cabal and a desire for regional significance lay behind Australian nationalism. Together they rendered the state as less holistic than current readings of the plight of minorities, routinely defined as non-white, would suggest.

Cultural identity

Current critiques of this mythic white nation frequently propose an ethnic minority cultural identity in opposition to a dominant national culture propped up by the nation-state. And yet immigrant ethnicities almost always have their own nationalist origins. Where these clash with legal forces then there is always a likelihood of singling out and marginalising the newcomer. This scapegoating occurs just as the notion of individual rights are compressed for all. The paradox of the western liberal state is that as individual rights rather than community-building become the basis for all civic and commercial ties, the state, in claiming to provide freedom for individuals, has to engage in even greater surveillance and restriction. Such restrictions on public places may be felt most keenly by the young and the visible minority, as discussed in Mike Dee's chapter below. But the use of CCTV and intrusive public order regulation govern all, just as electronic monitoring, whilst most heavily focussed on some groups, captures every citizen in its archived meta-data. In a neoliberal era, a patina of individual freedom exists beside a heavily anti-individualistic monitoring, from which few escape. The examples discussed in this collection could be replicated in any number of public spaces in western democracies, where the idea of a common, shared public space, engendering a sense of belonging, seems in itself to threaten both the state and commerce.

The problem with much of the argument about minority rights, then, is that those rights that enable cultural retention in a diverse Australia are guaranteed by a liberal western legality. And these ensure individual rather than communal or collective rights. Once other forms of rights are accepted, then the safeguards for ethnic minorities, as for others, fall away. The universal set of Human Rights as asserted in the United Nations Declaration of 1948, is made visible only in the absence of any universality beyond a very few westernised democracies. And in the post-colonial remnants of the British Empire, an adversarial legal system, presumptions of innocence, and the common law, are far more relevant protective mechanisms. As the role of these safeguards is queried by way of restrictions on double jeopardy, the euphemism of "truth in sentencing", offender stereotyping in day-to-day policing and inquisitorial anti-corruption agencies, the freedom of all, rather than simply that of minorities, is called into question.

Ebbs and flows in migration

Much of the unease about migration in the 21st century derives from a mistaken assumption about an "unprecedented" rate of arrivals. For all the fears about mass mobility in the 21st century, current flows have not yet become as transformative as those from Europe between the mid-19th century through to mid-20th century. Between 1821 and 1932 more than 30 million Europeans set sail for the United States alone. Over roughly the same timeframe nearly seven million departed for Argentina, more than five million for Canada and more than four million left for Brazil. Somewhat less than four million emigrants took the lengthy sea journey to Australia and New Zealand. In 1901 Australia had a higher percentage of overseas born than it did in 2011.

In the largest human migration in history, over 20 million Europeans were settled in new countries, as the catastrophe of the anti-Nazi war came to an end. Together, these Displaced Persons and later emigrants from Europe and Asia made up a massive body of settlers. Between 1945 and 2010, approximately 7.5 million immigrants settled in Australia – more than the total number of Australians at the end of World War II. The projected immigration intake for 2013-14 was approximately 190,000. In 1969-70 over 185,000 immigrants were settled in Australia, amongst a far smaller and far more unworldly local population than in 2013-14.[3] Whilst these demographic trends are generally understood, public debates continue to rely on uncertain statistical reference points. For example there are routine comments made about Australian immigration policy in the 19th century. There was no such policy, due to the simple fact that Australia as a nation-state did not exist. Some individual colonies in Australasia conducted their own schemes intermittently but movements from other parts of the world to the Australian continent were usually autonomous (those by the Irish and the Chinese troubled British loyalists the most). The first Australian official programs only commenced in 1919 and by 1939 over 700,000 immigrants had arrived in Australia.[4] With some obvious exceptions what is remarkable about the overseas born in Australia is how far the major countries of origin in the 21st century resemble those in 1901.

---

3 See generally Parliamentary Library of Australia, 2010, p. 5 and Phillips, Klapdor and Simon-Davies, 2001.
4 Ibid.

Overseas Born Australia. Major Countries of Origin as percentages
of all overseas-born

Country	1901	1921	1954	1971	1991	2006
Britain	57.7	67.7	47.9	40.6	30.0	23.5
China	3.5	1.8	-	-	2.1	4.7
Italy	0.7	1.0	9.3	11.2	6.9	4.5
Germany	4.5	2.7	4.0	4.3	3.0	2.4
Netherlands	-	-	4.0	4.0	-	-
Poland	-	-	4.4	2.3	-	-
Yugoslavia	-	-	1.8	5.0	4.4	-
Greece	-	-	2.0	6.2	3.7	2.5
India	0.9	0.8	-	-	-	3.3
Vietnam	-	-	-	-	3.3	3.6
Philippines	-	-	-	-	2.0	2.7
Ireland	21.5	12.5	3.5	1.6	-	-
New Zealand	3.9	4.6	3.4	3.1	7.2	8.8
Malta	-	-	1.6	2.1	-	-
South Africa	-	0.6	-	-	-	2.4

Source: Parliamentary Library of Australia, 2010, Table 7.

Current controversy then, needs to be set against a highly diverse
and for most part declining English (rather than British) migration
across the 20th century. With a couple of obvious exceptions, the
principal groupings in 2006 look remarkably like those of 1901. This
ongoing diversity is made more complicated by the fact that a blanket
"whiteness" is thrown over post-war and 19th century immigrants
obscuring the distinction between various European groups who

were more isolated than any migrant equipped with a 21st century smartphone; the young Italian travellers (rather than immigrants) discussed by Robert Pascoe and Michael Deery provide us with a clear example, their sense of belonging attuned to global digital networks rather than the material place around them.

Ethnicity and nation

Sociologists like Robert Park, William I. Thomas or Florian Znaniecki who pioneered the academic study of migration in the early 20th century, would no doubt find our current emphasis on cultural retention confusing. The early theorists of migration were certainly aware of the emigrant's desire for cultural continuity. They were more persuaded however by the over-riding economic ambitions of new arrivals in the United States. For the emigrant to rise through the ranks to a wealthy, suburbanised American lifestyle was seen as a uniting ambition. Recognition of cultural identity or the security of familiar connections were matters of which they remained aware although the process of emigration as a stage in economic advancement stood as the over-arching concern of the researcher as well as of emigrants. An Americanised host culture was rarely called into question – any subordination of host nation's interests to a transnational refugee convention they would no doubt have found bizarre. In recent research it seems as if these values have been reversed. A successful emigration program is judged as one in which the host state's nationalism allows for, and more likely promotes, immigrant cultural retention rather than economic mobility.

Researchers are aware of the impossibility of any holistic implanting of a traditional culture in the contemporary urban world. As a result, analysis often resorts to dualities, with the immigrant or more likely the second-generation members of an ethnic minority, caught between two cultures. It was this problem which Robert Park (drawing on Georg Simmel) identified in his account of marginality, and which is extended and complexified in the recent sociology of migration. Adam Weisberger for example, pointed to Park's linking of migration and marginality in the image of the "bewildered foreigner who is on the road to successful assimilation, joining the dominant culture and sacrificing his ethnic peculiarities to the melting pot".[5] This journey Park contrasted to the marginal migrant. And whilst in the 21st century marginality has become both more complex, understood as both debilitating and enabling (as a source of group- and self- assertion critical of dominant mores) Weisberger goes on to argue that:

> . . . the marginal person is caught in a cross-current, located within a structure of double ambivalence. This person is ambivalent toward his or her culture, wants to return but cannot, wants to leave but cannot do either, and is ambivalent toward the new culture.[6]

Ethnicity, the product of this cultural ambivalence is likewise subject to a critique. The "multicultural citizenship" of Kymlicka (discussed below by Paula Fernandez Arias) or Habermas's "constitutional patriotism" can be invoked to break the link between ethnicity and nation. Thomas Eriksen also suggested that the "emotional glue that binds nations together" might not need to be ethnic in character and that small daily rituals and gestures shared across ethnic divisions could make up for the lack of a common history, linguistic distinctiveness or a myth of descent.[7] He thought of a territorial identification as

---

5 Weisberger, 1992, p. 429.
6 Ibid.
7 Eriksen, 2004, p. 51.

critical, to go alongside the "bonds of mutual commitment and trust developed through endless encounters and acts of reciprocity".[8] No doubt these can exist alongside the cultural identity of a minority, although sustaining them requires a daily interaction, a sense of kinship and belonging in place, rather than any policy of multiculturalism or assimilation. In fact almost all immigrants find themselves assimilated or acculturated in some ways – often economically – in understanding home purchases, wage and banking systems as well as through their participation in mass consumerism. As to ethnicity, Eriksen further argued that "the very concept of the ethnic group appears as a child of nationalism".[9] As a "modern cultural construct", ethnicity relied on a process of mutually exclusive labelling, driven often by a small-group elite and connected to an assertion of nationhood. In fact, formal ethnic organisations in Australia, from 19th century Irish or Cantonese networks, to Polish and Hungarian opponents of Communist oligarchies in their home countries, all constructed an ethnicity for which nationalism was critical. It was not as if any of these groups reformed a cultural identity after emigration and then launched into nationalistic campaigns. Rather, they invented a distinct mythological identity out of nationalist activities, many of them driven by small elites. A contrast between the nation and cultural identity then does not seem all that sustainable. After nearly a century of massive immigration schemes, we are left with, for the most part, a bricolage of ethnic and immigrant tropes, some hybridised, others purified, and which are not typically articulated through any encoded, systematic sets of meanings, so as to meet an anthropological test of culture.

---

8 Ibid., p. 56.
9 Eriksen, 1993, p. 6.

There remain further complexities in the distinction between
nation and ethnicity, or what A.D. Smith called "ethnie".[10] For much
of the discussion about cultural identity, a set of meanings derived
from ethnicity is seen as opposed to the nation. In responding to a
shift from an assimilationist policy to one of multiculturalism and then
towards an embrace of difference, the rights of a cultural minority
are often asserted over the generally suspect claims of host-nation
ethnicity. But what is more significant is that the minority ethnic
culture, seen as more obtaining of rights than a national identity, is
itself a product of nationalism. The two seem linked in a way which
makes the practice if not the theory of a constitutional patriotism
challenging.

Place, belonging and symbol

Writing in 1952 in the very early phase of Australia's post-war
immigration program, James Roach reflected on male European
immigrants living in hostels, devoid of social contact beyond their
workmates, and with little opportunity to marry into Australian
families or even socialise with them. He wrote that in any Australian
town where there was a migrant hostel:

> . . . great numbers of new Australians may be observed
> wandering about the streets with no place to go and nothing
> to do . . . they become a little foreign community, speaking
> the old language, remembering and reliving the old days,
> misunderstanding and misunderstood.[11]

The "little foreign community" once seen as so debilitating, is now
of course a celebrated cultural memory. Roach's fears about absence

10 Smith, 1995.
11 Roach, 1952, p. 105.

of inter-ethnic marriage however have proved unfounded. Australia's post-war immigrants have inter-married with unique rapidity.[12] This cultural entanglement, no longer identified with segregated hostel living or the ethnic zones of the inner city identified by Park and others in Chicago, becomes now a source of belonging rather than an obstacle to it.

Place, once the locus of any sense of belonging, has, in turn, come to appear less important than a set of cultural symbols in art and artefacts. The Mixing Room exhibition discussed by Christopher Sommer below validates the experiences of young refugees in New Zealand and at the same time draws attention to their marginality for museum audiences. The Somali art exhibition discussed by Vivian Gerrand and Yusuf Sheikh Omar enabled a similar self-affirmation whilst offering a form of resistance, not to the dominant society, but to those within the ethnic community whose claims might intensify marginality. Symbols in exhibition and display, no doubt can both challenge and reinforce marginality. They can be innocuous and familiarising as well. As the Turkish novelist and private museum curator, Orhan Pamuk remarked "our museum has been built on the contradictory desires to tell the stories of objects and to demonstrate their timeless innocence".[13] The museum and the art exhibition certainly do symbolise and communicate innocence and identity, but one mediated by the expert, ethnic or otherwise.

Herbert Gans's definition of "symbolic ethnicity" refers to those established in a host society with few day-to-day ethnic connections but able to participate, even take leadership in the special occasions of a language group or ethnic community – art exhibitions, national day celebrations, visits from the home country's leaders, the openings

---

12 Koo, Birrell and Heard, 2009, pp. 15-28.
13 Pamuk, 2012, p. 141.

of museum and cultural displays. Their symbolic ethnicity is cost-free. It allows for those with little day-to-day involvement in communal struggles to adopt an instant identity and shed it just as quickly. The corporatising of multiculturalism is considered in this collection. Symbolic identity is perhaps an equally challenging issue, since it brings both expanded meaning to an ethnic identity and at the same time draws ethnicity into the transient recreational consumerism of our neoliberal era. Perhaps symbolic ethnicity does offer a response to that feeling of "being a stranger, a wanderer confronting an alien if not hostile culture (which) lies at the heart of marginality".[14] It nonetheless doesn't seem as significant a search for meaning and belonging as that at an individual, secular level, as discussed by Brigitte Lewis in this collection. Her research is an ethnography tracing alternatives to the modernising rationality that marginalises so many newcomers in the contemporary city.

The Janus complex evident in Australian migration policy afflicts immigrants themselves and the native-born as they seek to establish a sense of place and belonging in the digitally-connected and unpredictable 21st century. In their classic five-volume survey, which initiated the sociology of migration, Florian Znaniecki and William I. Thomas observed of Poles in Chicago that:

> As long as the Polish immigrant is isolated among Americans or immigrants of different nationalities he welcomes the arrival of any Pole. But even among people of the same nationality and the same class the desires for response and recognition are not satisfied . . . a Polish colony is divided into several distinct groups which, though more closely connected with one another than with their American milieu, still look at one another with some mistrust and even slight hostility.[15]

---

14 Weisberger, 2009, p.431.
15 Znaniecki and Thomas, 1918-20, pp. 1512-4.

The communal fissures, personal isolation, and desire for recognition which they saw in mass migrations across the Atlantic, now colour accounts of migration and settlement on all continents. It is not surprising then to find that some of the ways through which Chicago urbanists sought to understand emigrants are being returned to the centre of sociological inquiry, in another era of mass demographic movement. Robert Park's idea of marginality, E.W. Burgess's identification of the "zone in transition" and Cressey's predictions about spatial processes of succession and dominance, are all reworked to account for the migrant's desire for recognition, the personal impact of displacement and subsequent generations' eventual construction of meaningful, hopeful places.[16] The tension underlying these sociological explorations seems to fit an early 21st century experience where the shifting boundaries and nodal points of daily lives are no longer only geographic. Every inhabited locality is now shaped by a transient set of forces, few which incidentally support a sense of belonging in place.

Znaniecki, Cressey, Park and others were reflecting first and foremost on the era of mass European migration to North America, in which numerical scale overwhelmed an existing social order. The underlying concern of several of their research projects remained with "Americanisation" and the prevention of social disorder rather than with any immigrant cultural tradition. But if marginality and a sense of belonging are to be brought back to the centre of migration, place and ethnicity (as Weisberger, Eriksen and others seem to suggest) then so too might a concern for economic well-being, social mobility and social connection across boundaries of religion or race (the sort of intercultural dialogue discussed further in this collection). One 20th century sociological classic also drew on culture, ethnic boundaries

---

16 Jørgensen, 2010.

and identity but within a context of social class and neighbourhood. Herbert Gans's study of Italians in Boston's West End pointed to broad social disadvantage as well as to fragile networks of resilience rather than cultural celebration. As he wrote of this "urban village":

> The West End was not a charming neighbourhood of "noble peasants" living in an exotic fashion, resisting the mass-produced homogeneity of American culture and overflowing with a cohesive sense of community. It was a run-down area of people struggling with the problems of low income, poor education and related difficulties. Even so it was by and large a good place to live.[17]

"Low income, poor education and related difficulties" diminish the lives of native-born and immigrant, and remain largely unaltered by an emphasis on cultural retention and national migration policy. Perhaps in the end, Gans's criterion remains the only useful measure of migration policy, and a sense of belonging; that regardless of official statements about multiculturalism or embrace of difference, and in the face of continued marginality, a successful settlement is one that survives as "by and large a good place to live".

References

Calwell. Mary Elizabeth. (2012) *I am bound to be true – the life and legacy of Arthur A. Calwell.* Preston, Vic.: Mosaic Press.

Eriksen, Thomas Hylland. (1993) "The epistemological status of the concept of ethnicity". Conference paper. Amsterdam. December.

———. (2004) "Place, kinship and the case for non-ethnic nations". *Nations and Nationalism.* 10(1-2): 49-62.

---

17 Gans, 1962, p.16.

Gans, Herbert. (1962) *The urban villagers: group and class in the life of Italian-Americans*. New York: Free Press.

Gellner, Ernest. (1997) *Nationalism*. London: Weidenfeld and Nicolson

International Migration Digest. (1964) "The Janus Complex in Australia's immigration policy". *International Migration Digest*. 1(1). Spring: 67-8.

Jørgensen, Anja. (2010) "The sense of belonging in new urban zones in transition". *Current Sociology*. 58(3): 3-23.

Koo, Siew-Ean, Birrell, Bob and Heard, Genevive. (2009) "Intermarriage by birthplace and ancestry in Australia". *People and Place*. 17(1): 15-28.

Pamuk, Orhan. (2012) *The Innocence of Objects: The Museum of Innocence, Istanbul*. Translated from Turkish by Ekin Oklap. New York: Abrams.

Parliamentary Library of Australia. (2010) *Migration to Australia since Federation: a guide to the statistics*. Canberra: Australian Government Printing.

Phillips, Janet, Klapdor, Michael and Simon-Davies, Joanne. Statistical Section, Department of Immigration and Multicultural Affairs. (2001) *Immigration Federation to Century's End 1901-2000*. Canberra: Department of Immigration and Multicultural Affairs.

Roach, James (1952) "Australia's Immigration Program". *Far Eastern Survey*. 21(10).

Smith A.D. (1995) *Nations and Nationalism in a Global Era*. London: Routledge

Weisberger. Adam (1992) "Marginality and its directions". *Sociological Forum*. 3: 425-46.

Znaniecki, Florian and Thomas, William I. (1918-20) *The Polish Peasant in America and Europe*. First published in five volumes. 1918-1920. Reprint 1958. New York: Dover.

PART ONE:

Creating places and building hopes

1

Paula Fernandez Arias

Resettlement as an identity-building process

It comes as no surprise to hear that the world has shrunk, compressed, and been made accessible by the advances of science and technology; that individuals are no longer ruled by the tyranny of distance or bound solely to local networks, that identity has become a more nuanced endeavour that can be "streamed", "tweeted" or "liked". It would also be unsurprising to state that for many of the residents of wealthy western liberal nations, increased levels of mobility have become commonplace. International airports, once markers of wealth, elitism and a tropical holiday, are now places where regular international travellers transit en route to their next destination. People of all races and places traverse through the space of the airport and into the built environment of the city.

Mobile lives[1]

Western capitals, and to an extent their larger regional centres, have been populated steadily with a diverse range of races, ethnicities,

---

1 I borrow the title for my first section from A. Elliott and J. Urry, (2010) *Mobile lives,* London and New York: Routledge. Their exploration of the impact of advanced globalisation on the construction and deployment of the self and their concept of portable personhood is one that is both useful and thought provoking.

identities and creeds for the past fifty years.[2] This has meant that polyethnicity is no longer an imagined condition of the modern world but a highly visible reality for major cities in the west. Naturally, or at least consequently, these changes in the distribution and mobilisation of populations bring with them questions of identity, belonging, and community. With obvious difference has come the idea of diversity and with diversity there are efforts to organise people and groups into coherent categories so as to assign funding and develop government policies. Australia, as a migrant nation alongside Canada, Europe and the US, has been at the forefront of these diversity management strategies. One of the more popular strategies and by far the more persistent one has been multiculturalism. Australia, a nation once defined by the White Australia policy, has been officially multicultural since 1973.[3]

This paper will provide a glimpse of the current Australian humanitarian resettlement context, taking into consideration aspects of Australia's history and the official multicultural policy framework. It explores the possibility of reconstructing resettlement as a new locus for identity building and examines interculturalism as a response to the European challenges of mass migration, resettlement and community cohesion.

Australian story

Australia is known in popular lore as a migrant nation. Yet given the more recent changes in the treatment of asylum seekers, the swing towards a conservative government and the discussion of Australia's humanitarian role, it seems vital to remind ourselves that until

---

2 Hugo, 2011.
3 Uberoi, 2008.

1901 Australia consisted of a collection of self-governing colonies of the British Empire.[4] A considerable fragment of the imagined community of Australia represents a nation forged by the sweat and hard work of the brave (white) migrants who went to forge a new life in a distant land of great opportunities.[5] Yet we hear far less of the policy that defined Australia from 1901 until 1973. The reality that a racially based immigration policy was the defining factor of Australian national identity is rarely taken into account when speaking about, or analysing, the current state of racial tension or the backlash over the alleged problem with "boat people". Australia is a nation that speaks about itself as not having any racially based problems, it is multicultural and polyethnic.

Jatinder Mann is one amongst many scholars to make the broadly accurate claim that Australian national identity depended, from the late-19th century onwards, on the two overriding principles of "Britishness" and "Whiteness". To be British was to be White, and the best form of Whiteness was that of British Whiteness. Mann is arguing that Australia, though it had a name of its own and a history that was in the making, had until the early 1960s, constructed its national identity as decisively British. Australia was not an entity apart from Britain; it was an extension of Britain. Individual and collective identity, therefore, was intimately linked to the notions of racial purity and superiority, of a civilising mission and the overall triumph of "man" over nature.[6]

By the middle of the 20th century, radical change across the globe had begun to generate a shift in the understanding of interdependence between nations. The United Nations General Assembly's Universal

---

4 See for example Mogelson, 2013 and Liberal Party of Australia, 2013.
5 Arnold, 2006.
6 Mann, 2013.

Declaration of Human Rights (1948) gave expression to a new sense of human equality and dignity. Both Australia's geographical positioning and its political weighting became matters that could no longer be ignored. It also had to respond to the call for assistance with the millions of displaced people that war had created. Australia could no longer pretend that it was a solitary island floating in the southern hemisphere, unaffected by the pull of this new globalising and cosmopolitan era.

An important narrative shift occurred in the early 1960s, around the common history espoused by Australian governments. Robert Menzies in 1962 first addressed Australians as descendants of immigrants, in his speech to the Annual Citizenship Convention.[7] This linguistic change signalled two important features of Australian political discourse. Firstly, it was effectively re-writing the history of Australia, from a settler colony to a migrant nation. This heralded the beginning of an era that was to be defined by a narrative of sameness. It placed the new migrant and the old settler together within the same myth: that Australia has always been a diverse nation, that Australia is a nation of migrants and that it has been and will continue to be an example of success. This emergent narrative secondly served to eliminate the complexity of history. By generating a new myth on which to base national identity, Australian policy-makers sought to disengage from the long, protracted conflict with Aboriginal populations. "Terra nullius" could become "terra nostra", emptied of historical trauma, a place where everyone could look forward into the bright, diverse and multicultural future.

With the 1973 repeal of the Immigration Restriction Act the wheels of multiculturalism were set in motion. Subsequent changes

---

7 Ibid., p. 56.

in migration programs would bring with them, not only a different composition to the population, but also in the systems that had to deal with the needs of migrants. Australia has, since 1978, implemented a specific program to deal with and provide care to humanitarian entrants though the influx of humanitarian entrants stems from earlier than this.[8] The numbers, languages spoken and places of origin of humanitarian entrants have changed alongside the shifting international political scene. Where there is crisis, systems respond and liberal western democracies receive waves of humanitarian entrants from regions of the world affected by war, famine or disaster.

Australia as one of these liberal democracies has its own response system, the Department of Immigration and Border Protection, and a yearly quota that is filled with entrants from across the globe. In the current political climate considerable emphasis has been placed on how humanitarian entrants reach Australia and the legitimacy of their claims to asylum. However, focusing exclusively on this particular aspect of the program often skews the discussion about humanitarian entrants. It simply reduces humanitarian programs to a competition over acceptable methods of arrival and ignores the fact that resettlement is a complex process, commencing well before arrival and continuing for years afterwards.

Due to the anxieties generated by so-called illegal arrivals, a sense of context is important. According to the Humanitarian Program Outcomes for 2010-11, the humanitarian entrant program for that year was fully delivered, with 13,799 visas granted.[9] If this number were to be broken down into the different sub-classes that make up the program, we would find that of the total visas granted that year, 8971 were granted offshore and 4828 were granted onshore. Of the

---

8 Hugo, 2011.
9 Department of Immigration and Citizenship, 2011b.

latter only 2717 fell under the irregular maritime arrivals (IMAs), also commonly referred to as boat people category. Overall the single largest category is sub-class 200 Refugee, with 5211 visas granted; there were also 759 emergency rescue and 26 In-country special humanitarian visas. The total number of visas granted each year through the humanitarian program is less than one per cent of the total population of Australia.

Interestingly, despite the fact that Australia's largest immigrant group continues to be of European origin, the top ten ABS (2012) countries of birth – United Kingdom, New Zealand, China, India, Italy, Vietnam, Philippines, South Africa, Malaysia, and Germany – provide a glimpse into what has become and will continue to be a diversified population. And though the reality of a diverse Australia is tangible and present-day, it has not developed outside history or policy practice. Australia today, unlike many other immigrant nations, continues to proclaim itself as multicultural.

Multiculturalisms

Multiculturalism as a policy direction has manifested itself almost exclusively within western liberal democracies. Multiculturalism has, therefore, been deeply tied to the liberal values of individual rights, freedom and personal conceptions of quality of life. In the western world, liberal toleration came about as a way of finally resolving the religious disputes that plagued Europe during the 17th and 18th centuries.[10] Australia is today a multicultural nation, this is not merely a statement that refers to the polyethnic nature of the population but rather to a policy direction that the Australian government has been publicising and adapting to its needs since 1973.

---

10 Parekh, 2006; Kymlicka, 1995.

More recently the concept of multiculturalism has come under increasing scrutiny by the general population, the media and political institutions alike. In a post 9/11 world where difference is often exacerbated and the new right has increased its popularity considerably, it is possible to reflect upon the success and appropriateness of the hegemonic diversity management strategies of the last thirty years. Issues of definition have been at the heart of the multicultural debate; the concept is as Delanty notes "an essentially contested term taking many different forms".[11] It is this definitional challenge that perhaps has generated the diverse range of multiculturalisms present in different nations. It is also possibly one of its weaknesses. For even prominent intellectual voices within multiculturalism cannot generate a common understanding of what the term means and how it might best operate.

Tariq Modood points toward the importance of place when it comes to the manifestation of multiculturalism.[12] Modood compares the minority-rights struggles of blacks, gays and others, labelled multiculturalism in the USA, and the reality of post-colonial migration into Europe, which led to a push for diversity management, culminating in a European form of multiculturalism.[13] Modood's approach is practical and defines multiculturalism as "the political accommodation of minorities formed by immigration to western countries from outside the prosperous West".[14] European multiculturalism responds primarily to challenges posed for liberal democracies by the growing number of immigrants and more specifically to Muslim settlement in Europe. However, the political responses to the post 9/11 fears

---

11 Delanty, 2010, p. 71.
12 Modood, 2007.
13 Ibid.
14 Ibid., p. 5.

and demands of the mainstream population have been defined by national ideals and nation-based notions of identity.

Tracing the history of multiculturalism and what he sees as its rise and fall, Will Kymlicka frames multiculturalism as a result of the human rights campaigns of the 1950s and 1960s. Multiculturalism is thus deeply interconnected with the struggle for decolonisation and civil rights.[15] Yet for Kymlicka, multiculturalism is related to both indigenous claims and the manner in which historical national minorities produced what may be understood as a layered concept of multiculturalism. Arguably the most interesting part of his argument is the connection he makes between multiculturalism as a human rights based movement and the consequences for the groups who use the multicultural flag to advance their cause. Namely Kymlicka argues that because the belief in cultural rights equates to a belief in human rights, the groups that adhere to these ideals must themselves do away with, or have done away with, their own internal discriminatory practices. As inspiring as this conception of cultural rights may be, it is naïve to ignore the reality of the continuing of illiberal cultural practices by some groups.

Varun Uberoi in his exploration of the impact of multicultural policies and national identities attempts to define multicultural policies.[16] For Uberoi, multicultural policies have three common characteristics: a) they are measures that address issues such as race relations, discrimination, special exemptions and others relating to difference; b) they have a common origin in the rejection of assimilation; and c) they are an attempt to rectify inequalities and disadvantages produced by a monocultural hegemony.[17] Uberoi's

---

15 Kymlicka, 2010.
16 Uberoi, 2008.
17 Ibid., pp. 406-7.

definition of multicultural policies is a useful one as it allows for enough conceptual breadth to include different styles of diversity management, without being diluted to the point of impracticability. Finding unity in the common elements of what has proven to be a difficult-to-define theory adapted to disparate geographies, is probably the single most important characteristic of multiculturalism as it stands today.

The role, place and importance given to culture is another of the more contentious points within the multicultural theory debate. Culture, it is argued, is intimately linked to individual and collective identity. Defining culture it seems is also impracticable. However, for the purposes of this paper, culture as understood by the author, is a cohesive system of meaning, that organises the world of its members. Multiculturalism, in its many forms, has attempted to deal with the outcome of several cultures coming into contact with each other, within the hierarchical sphere of the nation-state. Prior to multicultural policy frameworks being established, assimilation into the dominant culture was the only option for immigrants.

Assimilation is frequently depicted as one of the many negative obsessions stemming from Social Darwinism. One aspect that many multicultural theorists agree on is that if minorities wish to be assimilated then they are free to do so, but that assimilation should not be a prerequisite for equal citizenship.[18] Multicultural societies, or multinational and polyethnic states require a broader concept of culture to operationalise the interactions between members.[19] Multiculturalism is an attempt to both manage and accommodate difference that is determined by the national, political and social realities of specific countries. This presents a challenge in terms of

18 Parekh, 2006, p. 197.
19 Kymlicka, 1995.

policy and practice as it will also determine how successful migrants will be in their new home. It also raises the question of whether it would not be better to have unified modes of operationalising policies that relate to diversity and migration, given that the problems in each separate nation seem to be increasingly similar.

Is resettlement a locus for new community and identity building?

The idea of re-settlement is one that conveys a sense of transference; a person or family transpose their old life into a new environment. How this process can be carried on more effectively and how the outcomes can be improved is a field of inquiry in its own right. However the degree to which one can re-create an old life in a new home is a contentious point and to assume that this is what effectively happens to all humanitarian entrants is a problematic hypothesis. In Australia, considerable research on settlement outcomes is mostly conducted or initiated by government and is primarily focused on quantifiable and measurable outcomes such as employment, health, housing, education, etc. A recent report by the Australian Survey Research Group (ASR) looked at settlement outcomes of new arrivals. ASR, when conducting their research, devised a conceptual framework to predict settlement outcomes where "many of the initially identified settlement indicators did not predict anything".[20] In other words, they found a marked difference between the Department of Immigration and Border Protection's definition of "good settlement", i.e. systemic outcomes, and the humanitarian entrants' own account of "good settlement", i.e. life outcomes.[21] Similarly Hugo's report on the contributions of

---

20 Australian Survey Research Group, 2011, p. 59.
21 Ibid.

humanitarian entrants and migrants categorises these contributions as economic, civic, social and demographic.[22] The report emphasises the real contribution made by immigration, and although this may take time, it is a benefit in every way. Such a conclusion is a welcome break from the reductionist view that immigration and the humanitarian program are burdens to be shouldered by the state. Both these reports reproduce the "transaction" dynamic of settlement. Put simply there is an exchange between the newly arrived and the state: one provides security, and the other generates gains.

Two interesting aspects emerge from such settlement-outcome studies. Firstly, that settlement like multiculturalism is a highly contested concept and has different meanings to different people and organisations. Secondly, that within settlement, there is no exploration of, or importance assigned to the possibilities for identity creation, generated when humanitarian entrants and migrants arrive in a new country. If we agree that one's culture and cultural membership provide meaningful options and an anchor for self-identification and belonging, and that contact with new or different cultures inevitably leads to the altering of one's own cultural composition, then why is so little importance given to this transformative aspect of settlement in reports generated by and for government?[23]

One answer lies in the nature of multiculturalism as a political theory and a policy direction. Multiculturalism with its battle flag of difference, cannot allow for any hybridisation, as it would signal that cultural identity, if it is subject to change, is perhaps less important than it has been made out to be and therefore less subject to special

---

22 Hugo, 2011.
23 Margalit and Raz, 1990, quoted in Kymlicka, 1995, p. 89.

protections and differentiated rights. In other words, there is a distinction between a "variety of cultures" and "cultural variety".[24] Australia's most recent multicultural policy was launched in February 2011 with claims that it "addresses the importance of the economic and social benefits of diversity, as well as our need to balance the rights and obligations of all who live here".[25] As with preceding policy documents, this latest document "values" cultural diversity and frames it in a positive light, at least to the point where the ideals of liberal democracy and unity reign over and contain diversity. The policy calls for the institutions of government to respond to diversity so that in turn, this will provide the nation with economic (especially trading) benefits. The government promises to uphold its end of the bargain by ensuring that it will act against intolerance and discrimination with the full force of the law. It is difficult not to feel that this policy has a contractual tone that speaks volumes about the state of multiculturalism in contemporary Australia.

The corporatising of Australian multiculturalism is perhaps a symptom of the dangers of constructing a polyethnic nation over the remains of a white supremacist state. The most viable survival strategy for the future of Australian multiculturalism is to frame the benefits within the economic and neoliberal supply and demand paradigm that has been customarily deployed.[26] Australia is not only a multicultural nation because it has ethnic diversity, it is a multicultural nation because that is the best bet for the future. The economic argument has become the number one justification for multiculturalism. Diversity is always positively framed in the narrative of government, and though the aim of this paper is not to dispute the legitimacy of this intention,

---

24 Bauman, 2002, quoted in Wilson, 2010, p. 24.
25 Department of Immigration and Citizenship, 2011a.
26 See for example Markus, 2012.

the extent to which those who come to Australia, or indeed those who would call themselves Australian, feel that their lived experience within diversity is beneficial, remains debatable.

Beyond multiculturalism?

We are all aware of the European crisis of multiculturalism and the consequent rise of right-wing extremism.[27] The increasing complexity of a globalised world is being felt in Australia with debates around integration in the mass media and the public sphere.[28] Or as Pardy and Lee would argue, "the public and policy reputation of multiculturalism, as well as its theoretical and interpretative force, has been considerably weakened in recent years".[29]

A European response to the crisis of multiculturalism, the increase of the perceived threat of terrorist attacks and rising levels of social disharmony have led to "interculturalism" and its practical arm, intercultural dialogue (ICD). Originally presented as part of the first EU-ECSA World Conference on Intercultural Dialogue and further developed in the Council of Europe's White Paper on Intercultural Dialogue, interculturalism has a solid grounding in the concept of human rights and social cohesion.[30] This White Paper was created through dialogue and consultation amongst the European member states, revealing a concern with certain key issues not unfamiliar to scholars of multiculturalism. Namely that "old" diversity management strategies were falling short of the task; that the ICD alternative was at

---

27 Bekemans et al., 2007; Council of Europe, 2008.
28 See for example: "Cambodians wary of Australia refugee deal", Sky News web-site; "Asylum seeker detention on Manus Island is constitutional, High Court rules", ABC, Australia, web-site.
29 Pardy and Lee, 2011, p. 298.
30 Bekemans et al., 2007; Council of Europe, 2008.

that stage too abstract and could not always be translated into policy; that there was a desire to adhere to some universal principles; and that the challenges of living in a diverse society could only be met if all could "live together as equals in dignity".[31]

The authors of the White Paper did not explicitly set out to generate a theory of interculturalism, although they did bring together basic requirements for such a theory to be expounded. The White Paper reclaimed the concept of integration and framed it in terms of a human rights endeavour whereby integration is a two-way process, in which all parties live together with "full respect for the dignity of each individual".[32] It put forward the idea that social cohesion was a common good to be pursued and that human rights were the foundations on which everything else was built, including the shared identity as Europeans. The White Paper clearly states that the "corpus of human rights recognises the dignity of every human being, over and above the entitlements enjoyed by individuals as citizens of a particular state".[33] The idea of the supra-national and the precedence of universal human rights over the nation-state is one of the defining features of intercultural theory. Such a clear-cut stand in relation to these issues goes against the grain of more accommodating views of cultural-minority rights.

The White Paper goes further, listing a series of conditions for ICD, but more broadly interculturalism, to take place. This explicit set of rules and common understandings is a move away from a multiculturalism that is bound by geopolitico-historical specificity. ICD can only take place if, alongside human rights, there is democracy,

---

31 Council of Europe, 2008.
32 Ibid., p. 11.
33 Ibid., p. 14.

the rule of law and gender equality. These conditions are not just to be met by the minority groups that have come to liberal democracies, but by all citizens within the European territories. Interculturalism presupposes that change is needed on both sides, but that change cannot come about unless there is a meaningful interaction on all sides. The burden does not lie solely with migrants and the responsibility is not just to be shouldered by the state, all citizens need to take part in constructing a shared vision of a humanity that takes bits and pieces from all members and where the whole is greater than the sum of its parts.

The dialogical aspect of ICD refers to the practice of engaging in a conversation with others with whom one would not normally speak in order to reduce barriers to further communication and prejudice previously related to those groups. ICD is a newer form of contact theory, originally espoused by Gordon Allport which the COE picks up on to generate a framework for different communities within Europe.[34] The importance placed on ICD stems from a growing body of evidence that points to the very isolated lives of some migrant groups and the negative effects this has had for levels of social harmony.[35] An interesting application of interculturalism has been put forward by Robin Wilson in his book on the Northern Ireland conflict.[36]

Wilson uses the principles of intercultural theory to argue for a model of reconciliation for Northern Ireland which he says has yet to be achieved.[37] Wilson contrasts interculturalism, a new paradigm, with multiculturalism, an old paradigm based on identity politics. Wilson's

---

34 Wood and Landry, 2008.
35 Cantle, 2001.
36 Wilson, 2010.
37 Ibid., p. 8.

arguments are not new, nor are they radical, but the application of
the intercultural principles to two groups of people whom to the
rest of the world, seem very similar, is creative to say the least. In
a few simple words the problem, as Wilson sees it, with the conflict
between Catholic and Protestant (or as they might see themselves,
Nationalist or Loyalist) Irish is that identities have been essentialised
to the point that there is no going between them or away from them.
Hatred for the other is based on an irreducible identity as "an-other",
of a different religion or system of belief. This irreducible, essential
identity becomes the defining and dividing factor of each faction,
and it enables further violence and long-standing stereotyping of the
members of the rival group. Although immigration implies different
difficulties in Australia and Europe, when looking at the transcripts of
the public hearings of the inquiry into multiculturalism in Australia,
the narrative of concern over the impact of immigration on the
Australian way of life sounds all too familiar.[38]

Conclusion

Australia is what Kymlicka would call a multinational, polyethnic
state, multinational because Australia has indigenous populations
and polyethnic because of the influx of diverse migrant groups.[39]
The fact that there is a border delimited by government implies
that immigration is a political act and as such invariably involves
Australia's relations with other countries.[40] Like many other migrant
nations Australia has a history that has been linked to systematic
forms of oppression, racial selectiveness and historical denial of its

---

38 Parliament of Australia, 2011.
39 Kymlicka, 1995.
40 Harris, 1993, p. 23.

indigenous peoples. Bringing history to the forefront is not an attempt at defamation but rather a recognition that immigration since the colonial era has been fraught with tension, and that these historical precedents shape the way in which resettlement and immigration are practiced today.

Australia has tried to right some of its former wrongs by investing resolutely in the idea of a diverse, vibrant migrant nation that welcomes all that come. However there is little research and possibly even less emphasis given to the study of the impact of re-settlement on identity and its later impact on community building. Bauman argues that the difference between the multicultural and intercultural divide lies in the understanding each has of culture, a distinction that summarises all critiques of multiculturalism.[41] Placing absolute importance on the value that individuals assign to cultural identity is a smart political manoeuvre, allowing for claims of recognition where there were none and giving these claims the political weight needed to become part of the institutions of the nation-state. On the other hand, the time of colour-blind states has come and gone and difference has become the critical issue to be addressed by politicians and the institutions of government.

References

Arnold, B. (2006) *Imagined Communities: Reflections on the Origin and Spread of Nationalism.* New York: Verso.

Australian Bureau of Statistics. (2012) *Australian Population Clock.* Canberra: Australian Bureau of Statistics.

———. (2012) *Year Book Australia.* Canberra: Australian Bureau of Statistics.

---

41 Bauman, 2002, as quoted in Wilson, 2010.

Australian Survey Research Group. (2011) *Settlement Outcomes of New Arrivals – Report of findings: Study for Department of Immigration and Citizenship*. Canberra: Department of Immigration and Citizenship.

Bekemans, L., Karasinska-Fendler, M., Mascia, M. et al. (2007) "General Introduction". In Bekemans. L., Karasinska-Fendler, M., Mascia, M. et al. (eds) *Intercultural Dialogue and Citizenship: Translating Values into Actions A Common Project for Europeans and Their Partners*. Venice: Marsilio Editori.

Cantle, T. (2001) "Community Cohesion: A Report of the Independent Review Team". London: Home Office.

Council of Europe. (2008) "White Paper on Intercultural Dialogue". Strasbourg: Council of Europe. Ministers of Foreign Affairs.

Delanty, G. (2010) *Community*. London: New York: Routledge.

Department of Immigration and Citizenship. (2011a) *Australia's Multicultural Policy*. Canberra: Department of Immigration and Citizenship.

————. (2011b) *Humanitarian Program Outcomes for 2010–11*. Canberra: Department of Immigration and Citizenship.

————. (2012) "Fact Sheet: Building a New Life in Australia Introducing the longitudinal survey of humanitarian migrants". Canberra: Commonwealth of Australia.

Elliott, A. and Urry, J. (2010) *Mobile lives*. London and New York: Routledge.

Harris S. (1993). "Immigration and Australian foreign policy". In Jupp, J., Kabala, M. and Bureau of Immigration Research. (eds). *The Politics of Australian Immigration*. Canberra: Australian Government Publishing Service.

Hugo, G. (2011). "Economic, social and civic contributions of first and second generation humanitarian entrants". Canberra: National

Centre for Social Applications of Geographical Information Systems, University of Adelaide.

Kymlicka, W. (1995) *Multicultural citizenship : a liberal theory of minority rights.* Oxford and New York: Clarendon Press; Oxford University Press.

Kymlicka, W. (2010) "The rise and fall of multiculturalism?". In Vertovec, S. and Wessendorf, S. (eds) *The multiculturalism backlash: European discourses, policies and practices.* London; New York: Routledge. p. 210.

Liberal Party of Australia. (2013) *Better Budget Management.* Available at: http://youtube/eJaAP7dF9h4

Mann, J. (2013) " 'Leaving British Traditions': Integration Policy in Australia, 1962-1972'. *Australian Journal of Politics and History.* 59: 47-62.

Markus, A. (2012) *Mapping Social Cohesion National Report.* Melbourne: Monash University and Scanlon Foundation.

Modood, T. (2007) *Multiculturalism: A Civic Idea.* Cambridge and Malden, MA: Polity.

Mogelson, L. (2013). "The Dream Boat". *The New York Times Magazine.* New York: The New York Times.

Pardy, M. and Lee, J.C.H. (2011) "Using buzzwords of belonging: everyday multiculturalism and social capital in Australia". *Journal of Australian Studies.* 35: 297-316.

Parekh, B.C. (2006) *Rethinking multiculturalism : cultural diversity and political theory.* Basingstoke, England and New York: Palgrave Macmillan.

Parliament of Australia. (2011) *Inquiry into Multiculturalism in Australia Schedule of public hearings, programs and transcripts.* Parliament of Australia. House of Representatives Committees. Parliament of Australia web-site.

Uberoi, V. (2008). "Do Policies of Multiculturalism Change National Identities?". *The Political Quarterly*. 79: 404-17.

Wilson, R. (2010) *The Northern Ireland experience of conflict and agreement: a model for export?* Manchester and New York: Manchester University Press.

Wood, P. and Landry, C. (2008) *The intercultural city: planning for diversity advantage*. London and Sterling, VA: Earthscan.

2

Dvir Abramovich

Exiled Citizens: Holocaust remembrance in the first decade of Israeli statehood and the gradual shift in attitudes in the 1980s

Although more than 60 years have elapsed since the end of World War II and the discovery of the harrowing facts, the presence of the Holocaust in the Israeli and Jewish psyche has not receded. For the vast majority of Israelis this event remains a calamity that cannot be relegated to the margins of history. As Terence Des Pres has noted, we seem to be living "in the unrest of an aftermath".[1] The operating mindscape today echoes the statement made by Israeli poet Nathan Alterman after the 1961 Eichmann trial – that the Holocaust, "is a basic powerful essence; its quality and image, the horror of its memories, are beyond life and beyond nature, an indelible part of the quality and image of the nation to which we belong".[2] This powerful sentiment was recast by Israeli writer Yehudit Hendel who declared that, "to the end of time it is forbidden to stop talking about it and telling it again and again, and if it is spoken about for a thousand years and recounted for a thousand years, still not everything will be told".[3] Yet, this was not always the case.

1 Des Pres, 1980, p. 13.
2 Holtzman, 1992, pp. 24-5.
3 Ibid.

41

The central aim of this chapter is to examine the attitudes in Israel of the 1950s towards the remnants of the Holocaust. It will analyse how, from its foundation in 1948, Israel adopted an official and collectivising position towards remembering the Holocaust and its dead. This effectively banished the personal stories of the survivors, undermined any genuine identification with their grief and caused the newly arrived immigrants to be displaced in their new home. Also explored are the gradual changes that took place following the 1961 Eichmann trial and the manner in which in the 1980s, Israeli society, culture and literature responded to these transformative shifts.

A case that encapsulates the damaging attitude exhibited towards the survivors in the formative years of Israeli statehood is that of Dr Boshminski. During the 1961 Eichmann trial, Boshminski, a Polish doctor, described on the witness stand how an SS officer with a truncheon had whipped a Jewish youth with 80 blows. Gideon Hausner, Israel's state prosecutor, asked him, "do you see the victim in the room"? The doctor pointed to Michael Goldman-Gilead, then a policeman, and part of the team investigating Eichmann's crimes. When Goldman was asked why he had never told anyone of the 80 blows, his response was: "When I got to Palestine I tried to tell people, but they didn't believe me. That was the 81st blow".[4] That phrase, "The 81st Blow", came to embody the doubt and disdain exhibited by Israelis towards survivors in the 1950s.

It is pivotal to understand that the Israeli state, in the first years of its establishment, sought to "emphasize the regenerative force of the Jewish people as demonstrated in the valiant founding and the heroic defence of the Jewish State" and as such, the glorification of Israel,

---

4 Michael Goldman-Gilead revealed that he did not even tell his wife and children about the incident; yadvashem.org, web-site; Goldman interview.

"superseded the grief and mourning of the Holocaust destruction".[5] A then nascent Israeli nation embraced and celebrated the ideal of the heroic "Sabra", as well as lionising and enshrining the doctrine of the "New Jew" – fierce, strong, courageous and self-reliant – who was now able to break away from the long history of Jewish suffering.

A consistent dilemma in Israeli culture of the 1940s and 1950s was the question of whether Israel should be considered a continuation of the historical Jewish past, or treated as a new beginning altogether. In other words, should Israelis reaffirm and acknowledge the ongoing tradition of Jewish heritage or disregard what came before and build on the present? The debate revolved around the subject of a Jewish national character, especially its endurance and vitality. Since it was being a Jew that sealed people's fate during the Nazi reign, a fundamental question for Israelis concerned Jewish cultural identity and whether it was, "a badge of shame, to be rejected and overcome? Or is it, on the contrary, to be the source of strength for those who have survived"?[6] The "New Israelis", who were shadowed by the troubling and anguished past of the diaspora, saw themselves anchored to the land rather than to the painful and somewhat uncomfortable memory of the Shoah. And herein lay the paradox. Israel was a nation born in the aftermath of genocide and with the promise of "Never Again". Yet, it acted to deny several aspects of that memory so as to renew and regenerate itself.

It should be noted that Hebrew culture had a substantive impact on the formation of Israeli national identity and its attendant values. Thus, during the determinative years of Israeli statehood, writers and commentators had a profound involvement in the evolution and construction of the New Jew. As Robert Alter has noted, "it is hard

5 Brenner, 2002, p. 10.
6 Ramras-Rauch, 1985, p. 13.

to think of another field of modern cultural activity that provides, as does Hebrew literature, such a luminous mirror both of the creative élan and of the deep perplexities of Jews trying to define some relationship to an age-old heritage in a radically unfamiliar new world".[7] All told, in various stories and essays, authors attempted to demonstrate the difficulties Israelis faced in remembering and commemorating the Holocaust, and the concomitant condemnatory sentiments of the young Israeli generation.

Knowledge of the Holocaust in 1950s Israel was fashioned in accordance with the popular themes of Israeli dogma, which considered and treated the diaspora with derision. In the dominant Zionist creed, the Holocaust was marshalled as proof that European Jews were actually responsible for their own fate.[8] Israelis growing up in the 1950s felt an intense sense of shame, even alienation, towards the millions who were exterminated, and whom they perceived as having offered no resistance. In their eyes, the 1948 War of Independence, in which the infant state repulsed the combined might of the invading Arab armies, reinforced the difference between Israel and the diaspora. This polarisation, between the Israeli "nature" and the Jewish "nature", became a pervasive element in excluding the victims' perspective.[9]

Such stigmatisation and suppression was coupled with an overwhelming desire by the survivors to forget. The fear in the survivors' community of re-opening unhealed wounds was just as strong as the desire of many to rehabilitate themselves and to create new family ties removed from the horrors of the Holocaust. The emphasis on the ethos of resistance was further amplified by

7 Alter, 1975, p. xi.
8 Yablonka, 1998, pp. 120-1.
9 Ramras-Rauch, 1985, pp. 3-18.

the weight given to images centred entirely on the heroic aspects of the Holocaust that provided the post-Shoah generation with comforting images of heroic partisans, forming an essential part of the overarching Zionist narrative. The Shoah was compacted into the overwhelming abstract number of six million, chiming with the statist model that aimed at stripping the catastrophe of its distinct and individual components. Not surprisingly, such a paradigm found its sharpest expressions in schools:

> It was quite common in the 1950s and 1960s, for example, for schools to commemorate Holocaust Day by sitting children as young as six in a darkened room for a slide projection show: black-and-white images of Jewish men being dragged by their beards, Jewish children piled onto trains . . . there were no preparatory talks . . . and no discussion afterwards.[10]

The 1948 War of Independence and the founding of Israel played critical roles in this model of suppression, overshadowing the historical narrative, including the Holocaust. Following the spectacular military success of 1948, a new identity of the strong and triumphant Israeli emerged. The Israeli-born at once claimed a mental and physical distance between themselves and the survivors, whom they denounced as embodying all those shameful qualities that their new nation must eschew. Appositely, Yigal Schwartz points out that the Holocaust's "theatre of shadows" clashed with the image of the young, confident Israel.[11] The survivors, in turn, longing to fit into their new home (which they viewed as the culmination of a journey from destruction to redemption) embraced new identities congruent with immigrants searching for a pathway forward. The evolving Israeli nation was so fixed on coming to grips with colossal nation-building challenges that it

---

10 Fox, 1998, p. 25.
11 Schwartz, 2005, p. 225.

had little time to attend to the needs of individual survivors and instead relegated memorialisation to official state ceremonies. It is thus not surprising that in this context, healing took a backseat.

In the first decade of statehood, Israeli society at large was enveloped by a national chronicle of the Holocaust in which personal accounts of survivors were sidelined. Through its Holocaust and Heroism Memory Law, the government generated an institutionalised position in memorialising the Shoah. Holocaust and Heroism Memorial Day, designed to commemorate the annihilation of the six million Jews in Europe, had, as its explicit goal, bracketing the Holocaust with other episodes in modern Jewish history, in particular the 1948 War of Independence.[12] It was held a week earlier than Israeli Memorial Day – dedicated to Israel's fallen soldiers – and Independence Day. The Holocaust thus came to be seen as the catastrophe that gave rise to the birth of the Jewish homeland. Put differently, the founding of Israel was framed as a redemptive act symbolising the journey from destruction to redemption. In addition, since Holocaust and Heroism Memorial Day was unequivocally identified with the anniversary of the Warsaw Ghetto Uprising in 1943, most associated that commemorative occasion with heroism. Yet, for a majority of survivors, the Warsaw Ghetto Uprising and its analogous symbolism was an event in which they had taken no part.

Here, the concept of "statism" or "Mamlakhtiyut", as instituted by Israel's first Prime Minister, David Ben-Gurion, is crucial. In the 1950s, "statism" strove to anchor a monochromatic and blinkered perception of the Holocaust in the Israeli consciousness. This crippling ideology sought to diminish and devalue Jewish life in the diaspora and chose in its place symbols and myths from the earlier periods of Jewish history,

---

12 Handelman and Katz, 1995, p. 75, p. 83.

particularly from the time of the Temple. In this statist concept, the Holocaust was the:

> ... most salient and deplorable symbol of the Jewish plight in the Diaspora ... thus, the memory of the Holocaust was greatly muted during the 1950s. The architects of Mamlakhtiyut sought to cultivate and emphasise the memory not of defeats – even glorious ones – but of victories, in accordance with the prevailing ethos of the new state.[13]

A manifestation of this doctrine can be seen in the founding of Yad Vashem (Israel's official Holocaust Martyrs' and Heroes' Remembrance Authority and Museum) by Israel's parliament in 1953. In various ways, this governmental body encased mixed messages. It central purpose was to honour and memorialise the incredible courage of European Jewry. By stressing the element of valour, Yad Vashem moulded Israeli attitudes towards the Shoah and its remnant. At the same time, this stance impaired genuine identification and comprehension of the world of the diaspora Jew, for whom survival of the Nazi onslaught and imprisonment in the extermination camps was as much an act of heroism as was armed resistance. For that reason, the vast majority of European Jews who were either murdered in Nazi-occupied Europe or survived and emigrated to Israel, were tagged as passive weaklings who submissively allowed their Nazi persecutors to lead them to their death. In these early years, victims of the Nazis were called "sheep to the slaughter", implying that they had a choice, and that this choice was one of revolt and heroism; the phrase was not meant as a description of their situation, but as a harsh judgment on the victims and survivors, who were constantly asked: "Why didn't you fight"? Children of survivors thus had to deal with their parents' wartime experience and

---

13 Weitz, 1995, p. 143.

its effects on their home life, as well as with the surrounding society's ignorance. Year after year, they were exposed to a Holocaust education that had little to do with what they heard from their own parents.[14]

In the 1950s, common attitudes held that survivors could adjust if only they kept their tortured memories in check. A recurring element in post-Holocaust families was the parents' incapacity to mourn for those they had lost, a catharsis that would have allowed for some relief. Consequently, the survivors elected to remain silent, and a candid conversation with the Israeli nation was rendered impossible. Further, the survivors justifiably believed that the inferno they had endured and the sorrow they felt were far too intimate to disclose, especially in light of the antipathy of other Israelis. Finally, not wanting to remain perennial outsiders, the survivors sought to integrate into Israeli society through a life of lacerating denial and stillness. In the words of Holocaust survivor and author Aharon Appelfeld:

> So we learned silence. It was not easy to keep silent. But it was a good way out for all of us. For what, when all is said and done, was there to tell . . . there was a desire to forget, to bury the bitter memories deep in the bedrock of the soul, in a place where no stranger's eyes, not even our own, could get to them . . .[15]

In her groundbreaking book *Nos'ei Hachotam*, Dina Wardi (one of the first Israeli psychotherapists to utilise group therapy in treating the post-war generation) coined the term "Carriers of the Mark" (in English the term was rendered as "Memorial Candles") to explain the roles which Holocaust survivors demanded of their children.[16] The Holocaust,

---

14 Fox, 1998, p. 25.
15 Appelfeld, 1994, pp. 150-).
16 The direct translation is "Carriers/Bearers of the Mark". When Wardi's book was published in English this designation was translated as *Memorial Candles*.

in Wardi's view, imprinted its own stamp on the second generation, unloading its victims' burden onto the shoulders of children and in doing so creating guilt, excessive anxiety, fear of separation and a lack of independence. Not infrequently, those children displayed symptoms directly paralleling their parents' pathology. Additionally, the children of Holocaust survivors were expected to bring light and meaning into the darkness enveloping their parent's existence. As Wardi observes:

> These little children were given the role of lifesavers for the confused soul of their parents. But the parents saw the children not only as lifesavers, but also as new content for their lives . . . one must stress the intensity of the survivor parents' expectation from their children – that they would infuse content into their empty lives and serve as compensation and a substitute for their relatives who had perished, their communities that had been wiped out and even for their own previous lives. For if they could not consider their new children a continuation of the loved ones they had lost, all their suffering and their efforts to survive would have seemed to them a worthless exercise . . . they were not perceived as separate individuals but as symbols of everything the parents had lost in the course of their lives.[17]

In seeing the children as offshoots, parents fulfilled a basic need for identity. The Memorial Candles, to borrow Wardi's appellation, carried the inescapable and unbearable burden of mending the severed link in the chain between their parents and their deceased families. Understandably, when the children of the survivors wrote about their experiences, they concentrated on:

> Areas that a young Israeli writer can approach directly and faithfully on the basis of his authentic life experience. Fiction

---

17 Wardi, 1992, p. 27.

of this kind, generally realistic, asks relatively modest questions such as: how are echoes of the Holocaust audible in Israeli life today, especially in the lives of young people? Do the children of survivors undergo some special experience different from their peers? What does the survivor generation look like to its children?[18]

In examining Israeli society's response to the trauma of the Holocaust, the model that Eric Santner has titled "narrative fetishism" is instructive.[19] Santner differentiates between "narrative fetishism" and Freud's "work of mourning". Both are story-telling stratagems whose key objective is to deal with a past which, because of its very nature, resists and repudiates any bid for effacement. By contrast, in Freud's "work of mourning", the experiential damage and trauma are integrated and transmitted through ongoing remembrance, metaphorically and dialogically. Hence, the Holocaust is acknowledged and admitted into the cultural timber without masking its echoes and imprint, sharply diverging from "narrative fetishism", the typical thread of the early Zionist quilt, which was a strategy of:

> Undoing, in fantasy, the need for mourning by simulating a condition of intactness, typically by situating the site and origin of loss everywhere . . . it releases one from the burden of having to reconstitute one's self-identity under "posttraumatic condition" . . . the post is indefinitely postponed."[20]

Obviously enough, narrative fetishism as a process of repair and emotional healing, is fraught with problems and dilemmas. For rather than affording the individual with the space for the recuperation and working through the piercing misery, it provides them with a misplaced

---

18 Holtzman, 1992, pp. 24-5.
19 Santner, 1992, pp. 143-54.
20 Ibid., p. 144.

sense of comfort that conveys the message that there never was a cause for anxiety. And because traumatic anxiety is unrecovered and not mourned, communal identity is therefore neither revitalised nor regenerated. The past continues to overhang the suffering self so that only by re-telling the story and transferring it to the second generation, can "working through the trauma" be actualised. According to Santner, a restorative pathway for post-Holocaust societies lies in "radical rethinking and reformulation of the very notions and boundaries and borderlines … to shift one's theoretical, ethical and political attention to the psychic and social sites".[21]

The eventual shift in attitudes in Israel is directly related to the 1961 Eichmann trial. During the trial, survivors were afforded the opportunity to testify about their personal inferno, and to demonstrate "that Holocaust victims and survivors were part of the Israeli experience and had as much literary (and social) legitimation as the new 'Hebrews' ".[22] The Holocaust stereotype that had eclipsed public understanding in the previous decade was fractured, as scores of young Israelis (including of course children of survivors) watched one witness after another tell an individual story on the stand, in the Israeli court, in Jerusalem. Notably, the Holocaust was transformed, albeit momentarily, from a national calamity to a personal trauma, endowing the tales of horror with individual faces and spurring a wave of Holocaust scholarship. Contempt for the European past gave way to unshakeable respect for the victims so that reconciliation between survivors and Israeli society was reached, at least partially, by the 1980s.[23]

Immediately after the Eichmann trial, Israeli poet and author Haim Gouri, who had covered the event as a reporter for the newspaper

---

21 Santner, 1992, pp. 152-3.
22 Shaked, 2006, p. 44.
23 Porat, 1998, pp. 785-98.

Lamerchav, epitomised the transformation felt by many Israelis.[24] Gouri's riveting account of the testimonies and trial entailed a personal transformation for the journalist, who, in the following passage, acknowledges the attitudinal shift toward the catastrophe and its victims which he and his fellow countrymen experienced:

> If a new leaf has been turned over, it is inside us. We now
> see things differently. We have set aside a Memorial Day for
> the Holocaust and Heroism, and in doing so we have drawn
> a subtle distinction between the two, as if we had juxtaposed
> them as complementary but different. The Holocaust was a
> source of shame for us, like some awful blemish, visible to
> all. But the heroism we embraced as a shred of pride, has
> given us the right to hold our heads high . . . but we must
> ask the forgiveness of the multitudes whom we have judged
> in our hearts, we who were outside the circle. And we often
> judged them without asking ourselves what right we had to
> do so.[25]

This end to silence depended on a number of additional elements. One was the overcoming by the survivors of the guilt and shame they felt for staying alive. The second was their willingness to talk to others about the cruelty they endured. Both owe much to the coming of age of the survivors' children.

Following an extended spell of silence, coming to terms with the Shoah reached its highest point in the 1980s, in what has been termed "a period of obsession".[26] This impassioned engagement makes closure now impossible, as Israeli historians and artists plainly declaim that

---

24 The book appeared in English as *Facing the Glass Booth: The Jerusalem Trial of Adolf Eichmann*, Detroit. Wayne State University, 2004. The translations in this essay are taken from the English-language edition.

25 Gouri, 2004, p. 274.

26 Hartman, 1996, p. 29.

memory and its preservation should be at the forefront of Israeli culture. In the 1980s and 1990s a poetical direction known as "bearing witness" fiction conspicuously and visibly surfaced. A cadre of second-generation writers appeared. Born after the war, they overcame the dual moral obstacles of describing a reality that they did not directly experience, and making art of a subject that still defies human comprehension. Moreover, the much derided portrait of the diaspora, as the locus of oppression, persecution, and passivity was now accommodated and incorporated into the arena of Israeli consciousness so as to become a vital part of the country's persona. Indeed, it was in the 1980s that "bearing witness" literature flowered into a fully-fledged literary genre. As Gerald Jacobs notes:

> With distance – and doubtless imitations – has come the ability to confront at last the ugly, cruel and contagious abandonment of morality that erupted in the middle of the century and of a civilisation emblematic of human progress with distance too, has come a willingness to engage the creative imagination with that same period of history in order to search for meaning, warning or consolation.[27]

Crucially, Holocaust literature undermines and dismantles assumptions about post-Shoah identity. Above all, these texts serve as testament to the fact that within the domain of Jewish culture, representations of the Holocaust have now transcended generational, tribal or national limitations. In the main, one of the chief tasks of second-generation fiction is to inscribe, externalise and incorporate the Holocaust back into the shared national identity by providing the uninitiated reader with a textual space to enter, both emotionally and intellectually, into this horrific realm, from which they were psychologically removed

---

27 Jacobs, 1998, p. 67.

by the incapacitating impact of suppression. One may suggest that the second-generation writers understand, as did Dominick LaCapra that:

> The Shoah calls for a response that does not deny its traumatic nature or cover it over through a "fetishistic" or redemptive narrative that makes believe it did not occur or compensates too readily for it . . . what is necessary is a discourse of trauma that itself undergoes – and indicates that one undergoes – a process of at least muted trauma insofar as one has tried to understand events and empathise with victims.[28]

Moreover, "bearing witness" writing tackles the dark, counterfactual question that constantly overhangs the second generation: "If I would have been there, what would I have done?" Indeed, Aharon Megged, himself a Holocaust novelist, finds the staggering fixation with the Holocaust since the 1980s to be an "unpredicted phenomenon".[29] It is little wonder then that the psychological legacy is a cardinal preoccupation of Israeli novelists. In coming to grips with the hurt of the past and, refusing to partake in the process of collective repression, this generation reminds Israeli society of the function of memory. As Alice L. Eckardt puts it, "memory and knowledge of the awful, the terrifying, or the shameful, can be a positive force in redeeming the future, even if the past can never be redeemed".[30]

Over time, the fictions of the imaginative writer have taken centre stage in Holocaust discourse. Undoubtedly, Ideology has seceded authority to Literature. It is the "novelist's crucible" that is shaping future Holocaust images rather than the "historian's anvil".[31] Gabriel

---

28 Lacapra, 1994, pp. 220-1.
29 Megged, 1988, p. 97.
30 Eckardt, 1993, p. 3.
31 Yerushalmi, 1989, p. 98. For some new perspectives on the ethics of imagining the Holocaust, see Schwartz, 1999.

Josipovici concurs with this assessment: "Historians are becoming more and more aware of this and recognise that writers of fiction have an important role to play here, giving voice to the partial and uncertain".[32] Likewise, Geoffrey Hartman has argued that aggregated Jewish memory of the Holocaust is in decline and that a breach between history and narrative has occurred. Hartman feels that novels, quietly obeying their own logic, and unrestrained by the boundaries of ritual and practice, are able to penetrate surface attitudes and investigate our deepest truths, sometimes hidden by the historicity of the past. Hartman writes: "We have learned that stories cannot be abbreviated by an intellectual method, or foreclosed by spiritual hindsight".[33]

For some, like author Norma Rosen, post-Holocaust fiction is a "call to the imagination of a people to repair the work of reality – to recreate a destroyed world by infusing meaning into the very events that destroyed it – what else could be more moving?"[34] Rosen maintains that the creative power of stories written by those she terms "witnesses through the imagination" provides the keys of awakening and experiencing for those unaffected by the trauma. Rosen cautions against turning away from engagement with the Holocaust and asks that writers and readers alike, open a space in their consciousness to the "second life" that stirs in our soul when we encounter the intense images of that event.

No doubt, novels and short stories can grant an open space for independent and meaningful rumination about the Nazi nightmare in a way that history books cannot. "While over the last few years the Shoah seems more present than before in Israel and wider Jewish conscious-ness", wrote Saul Friedlander of the mood in the 1980s, "its interpreta-

---

32 Josipovici, 1998, p. 12.
33 Hartman, 1996, p. 29.
34 Rosen, 1992, p. 47.

tion is increasingly multifaceted and lacking in consensus interpretation
. . . a long-term trend seems to subvert the early ideological stances . . .
this non-integration of the Shoah at the level of collective consciousness appears as a new phenomenon within Jewish tradition".[35]

Inevitably, we are compelled to ask: How does one write after
Auschwitz? How do those who mercifully were spared the catastrophe
imaginatively fill in the blanks? And how do they translate the trauma that
has been transmitted with empathy and affinity? The backward glance
over the shadow of the past that characterises the new Israeli culture
and fiction, embodies the principal motif of mourning, of working
through the inherited pain and trauma. According to Friedlander,
"the voices of the second generation are as powerful as the best work
produced by contemporaries of the Nazi epoch".[36] As a matter of fact,
in his examination of narrative perspectives in Holocaust literature,
Leon Yudkin refuses to endow any particular genre with a unique or
overriding legitimacy. Indeed, Yudkin forcefully states that, "Holocaust
literature is no less legitimate for not being written by those directly
affected".[37]

The post-Holocaust writer seeks to portray the various states of
minds of the children of the survivors, burdened by a collective and
personal memory. They weave into their stories a tone of frustration
that is compounded by the desire to know the unknowable, to actualise
through their imagination what is lacking, casting a searching eye in
the midst of the storm of their family and national silence. For the
second generation, penning their family's past becomes a psychological
archaeology, excavating slowly through the layers of events they cannot
comprehend in the hope that they can etch the victim's agony into the

---

35 Friedlander, 1992, p. 255.
36 Ibid., p. 263.
37 Yudkin. 1993, p. 21.

world of today. We are reminded that contemporary post-Holocaust authors are confronting a nightmare that more than sixty years later stubbornly refuses to disappear. The main point, the second generation declares, is that silence is not the only response to the Holocaust, or that to write poetry after Auschwitz is not barbaric as Adorno's dictum suggested.[38]

The post-war generation may have to ultimately admit that the Holocaust lies within a terrain that it can never traverse or fathom. Yet, as Langer contends, the young writers of today, setting out to bring their unique imaginations of Holocaust miseries to light, need to reject, not adopt, the techniques and approaches of their progenitors.[39] In a similar vein, Yael Feldman avers that in the transmission of memory from one generation to the next, the authors of the second generation reject:

> The collective model of representation that they inherited from their parents and cultural mentors . . . contemporary writers seek a subjective encounter with the experiences that the ideology of this model suppressed. That they thereby undermine the historical closure assumed by that model is only too obvious.[40]

Quite clearly, when literature intersects with genocide, a writer must inexorably confront the perils of their undertaking. Such challenges plague any author seeking the most fitting architecture of language and narrative. In his book *The Imaginary Jew*, Alain Finkielkraut examines the predicament in which he, along with the post-war generation, find themselves. Employing the metaphor of one glancing at a screen of the past but powerless to act, Finkielkraut speaks of his own struggles:

---

38 Adorno, 1974, p. 422.
39 Langer, 1998, p. 65.
40 Feldman, 1992, p. 238.

> This murdered world moves me, haunts me, precisely because
> I am completely excluded from it. Instead of examining the
> past for images of myself, I search for what I am not, what
> is now impossible for me to be. Far from ending my exile,
> memory makes it deeper by making it more concretely felt.[41]

Yet, despite these inherent difficulties, fictional writings about the Holocaust have brought about significant constructive and positive transformations:

> Instead of the shame, the repression, the reservations, a much
> better understanding of the parents' generation has developed,
> as well as an ability to identify with them . . . the stories have
> brought about not only an opening of a real dialogue with the
> parents' generation and the past, with the "there" and "then",
> but chiefly with ourselves. Through the works of the second
> generation, the terms "Jew" and "Israeli" assume their deep
> and profound meaning among the generation as a whole. The
> isolated personal memory of the past becomes a collective
> one, part of a combined Israeli and Jewish identity.[42]

The heirs to the heritage of Holocaust imagery feel they have an obligation, as part of the chain of transmission, to testify to what took place through their works. In doing so, they help readers admit and integrate the Shoah's category-rupturing facts into their consciousness. Further, postmodernism proffers the children of survivors and authors with an effective and liberating index of literary tools to aid in this retrieving of suppressed memory. Writers often rummage the artistic paintbox to uncover the most fitting approaches that will enable them to safeguard the memory of the Shoah by crafting the victim's individual tale into a narrative. They painfully accept their post as emissaries,

---

41 Finkielkraut, 1994, p. 39.
42 Govrin, 1985, pp. 9-10.

transmitting the cicatrices of the tortuous past to those removed from the realm of "then". In the process, Israeli authors also empower those who feel incapable of identifying or empathising with their forebears when the memory of the horror reaches its crescendo.

Over the last 30 years, Israeli society has undermined and deconstructed predominant national assumptions about post-Shoah identity. Saul Friedlander rightly avers that in the 1980s, the Holocaust has " . . . come back into Israeli consciousness in the most vivid way . . . there are today more books in Israel about the Shoah than about probably any event in Israel's history".[43] Hence, Israeli cultural works question the adequacy of the official and sacrosanct frameworks produced by the state to portray the Holocaust. Moreover, they offer alternate ways to depict the legacy of the Holocaust. One now finds a gritty spirit of rebellion against the statist appropriation of the Shoah and a vigorous desire to de-nationalise the Holocaust narrative so as to reclaim its personal and intimate dimension. In other words, what is at play here is an effort to privatise the traumatic memories of individuals that had been collectivised by the state. Ideology has indeed ceded authority to Literature. If before, the state was the repository of collective memory, enlisting its institutions in service of a mono-ideology that dictated the terms for local memory of a specific experience, the Holocaust, this oppressive coherence no longer exists. The notion of a totalising version of the Holocaust has today been completely dismantled.

---

43 Friedlander, 1988, p. 288.

References

Adorno, Theodor W. (1974) "Engagement". In *Gesammelte Schriften*. Frankfurt A. M.: Suhrkamp.

Alter, R. (ed) (1975) *Modern Hebrew Literature*. New York: Behrman House.

Appelfeld, Aaron. (1994) "The Awakening". In Hartman, Geoffrey H. (ed) *Holocaust Remembrance: The Shapes of Memory*. Cambridge: Blackwell.

Bergman, Martin S. and Jucovy, Milton S. (eds). (1982) *Generations of the Holocaust*. New York: Basic Books.

Brenner, Rachel Feldhay. (2012) "Discourses in Mourning and Rebirth in Post-Holocaust Israeli Literature: Leah Goldberg's *Lady of the Castle* and Shulamith Hareven's 'The Witness' ". *Women in Judaism*. Spring: 1-12.

Des Pres, Terence. (1980) "The Dreaming Back". *Centrepoint: A Journal of Interdisciplinary Studies* (City University of New York Graduate Center). 4(1): 13-14, 17.

Devoken, Ezrahi, Sidra. (1980) *By Words Alone: The Holocaust in Literature*. Chicago: University of Chicago Press.

Eckardt, Alice L. (1993) *Burning Memory: Time of Testing and Reckoning*. New York: Pergamon.

Feldman, Yael S. (1992) "Whose Story Is It, Anyway? Ideology and Psychology in the Representation of the Shoah in Israeli Literature". In Friedlander, Saul (ed). *Probing the Limits of Representation: Nazism and the "Final Solution"*. Cambridge: Harvard University Press. 1992: 223-39.

Fox, Tamar. (1998) "Stories from the Second Generation: An Interview with Savyon Liebrecht". *Jewish Quarterly*. 45(2) Summer: 45(2-170): 25-8.

Finkielkraut, Alain. (1994) *The Imaginary Jew*. London: University of Nebraska Press.

Friedlander, Saul. (1992) *Probing the Limits of Representation: Nazism and the "Final Solution".* Cambridge: Harvard University Press.

_____. (1988) "Roundtable discussion" in Lang, Beril. (ed). *Writing and the Holocaust.* New York: Holmes and Meier.

Govrin, Nurit. (1985) "Kafo Alay Chaim Shel Acheret," in Semel, Navel. *Kova Zehuhit.* Tel Aviv: Sifriyat Hapoalim.

Hartman, Geoffrey. (1996) *The Longest Shadow: In the Aftermath of the Holocaust.* Bloomington: Indiana University Press.

Hass, Aaron. (1995) *The Aftermath: Living with the Holocaust.* Cambridge: Cambridge University Press.

Hendelman, Dov and Katz, Elihu. (1995) "State Ceremonies of Israel: Remembrance Day and Independence Day". In Shlomo Deshen, Charles S. Liebman and Moshe, Shokeid. (eds). *Israeli Judaism.* New Jersey: New Brunswick.

Holtzman, Avner.(1992) "The Holocaust in Hebrew Literature: Trends in Israeli Fiction in the 1980's". *Modern Hebrew Literature.* 8-9. Spring/ Fall: 23-8.

Jacobs, Gerald. (1998) "The Jewish Literary Quarterly Awards". *Jewish Quarterly.* 45(1) Summer: 66-7.

Josipovici, Gabriel.(1998) "Writing the Unwritable: A Debate on Holocaust Fiction". *Jewish Chronicle.* 45(2-170) Summer: 4, 12-5.

Karpf, Ann. (1996) *The war after: Living with the Holocaust.* London: Heinemann.

LaCapra, Dominic. (1994) *Representing the Holocaust.* Ithaca: Cornell University Press.

Langer, Lawrence L. (1998) *Preempting the Holocaust.* New Haven: Yale University Press.

Megged, Aharon. (1985) "I Was Not There". In Cohen, Asher, Gelber, Yoav and Wardi, Charlotte. (eds). *Comprehending the Holocaust: Historical and Literary Research.* Frankfurt and New York: Peter Lang: 98-106.

Porat, Dina. (1991) "Attitudes of the Young State of Israel toward the Holocaust and Its Survivors: A Debate Over Identity and Values". In Silberstein, Laurence J. (ed). *New Perspectives on Israeli History: The Early Years of the State*. New York and London: New York University Press.

Ramras-Rauch, Charlotte, Michman-Melkman, Gila and Joseph. (eds). (1985) *Facing the Holocaust: Selected Israeli Fiction*. Philadelphia: The Jewish Publication Society: 3-18.

Rosen, Norma. (1992) *Accidents of Influence*. Albany: State University of New York Press.

Santner, Eric. (1992) "History beyond the Pleasure Principle: Some Thoughts on the Representation of Trauma" in Friedlander Saul. (ed). *Probing the Limits of Representation: Nazism and the "Final Solution"*. Cambridge: Harvard University Press.

Schwartz, Yigal. (1993) *Ma Sheroim Mikan: Sugiyot Ba-historiographia shel Ha-sifrut Ha'ivrit Ha'hadasha Or Yehuda: Zmora Bitan, Dvir.Shaked, Gershon*. Tel Aviv: Keter.

Wardi, Dina. (1992) *Memorial Candles*. London and New York: Routledge.

Weitz, Yechiam. (1995) "Political Dimension of Holocaust Memory in Israel During the 1950's". *Israel Affairs*. 1(3) Spring: 129-45.

Yablonka, Hanna. (1998) "The Formation of Holocaust Consciousness in the State of Israel: The Early Days". In Efraim Sicher. (ed). *Breaking Crystal: writing and Memory After Auschwitz*. Urbana: University of Illinois.

Yerushalmi, Haim Yosef. (1998) *Zakhor: Jewish History and Jewish Memory*. Seattle: University of Washington Press.

Yudkin, Leon. (1996) *A Home Within: Varieties of Jewish Expressions in Modern Fiction*. Middlesex: Symposium Press.

3

Irene Bouzo

Adaptation after displacement:
A case study of the Temple Society Australia

Adaption after displacement involves a lot more than finding
employment and a place to live.[1] For all immigrants there are
the rich narratives of how specific ethnic groups of immigrants
and their offspring adjusted, the decisions they made and how their
identities were transformed. The extent to which public policies
around migration and diversity impacted on immigrant communities
from the 1950s onwards has been too often forgotten. German-
speaking Templers, many displaced and non-repatriable, arrived
in Australia from the 1940s to the 1960s. This study includes their
locally born partners and children, and shows that immigrants do
not simply arrive in a new place, get jobs, find houses and send their
children to school. Rather it demonstrates that they go through a far
more complex process, incorporating nine ways of thinking about
settlement adaptation.

This chapter explores the rich community languages resources and
multiple identities of an immigrant community that has shaped, and
been shaped by Australian institutions for over 60 years. Ordinary

---

1 Bouma, et. al 1996; Bouzo, 2008.

Templers, otherwise known as members of the Temple Society
Australia, tell the extraordinary stories of how they adjusted after
displacement, the cultural and linguistic choices that impacted on
their community building, and how they developed an intercultural
sense of belonging whilst forming transnational identities.

Studies about the long-term impact of diversity and migration
polices have been largely neglected in Australia.[2] This case study
of the Templers in Melbourne is located in the post-war era when
Australia accepted over a quarter of a million refugees and Displaced
Persons mainly from Central and Eastern Europe.[3] It challenges the
assumption that the first large-scale groups of established European
immigrants in Australia, such as the Templers, during the mid-20th
century, assimilated automatically. Their settlement struggles have
been forgotten.[4] Their triumphs and tragedies, their shattered hopes
and dreams in a country that was unprepared for such large numbers
of non-English speaking people are no longer fully understood.
Markus and Clyne point out that those immigrants successfully
built up ethno-specific community centres, clubs, religious centres,
community languages schools and aged-care facilities with tenacity
and drive. Many saw opportunities in the market and used their
overseas experience to open spectacularly successful businesses.
I explore one group's everyday attitudes and settlement decisions
concerning adaptation.

The first Templers, a group of 665 civilians, came to Australia
involuntarily in 1941 via deportation from British Palestine to a
family internment camp in Tatura in central Victoria.[5] After the war,

---

2 Jupp and Clyne, 2011.
3 Jupp, 2002; Clyne, 1991, 2003.
4 Murphy and Smart, 1997.
5 Ruff and Beilharz in Jupp 2001; Kaplan in Ibid; Clyne, 2003; Hope, 2004; Glenk, 2005.

Migration and belonging in an unpredictable era 65

they remained in Australia to be joined in the 1950s and 1960s, by other Templers who had been scattered throughout the world due to wartime displacement. The Templers are best described as "accidental immigrants" a term first used to describe people who were forced into geographic displacement or involuntary migration, such as civilian internees in Canada.[6] As a study group, they represented a microcosm of many other migration and refugee groups in Victoria since they were a faith-based group from a culturally and linguistically diverse background with a preference for living in communities. Australian research on the Templers is fragmented. The majority of Templers in Australia were never officially recognised as refugees, exiles, Displaced Persons or even migrants. They have been studied sporadically within the broader context of the diversity of German-speakers and immigrant settlement in Australia.[7] In socio-linguistic studies they are characterised by their close-knit social networks, closed culture and remarkable German-language retention.[8]

The Temple Society Australia was officially founded in Melbourne as an independent religious community in 1950 and as an autonomous regional branch of the Temple Society that includes the "Templegesellschaft" in Stuttgart, Germany.[9] The unique background of the Templers is described in Sauer's comprehensive historical study. Founded at Kirschenhardthof in southern Germany in 1861, the Temple Society is a faith community that arose out of the 19th century pietism and was later excommunicated from the Lutheran Church in the State of Württemberg, Germany for its theological differences.[10] The group was seeking to practice Christianity without

6 Farges, 2004, p. 2; Draper, 1978; Knowles, 2000.
7 Clyne,1991, 2001, 2003, 2005; Christa, 1995; Seitz and Foster, 1988; Jupp, 2001, 2003.
8 Kaplan in Jupp, 2001; Clyne, 1991, 2003; Ruff and Beilharz in Jupp, 2001.
9 Sauer, 1991.
10 Ibid.

an institutionalised priesthood. Following religious persecution, the Templers migrated from Germany during the mid-to-late 19th century, to establish pioneer settlements throughout Turkish Ottoman Palestine, later to become the British Mandate of Palestine. They were joined there by other traumatised German-speaking Templers from Mennonite settlements in Russia, and were subsequently deported twice by the British during the two world wars to Egypt and Australia respectively. Following the outbreak of World War II, they were deported to camps in Cyprus, East Africa, Australia and some were subsequently trapped in war-torn Germany.[11]

After their release from internment in Australia, the Templers were devastated by the British-Palestine Custodian's prohibition of their return to their pre-war Middle Eastern settlements. They were further incensed by unreasonable offers of repatriation to a ravaged Germany, where many Templers had never lived, and by offers to settle in Kenya.[12] In the late 1940s Arthur Calwell, the Australian Minister for Immigration, and his successor Harold Holt, both supporters of German immigration, became strong advocates for Templer settlement in Australia and opposed their post-internment and overseas repatriation.[13] Calwell succeeded in creating a parliamentary statutory bill, the "Temple Society Trust Fund Act 1949". This allowed for the transnational transfer to Australia, of the Templer compensation payments for their extensive confiscated properties in pre-war Palestine. In addition Calwell exonerated the Templers from any wartime stigma. He gave Judge Hutchins of the Supreme Court Tasmania the task of political examination of the Templers and so further smoothed their entry into Australia.[14]

---

11 Sauer, 1991; Glenk, 2005; Ruff and Beilharz in Jupp, 2001; Christa in Jürgensen, 1995.
12 Sauer, 1991.
13 Calwell, 1949; Gohl, 1991; Sauer, 1991.
14 Christa in Jürgensen, 1995; Gohl, 1991; Sauer, 1991.

For many decades in Australia the Templers had a strong desire to keep their cultural traditions so that during the assimilation era, when being different was frowned upon, an outsider observed of the Templers, that ". . . [so] quietly have these believers been absorbed into Australian life while still retaining intact their religious identity that it is fair to say that their origins are unknown to most of their fellow Australians".[15]

Adaptation is never finished

Immigration is never easy. Most immigrants arriving in a new country try to adapt. They go through an arduous, but natural, transformation process, one that is never finished.[16] Immigrant adaptation involves coping behaviour, often fraught with subsequent dilemmas. The definition of adaptation provided by Eckermann is deemed the most suitable application in this study of Templer settlement in Australia where a focus is on a "cultural ecology", whereby people constantly make choices and daily decisions in order to cope.[17] Eckermann further notes that the more rapidly socio-cultural or economic-political change occurs, the more it tends to be imposed from the outside. One example of such top-down control is the assimilation policy in Australia in the 1950s and 1960s that pressured immigrants to forget their language and culture and fit in as quickly as possible.[18]

The social and economic hardships that Templers suffered after internment, in the early decades of their settlement in Australia, ranged from xenophobic hostilities to enforced agricultural job placement

---

15 Van Sommers, 1966, pp. 228-9.
16 Eckermann,1994, Kuzmickaite, 2000, Markus, 2001.
17 Eckermann, 1994, p. 23.
18 Castles et. al., 1992.

in remote areas.[19] Despite these restrictions they took up whatever jobs they could find with the enthusiasm of a group suddenly freed from internment behind barbed wire.[20] Eventually, despite enormous obstacles in the 1950s and as far as constraints allowed, the Templers regrouped and established small but well-connected local community networks in the outer Melbourne suburbs of Bayswater, Boronia and Bentleigh along with smaller offshoots in Sydney and Tanunda (in South Australia). They found themselves in a climate where multiculturalism celebrated differences but where entrenched attitudes persisted. Many had already learnt to switch their cultural behaviour on and off. After 60 years the Templers are still going through their adaptation processes. Nine ways of thinking emerged from this study. They represent the complexity of the immigrant settlement and adaptation process with varied perceptions and dilemmas across three generations as Templers attempted to adjust to the new society.

The first generation of Templer immigrants who arrived as adults with an already-established life experience, were in their seventies and eighties at the time of these research interviews. They represented the pioneers. The "one-and-a-half generation" a term coined by Kandiyoti was the in-between generation represented by those who were children and teenagers on arrival and grew up both overseas and in Australia.[21] The majority of the Templers spent between five and seven years in the Tatura family internment camp. Consequently many children spent a large part of their youth in detention where they went to school, studied German, and lived in a close-knit Templer environment, as well as later living outside under assimilation pressures. They were in

---

19 Clyne, 1991; Sauer, 1991; Gohl, 1991; Beilharz, 2000.
20 Vondra, 1981; Bouzo, 2005; Beilharz, 2000.
21 Kandiyoti, 2003, p. 2.

their fifties, sixties and seventies at the time of interview. The third cohort was represented by the Australian-born Templers, the second generation under fifty years of age when interviewed.

Nine ways of thinking about adaptation

An analysis of the everyday stories told about the settlement experiences of ordinary Templers shows that they went through nine ways of thinking about immigrant adaptation. These were: assimilationist thinking, re-establishment thinking, idealised thinking, religious thinking, ethnicity thinking, bilingual thinking, diaspora thinking, transnational thinking and community-building thinking. The first adaptation strategy of the research participants was assimilationist thinking. In the 1950s and 1960s public pressure was placed on newcomers to be the same, and to assimilate as rapidly as possible. Indicators of successful assimilation were losing the immigrant language, geographic dispersal in the early years of the policy, naturalisation and invisibility.[22] Refusal to accept their qualifications generated much bitterness amongst the better educated and in some cases led to serious mental health problems.[23]

After years of internment, Templers talked about "coming out" of the camp, rather than arriving in a new country. They did not understand assimilation, tried hard to fit in, and thought this meant being accepted. They became naturalised for pragmatic reasons not civic loyalty, afraid to appear ungrateful at work and school if they rejected the Australian way of life. Despite feeling assimilated, many preferred to conduct their case study interviews in German. One person commented: "Jetzt sind wir assimiliert. Jetzt sind wir

22 Galligan and Roberts, 2003; Castles et. al. 1992, 2002; Kaplan in Jupp, 2001; Clyne, 2003.
23 Kunz, 1988; Birrell, 2001; Bouzo, 2005.

akzeptiert, aber immer noch, die wissen das . . . wo wir herkommen, ja". ("Now we are assimilated. Now we are accepted, but still, they know where we come from"); [CASE047].

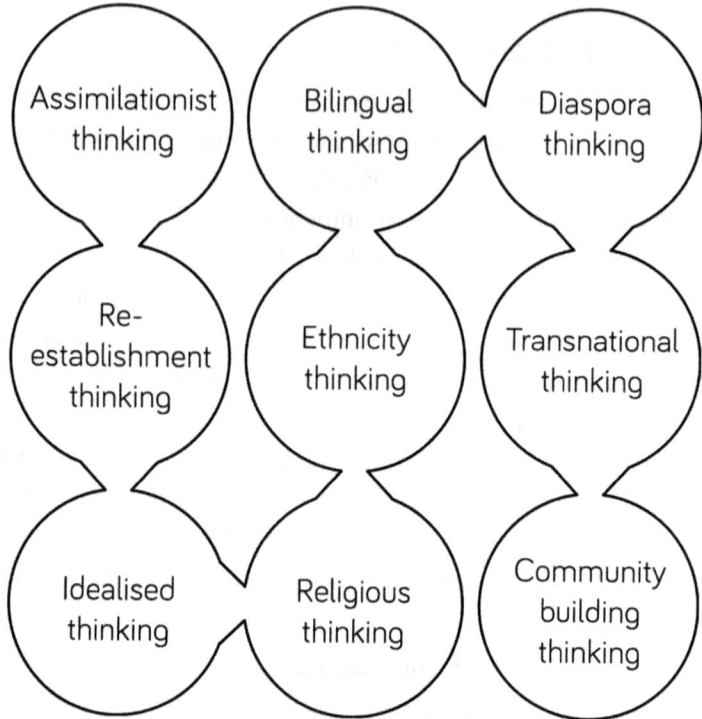

Figure 1. The nine ways of thinking about adaptation

The older, first generation of immigrants born overseas could not give up their language and ethnicity and became the "insider-lookers". The teenagers who were the "one-and-half generation" wanted to fit in and live up to expectations at school even at the expense of becoming alienated from their parents. They became the "assimilation experts". Those born in Australia became the "adapters" and learnt to move in and out of two worlds. Despite the assimilation pressures and early hardships, Templer families were determined to re-establish their community in Australia. The second insight from the stories of ordinary people is re-establishment thinking. Templer families tried hard to stick together and were determined to re-establish their religious community in Australia. They shifted closer together following the relaxation of dispersal policies.

Strong social ties and closed networks of family and friends inside their ethnic group lead to an urban village life. As a result they had weak ties with the outside world. Over time they lost the skills to open up to the outside, restricting their access to new ideas, opportunities and resources.[24] The Templers had an impressive record of community service they called "Mitmachen" (participation). They made sacrifices and built new community buildings almost entirely with volunteer labour. Even school children dug the foundations. Geographic distance was a barrier to Templer participation. One woman said, "We definitely drove around the world two or three times. We took our children to every Christmas celebration; every event. We tried so hard to bring up the children in the Temple"; [CASE046].

Whilst the Templers attempted to re-establish their community without government support, it became increasingly clear that they were not able to replicate their settlements in Palestine. For many the psychological adaptation from their pre-migration experiences was a dilemma. For older Templers pleasant, accumulated memories of the past became idealised thinking, the third adaptation process. The sudden rupture of home and host countries due to political upheavals that prohibited return to their homeland in former historical Palestine, led them to form life stories based on constant before-and-after or there-and-here thinking. Happy memories of the past became

---

24 Rose, 1999.

glorified and idealised. Their country of origin no longer existed on the world map, only in their memories.

Older Templers used the unforgettable German colonies "over there", in the Middle East, as a benchmark for setting up activities in Australia. Second-generation Templers resented this constant backwards-benchmarking as it created unrealistic pressures on community-building here. During internment people had their lives put on hold. The camps were dismantled after the war, leaving only empty paddocks as reminders. When people are denied memories of displacement experiences they lack the competence to come to terms with past-future dynamics.[25] Nostalgic memories and symbolic homecomings accumulated across generations. Children felt the intensity of their grandparents. One woman in her eighties, talked about going "home" when she revisited the internment camp decades later. Another confided, "I call the trip to Tatura a pilgrimage". Public recognition helps reconnect people with the past and ground them in the present such as the exhibition "Templers in the Holy Land – Chronicle of a Utopia" which opened in Tel Aviv in March 2006 and was visited by several Australian Templers.[26] One intention of their here-and-there thinking was to set up a faith community in Australia.

The fourth adaption insight is religious thinking. Language, ethnicity and religion are closely intertwined.[27] Keeping the faith for the Templers brought sacrifices between their core values of cultural and religious continuity. Eventually they were forced to attach less importance to language and culture and more to religious values to preserve their faith community. A first-generation woman felt her son grew away from the Temple Society because of a lack of translated

25 Hoerder, 2004.
26 Taylor, 1994; Blaich and Haering, May 2006, p. 39.
27 Ata, 1990.

resources about the Templer religion. She said, "we lost them especially where inter-faith marriages occurred". Extensive efforts by the one-and-a-half generation provided English language translation of essential religious thinking.

The fifth adaptation insight was ethnicity thinking. The Templers avoided the ethnic label and focussed on their spiritual identity. A typical comment was, "we are the Temple Society and not the German society". After all, assimilation policies pushed them to discard their cultural capital as if it was unwanted baggage. Nevertheless they said the notion of ethnicity gave immigrants a voice and allowed them to identify themselves by common factors such as their history, language, culture, nationality and religion.

It is important to note that the Templers were resented by German Nazism due to their religious ties, their focus on the Holy Land, their anti-Nazi writings and passive resistance.[28] All the same, a shadow of negative post-war stereotyping lingered over the Templers who were after all German-speakers in Australia.[29] Some preferred the hyphenated identity "Palestinian-Germans". Adaptation was a balancing act of being German at heart and at home in Australia. The Australian-born second generation expressed negative feelings about their German background especially in monolingual company. The result was a community that "kept quiet" until its ethnic vitality became invisible in the broader society.[30]

The process of cultural and linguistic identification involves continual shifting, affirming and contesting of identities as expressed through linguistic practices such as "culture-switching" or

---

28 Van Sommers, 1966.
29 Rutland, 2005.
30 Kaplan, 1996.

biculturalism; a process more difficult than code switching.[31] "Culture switch" is a process of adaptation that encompasses "the mosaic of contemporary community life" where people see themselves as part of many communities.[32] It implies making decisions about what behaviour is appropriate in different social situations. By way of comparison, Aboriginal people who experience the dilemma of multiple identities that are not acknowledged by public authorities, may try to "orbit" in and out of their different life spheres.[33] Some people adopt culture-switching as an adaptation strategy to overcome negative feelings such as self-doubt and varying behaviour expectations about their traditions and beliefs.[34]

Second-generation Australian-born Templers learnt to culture shift and orbit in and out of their different cultural domains. When multiculturalism recognised cultural diversity, the second generation began to express their ethnic identity with increasing confidence, "When I was younger I was always embarrassed. I didn't speak in public at all because we had to speak German. But now the community is far more accepting of that." [CASE018]. The greater the overlap in different social settings, the less the need to culture switch.[35] Adaptation over a period of time led Templers to develop a strong sense of belonging to their new home country. An ethnic presence however suggests a multilingual presence involving the use of community languages as well as English.[36]

The sixth adaptation strategy was bilingual thinking. Templers

---

31 Eckermann, 1994, p. 226.
32 Black and Hughes, 2001, p. 3.
33 Sutton, 2001, p. 15; Pearson, 1994.
34 Eckermann, 1994.
35 Black and Hughes, 2001, p. 4.
36 Fishman, 2001.

preferred their bilingual identity over their ethnic identity. They put enormous resources into German Saturday Schools. They did a better job than all other post-war German-speaking groups at language retention and transmission to their offspring for over 50 years.[37] Choosing English for religious activities was a difficult decision as they moved to bilingual religious services and eventually to English. The continued use of German for much of their hymn singing acted as a symbolic marker of group solidarity and a subtle form of language retention.

The Templers felt good about their century-old version of the Swabian German dialect. They practised a kind of ritualised code-switching and developed a quirky ethnolect that consisted of made-up and foreign words. Clyne pointed out that these were simultaneously indicators of in-group solidarity, bicultural identity and language maintenance, as well as language shift. At a typical Templer dinner table, family members used a form of insider-talk, skilfully code-switching between Swabian, English and Palestinian Arabic, without losing the grammatical flow and structure of their language. During the 1990s however a language shift to English rapidly gained ground amongst the second generation. The monolingual mindset of Australians set up social barriers hindering the maintenance of community languages, and undervalued the advantages of bilingualism in an increasingly multicultural and multilingual world. Increasingly young people think of themselves as "world kids" who feel they need bilingualism and intercultural skills for global participation, as evidenced by some language revival activities amongst younger Templers.[38]

The seventh way of thinking about adaptation was diaspora thinking. The term diaspora meaning dispersed person has made

---

37 Clyne, 1991, 2006, personal communication.
38 Lo Bianco, 2005, p. 3.

a dynamic comeback in debates about people's multiple sense of belonging and loyalties beyond national boundaries. Immigrants and displaced people are able to maintain a sense of ethnicity and community through transnational networks, regular communication and frequent contact without relying on returning to their distant homeland.[39] Many diaspora ethnic Germans have a multi-dimensional sense of belonging to different places due to forced migration over several centuries, experiencing dual "Heimat" loyalties.[40] A large number of diaspora communities left Swabia in the 18th and 19th centuries at a time when Germany looked a lot different to the unified country it is today, consisting of hundreds of small German states, principalities, and duchies. The Swabian Templers, not unlike many other diaspora Swabian groups in Eastern Europe and America, still identify with the 19th century local community of Swabia in Württemberg.[41]

Each migration to a new country involves a migration of identity. The Templers lived outside Germany for 150 years and those from Russia for over 200 years. As diaspora immigrants they developed multiple loyalties to many homelands and places rather than nation-states. For them belonging was about social and emotional attachments wrapped in kinship, responsibility to their community, emotional heritage ties and one's "beloved language". Grandparents encouraged their offspring to visit ancestral places they called home in different countries, such as Jerusalem, Stuttgart and Tatura. The grandparents and parents were the exile generation. The second generation had become the "new internationals". Diaspora groups such as the Templers are accustomed to living their everyday lives within a mindset of transnational belonging

39 Georgiou, 2001.
40 Wolff, 2001, p. 28; Farges 2004, p. 15; Hoerder, 2004.
41 Sauer, 1991; Medick, 1998.

across the world in terms of family relationships, social and religious affiliations, and consequently have highly developed intercultural skills.[42] The paradox of diaspora thinking is that dwelling in one place assumes a solidarity and connection in another. It is not necessarily the single place that is important but rather connections across a map of places so that diaspora becomes the historical precursor to present-day transnationalism.

The eighth adaptation insight of this study is transnational thinking defined as "a certain elasticity of belonging and identification" across countries and continents.[43] It involves constant travels to multiple homelands to support emotional, social, cultural, religious, family and financial networks that are not linked to any form of political and national infrastructures.[44] Each year individual and groups of Templers travel from Australia to Germany and Israel to meet other Templers and visit places of significance to Templers. It is "a circular mode of living".[45] It can be considered as one "single, social continuum" rather than a form of "from here and there" global movement.[46] The Templers talked about religious tourism across the oceans between Melbourne, Australia and Stuttgart, Germany with a "just around the corner" familiarity. Members of all three generations regularly attended religious events and community celebrations in the different countries supported by Temple Society–organised religious elder exchanges, youth exchange schemes and heritage study tours in collaboration with Israeli historians.

A transnational sense of belonging assisted language revival amongst the second generation.

---

42 Vertovec, 1999.
43 Kandiyoti, 2003, p. 1.
44 Sahoo, 2004.
45 Kandiyoti, 2003, p. 1.
46 Guarnizo et. al in Kandiyoti, 2003, p. 1.

Collective memory, sometimes of fractured memories, about another place and time, created new maps that became transnational heritage trails. "Back home tourism" included groups of young Templers from Germany and Australia travelling to Israel as volunteers to maintain their cemeteries in Haifa and Jerusalem and provide support for heritage museums and archives in various places across the continents.

Transnational thinking had an important impact on networking and bonding within the Templer Society through their common ancestry and in building bridges with present-day communities in their source countries. This has contributed to the Temple Society's strengths and sustainability in its community building in Victoria.

The ninth part of the journey through immigrant adaptation was community-building thinking. The Templers constantly engaged in community building activities. After decades of hard work, the Temple Society Australia established a sophisticated infrastructure of self-sufficient communities in the southern and south-eastern suburbs of Melbourne. These communities are characterised by "dense networks based on in-marriage and a strong institutional infrastructure" that includes religious centres, German community language schools, a German-speaking residential aged care facility, and other extensive social and cultural networks.[47] As the years progressed, the older people were anxious about who would take over. There was no more migration to replenish membership. Community strength depends on who will replace the pioneers of the ethnic community organisations; on keeping up high levels of connectedness; as well as challenging decisions about which aspects of language and culture will be carried on by subsequent generations.[48] Community building thinking involves

---

47 Clyne, 2003, p. 12; Uhlenbruch, 2004.
48 Jupp, 2003; Lo Bianco, 2005; De Fazio, 2005.

each generation finding meaningful connections with its roots, and establishing social networks within the immigrant community.

Assimilation had encouraged fragmentation and suppressed cultural differences. Multiculturalism celebrated diversity. It allowed immigrants' identities to emerge naturally. In the 1990s, the climate was right. Templer leaders did some innovative thinking. They engaged consultants. The community underwent a massive "infrastructure takeover and makeover". It worked and gradually the Australian-born generation became more engaged in Templer volunteering activities. Bonding and bridging, terms coined by Putnam, created meaningful and functional participation for the Australian-born members of the second generation.[49] Distant, younger members and fringe-dwellers found new opportunities to strengthen their internal bonding. The Templers then found additional resources to focus on building bridges and strengthening networking with outside groups, community organisations and local government. They kept their focus on faith and joined inter-faith groups. They partnered with Australian historical societies and developed nostalgia publishing, exhibitions and museums. They pooled resources with other ethnic communities to run aged care services and obtained government accreditation and community grants to upgrade their community languages schools and community events under the government's multicultural policies. They adapted, changed and adjusted to life in Australia and succeeded in their primary aim, to re-establish their faith community.

Positive identity formation

Identity formation is a collective and an individual matter. The in-terviewees demonstrated a complexity of multiple, collective identi-

---

49 Putnam, 2000.

ties that emerged from the nine ways of thinking about adaptation. In summary, the Templers had many complementary homelands or places-called-home. Their religious identity was the most prominent. Their diaspora and ethnicity identities were fragmented. Their bilingual identity was under-stated. Their transnational identity was subliminal even though it functioned well. The interviews demonstrated that identity formation has three characteristics. When a community cannot clearly articulate or define its identity, it risks losing its group cohesion. The group that defines its identity, but does not feel good about it, is in danger of an identity crisis. The group that lacks the ability to make a commitment to its various identities diminishes its sustainability. Positive identity formation is essential for individual wellbeing. A simple, positive identity-formation framework in three steps emerged from this study as follows. Firstly a person should be able to define their identity and say it aloud. Secondly a person needs to feel good about their identity. Thirdly they should make a commitment to their identity or multiple identities in whatever way they see fit. Immigrants who can define their identities with clarity and confidence have higher levels of well-being and personal happiness. People who feel good about their identification processes have better self-esteem and social connectedness.[50] The individual that makes a commitment and fulfils all three steps strengthens their sense of belonging.

The three generational cohorts of Templers consisted of inside-lookers, assimilation experts and adapters. Many Templers' attitudes were locked into the 1950s myth that a quiet, even invisible community was a well-assimilated group. The oldest cohort, the first generation of immigrants, represented the disoriented, suppressed

---

50 Black and Hughes, 2001; Department for Victorian Communities, State of Victoria, 2004.

newcomers who were dispersed, and worked hard to re-group and re-establish their faith community. Their sacrifices were many. They were the silent generation, who tried to live up to the assimilationist pressures not so much to fit in, but rather to gain overt acceptance in the wider society without completely discarding their language and culture. They retreated into their community for support with the hope to keep their faith alive. They were the inside-lookers. The one-and-a-half generation, whilst born and schooled overseas, had the benefit of also growing up in Australia. They mastered both their immigrant community languages of the Swabian dialect and standard German, as well as the English language. They voluntarily tried to live up to assimilationist expectations to take on the Australian way of life. Consequently they became the assimilation experts. Some made an overt demonstration to diminish their "Germanness", playing a balancing act to find a third way of remaining German in English. Many in this group had highly proficient bilingual skills and became masters of translation and nostalgia publications of Templer historical and religious literature as part of a drive to pass on the culture and faith via the English language to the next generation.

The second generation of Templer immigrants were born, grew up and went to school in Australia. Many experienced their schooling during the assimilationist years when their parents and grandparents were preoccupied with building up the Templer communities. English was their first language. Many of the older ones in the group felt uncomfortable about their German heritage and had limited motivation to maintain formal levels of advanced German language education. Some were fluent in Templer, Swabian insider talk but struggled with German proficiency when they mixed with outsiders from a German background. Others went to school during the years when cultural diversity was celebrated in Victoria and were more enthusiastic about finding more extensive German-language learning opportunities. In recent years this group demonstrated a renewed interest in their ancestral, multiple diaspora heritages. A symbolic rediscovery of their Templer identity led to a recovery from the negative effects of assimilation. In that sense the second generation represented the recovering victims of that long forgotten government policy.

They were at ease as Australians and felt comfortable orbiting in and out of Templer circles. They were the adapters, able to fit in and feel part of both communities without appearing different. Several sought out new ways of connecting as Templers and a significant number took an active role in the participation in the takeover of operational infrastructure of the Temple Society Australia with renewed enthusiasm.

Conclusion

The Templers in their journey of resettlement in Melbourne faced the challenges of dispersal and re-grouping as a community; the dilemma to be the same or different; to speak German and not want to; as well as dealing with the competing core values of religious and language continuity, and who would take over the community leadership. Adaptation does not mean the renouncing of attachments to past traditions and places. It is about the strategies that immigrants find to adjust whilst attempting to preserve some degree of attachment to their past cultural values. Nine ways of thinking about adaptation represent the complexity of the immigrant settlement process that participants face on the way as they attempt to establish themselves in their new society. Through their massive dedication, collectively and individually, the Templers never lost sight of their hopes and dreams.

Their faith community survived and flourished in Melbourne as they adapted to change. Community continuity depends on a sense of well-being and belonging and the development of a positive self-ascribed identity. The nine ways of thinking are helpful in understanding the process of adaptation that immigrants go through in a new country. Whilst they describe the adaptation story of Australian Templers as a religious ethno-linguistic group, the application of the nine adaptation strategies to other displaced and immigrant groups, such as established long-term immigrants, newer arrivals, new and emerging communities, refugees, and asylum seekers has the potential to provide valuable insights into their settlement behaviour.

References

Ata, A. W. (ed). (1990) *Religion and Ethnic Identity: an Australian Study.* Three volumes. Richmond, Victoria: Spectrum.

Birrell, Robert. (2001) "Multicultural Literature". In Jupp, James. (ed). *The Australian People: An Encyclopedia of the Nation, its People and their Origins.* Oakleigh, Vic.: Cambridge University Press: 815-8

Black, A., and Hughes, P. (2001) "What is meant by 'Community Strength?' " In Browne, C., Edwards, K., Watson, V. and van Krieken, R. (eds). *TASA (The Australian Sociological Association) Conference Proceedings.* Sydney. University of Sydney: The Australian Sociological Association.

Blaich, H., and Haering, M. (2006) "Relations Strengthened Between Israel and the Templers". *Templer Record.* 683 May: 39-40.

Bouma, G. D. (ed). (1996) *Many Religions, All Australian: Religious Settlement, Identity and Cultural Diversity.* Adelaide, SA: Department of Immigration and Multicultural Affairs, Australia.

————. (1999) *Managing Religious Diversity: From Threat to Promise.* Nunawading, Vic.: Christian Research Association.

Bouzo, Irene. (2005) *Gingerbread Men of Moorabbin: The Story of Erica Specialties 1957-1999.* Melbourne: Richter Family.

————. 2008. "The Dilemma of Adaptation and Assimilation: a Case Study of the Temple Society Australia", Doctor of Philosophy Thesis. University of New England. NSW. Australia.

Calwell, A. (1949) *Hansard, Commonwealth of Australia, Parliamentary Debate, Senate and House of Representatives – Second Session of the Eighteenth Parliament.* Fourth Session. Volume 1. 23 September. Canberra: Commonwealth of Australia.

Castles, S. (2002) "Migration and Community Formation under Conditions of Globalization". *International Migration Review,* 36(4): 1143-69.

Castles, S., Kalantzis, M., Cope, B., and Morrissey, M. (1992) *Mistaken Identity.* Sydney: Pluto Press.

Christa, C. M. (1995) "The German Templers in Australia". In Jurgensen, M. (ed). *German-Australian Cultural Relations since 1945.* Bern: Peter Lang: 130-9.

Clyne, M. (1991) *Community Languages: The Australian Experience.* Melbourne: Cambridge University Press.

————. (2001) "German Language" in Jupp, James (ed). *The Australian People: An Encyclopedia of the Nation, its People and their Origins.* Oakleigh, Vic: Cambridge: 385-7.

————. (2003) *Dynamics of Language Contact: English and Immigrant Languages.* Cambridge: Cambridge University Press.

DeFazio, T. (2005) "Culture is Cool: Developing Cultural Awareness in the Ethnic School Classroom". Doncaster, Vic.: Paper presented at the Victorian State Community Languages Schools Conference, Doncaster.

Department for Victorian Communities. (2004) *Indicators of Community Strength in Victoria, Strategic Policy and Research Division.* Melbourne: State of Victoria.

Draper, P. J. (1978) "The Accidental Immigrants: Canada and the Interned Refugees, Part I". *Canadian Jewish Historical Society Journal.* 2(1) Spring: 1-38.

Eckermann, A-K. (1994) *One Classroom, Many Cultures: Teaching Strategies for Culturally Different Children.* St Leonards, N.S.W.: Allen & Unwin.

Farges, P. (2004) " 'Which Church Do You Go To?' The Difficult Acculturation of German-Jewish Exiles in Canada, 1933-2004". Paper presented at the Assimilation, Integration, Acculturation Conference. The German-Canadian Case. Winnipeg: University of Winnipeg.

Fishman, J. (ed). (2001) *Handbook of Language and Ethnic Identity.* Oxford: Oxford University Press.

Galligan, B., and Roberts, W. (2003) "Australian Multiculturalism: Its Rise and Demise". Paper presented at the Australasian Political Studies Association, School of Government. University of Tasmania. Hobart: Australasian Political Studies Association.

Glenk, H. (2005) *From Desert Sands to Golden Oranges: The History of the German Templer Settlement of Sarona in Palestine 1871-1947.* Victoria, BC, Canada: Trafford.

Georgiou, M. (2001) "Thinking Diaspora: Why Diaspora is a Key Concept for Understanding Multicultural Europe". *The Multicultural Skyscraper Newsletter.* 1(4): 3.

Gohl, E. (1991) *The Transportation of Members of the Temple Society to Australia for Internment.* Turramurra North, NSW: C. H. Gohl.

Hoerder, D. (2004) "Local, Continental, Global Migration Contexts; Projecting Life-courses in the Frame of Family Economies and Emotional Networks". Winnipeg: Paper presented at the Assimilation, Integration, Acculturation Conference. The German-Canadian Case. University of Winnipeg.

Hope, S. (2004) "Exodus to the Holy Land". *Geographical.* 76(7) July: 63-6.

Jupp, James. (ed). (2001) *The Australian People: An Encyclopedia of the Nation, its People and their Origins.* Oakleigh, Vic.: Cambridge.

————. (2002) "The Polish Impact on Australian Society – speech delivered to the Australian-Polish Community Services". Canberra.

Jupp, J. and Clyne, M. (eds). (2001) *Multiculturalism and Integration – a Harmonious Relationship*. Canberra: ANU E-Press.

Kandiyoti, D. (2003) "Multiplicity and its Discontents". *Genders*. 37: 18.

Kaplan, G. (1996) *The Meagre Harvest. The Australian Women's Movement 1950s-1990s*. Sydney: Allen and Unwin.

Kaplan, G. (2001) "Post-war German Immigration". In Jupp, J. (ed). *The Australian People: an Encyclopedia of the Nation, its People and their Origins*. Oakleigh, Vic: Cambridge: 377-9.

Knowles, V. (2000) *Forging our Legacy: Canadian Citizenship and Immigration 1900-1977*. Canada: Public Works and Government Services Canada.

Kuzmickaite, D. (2000) "The Adaptation of Recent Lithuanian Immigrants in Chicago". *Lithuanian Quarterly Journal of Arts and Sciences*. 46(2) Summer: 6.

Lo Bianco, J. (2005) "Quality and Controversy: What Does Australian Society Want from Community Language Schools?" Doncaster, Vic.: Paper presented at the Victorian State Community Languages Schools Conference, Doncaster, Victoria.

Markus, Andrew. (ed). (2001) *Building a New Community: Immigration and the Victorian Economy*. Crows Nest NSW: Allen and Unwin.

Medick, H. (1998) "The Swabians and Modernity". *Journal of Social History*, 32(1): 196-9.

Murphy John and Smart, Judy. (eds). (1997) *The Forgotten Fifties: Aspects of Australian Society and Culture in the 1950s*. Carlton, Vic.: University of Melbourne Press.

Putnam R. D. (2000) *Bowling Alone: The Collapse and Revival of American Community*. New York: Simon and Shuster.

Rose, D., Carrasco, P., and Charboneau, J. (1999) "The Role of 'Weak Ties' in the Settlement Experiences of Immigrant Women with Young

Children: The Case of Central Americans in Montréal". http://ceris. metropolis.net/virtual%20library/ web-site.

Ruff, D., and Beilharz, R. (2001) "The Templers" in Jupp, James (ed). *The Australian People: An Encyclopedia of the Nations, its People and their Origins.* Oakleigh, Vic.: Cambridge University Press: 375-7.

Rutland, S. D. (2005) "'Buying out of the Matter': Australia's Role in Restitution for Templer Property in Israel". *The Journal of Israeli History.* 24(1) March: 135-54.

Sahoo, A. K. (2004) "Transnational Networks of Indian Diaspora in Australia". *Journal of Contemporary Asia and Europe, Centre for Asian and European Studies.* 1(2): 120-34.

Sauer, P. (1991) *The Holy Land Called.* Translated by Gunhild Henley. Melbourne: Temple Society Australia.

Seitz, A., and Foster, L. (1985) "Dilemmas of Immigration – Australian Expectations, Migrant Responses: Germans in Melbourne". *Australian and New Zealand Journal of Sociology.* 21(3) November: 414-30.

Taylor, C. (1994) "The Politics of Recognition". In Gutman, A. (ed), *Multiculturalism.* Princeton, NJ: Princeton University Press: 25-74.

Uhlenbruch, W. W. J. (2004) *50 Years of Serving Those in Need: A History of the Australian-German Welfare Society Inc 1954-2004.* Melbourne: Design Print Integration.

Van Sommers, T. (1966) *Religions in Australia.* Adelaide: Rigby.

Vertovec, S. (1999) "Conceiving and Researching Transnationalism". *Ethnic and Racial Studies.* 22(2).

Vondra, J. (1981) *German Speaking Settlers in Australia.* Melbourne: Cavalier Press Pty Ltd.

Wolff, S. (2001). "German Expellee Organizations between 'Homeland' and 'At Home': A Case Study of the Politics of Belonging". *Refuge.* 20(1): 52-65.

4

Gemma Tulud Cruz

Living in the Interstice: An Asian case of contestations against marginalisation

Introduction

In the past few decades Asia has been the site of intense movements of people, particularly for those who are moving for economic reasons. This is not surprising given that Asia is home to the world's second and third largest economies (China and Japan) as well as some of the more stable (Singapore) and fastest-rising economies (India). This intensity of human mobility in Asia is also not surprising in view of the fact that Asia is home, as well, to some of the world's poorest populations. Without a doubt this forms the backbone of Filipina migration to Hong Kong as domestic workers.

Filipina migration to Hong Kong as domestic workers started in the 1970s but the profile of these migrants consistently remains somewhat the same: young, single, and educated women. In a study conducted by Carolyn French in the 1980s, for example, the respondents were mostly single women, in their twenties to thirties, and with a high level of education.[1] More than a decade later, in Rita

---

1 See French, 1986, pp. 7-15.

Ybanez's study the respondents were again mostly single (75 per cent for the in-depth interviews and 54 per cent for the survey), young, and highly educated. In Ybanez's study the respondents were mostly 20 to 40 years old (the mean age among the respondents for the in-depth interviews is 32.2 years old, while that for the survey is 33.8 years old). Many of the respondents also reached the college level or successfully finished an undergraduate course (50 per cent for the in-depth interviews and 66 per cent for the survey).[2]

Today, although their numbers are dropping, the Filipina DHs (as they are more popularly called) make up a significant segment of Hong Kong's more than 300,000 foreign house-help. In 2013, for example, there were some 320,000 foreign domestic helpers in Hong Kong, of which 50 per cent were from the Philippines, 47 per cent from Indonesia, and the rest from Thailand, Myanmar, Bangladesh, Nepal, Pakistan and Sri Lanka.[3] Life for the Filipina domestic workers in Hong Kong, however, is marginalised. Using existing studies on the Filipina domestic workers in Hong Kong together with informal interviews in centers and shelters for domestic workers in Hong Kong, this chapter explores the struggle of the Filipina domestic workers in Hong Kong against their marginalisation.

Geographies of marginalisation

At the outset it is noteworthy to point out that the DHs' experience of marginalisation, in general, happens across borders. It is inflicted by various groups from their recruiters to their employers, the Philippine government to the Hong Kong government, as well as their compatriots and their very own friends and family members.

2 Ybanez, p. 30.
3 See "Foreign Domestic Workers in Hong Kong", *South China Morning Post,* on-line edition.

As migrant domestic workers, the DHs' labour is, first and fore-most, "bought". Hence, it is subject to control. Curfew is imposed even on off-days. The study by Ybanez sheds light on the various ways in which the mobility of the DHs is controlled. These include the use of spy cameras or alarms, not being allowed to use the phone to talk or interact with other workers, and keeping close watch of the DH's every move. One respondent said that when she went to the bank to remit money to the Philippines, her employer would accom-pany her while another respondent complained of how her employ-er's mother kept a tight watch over her so she (DH) has to be doing something all the time. She revealed how she got her moment's rest by going to the bathroom and just sitting on the bowl to cry over her situation.[4] Some employers even phone to check on the DH periodi-cally as they expect the DH to be always working.

As it is, domestic work is replete with ambiguities because it blurs the boundaries between the public and the private. "Work" which is usually done in public is done in private, and "home" which is supposed to be the realm of the private, becomes the DH's work (hence public) place. "Daily she [the DH] rubs with the family, roams about the house, pokes into drawers and the refrigerator, and picks up on the family's most closely guarded secrets. She is an insider. Her workplace is her employer's home, her colleagues are his family. She is in a very deep sense a 'part of the family' ".[5] But, in reality, she is not. "Home", which is supposed to be her haven and refuge, is the very site of her marginalisation. It does not help that women migrant domestic workers are not judged for their "intimate labor" but as women who leave their own families to sell their services abroad for economic gain.[6]

---

4 Ybanez, 2000, p. 33.
5 "Surrogate Parent?", *TNT Hong Kong*.
6 Chang and Groves, 2002, p. 74.

Cultural and language differences also marginalise the DHs. Inability to speak Cantonese severely delimits the DHs in their daily interaction with the local people and their employer. Moreover, the Chinese way of speaking English adds to the DHs' communication problems with their employers as English spoken with a Cantonese accent can be hard to decipher. In addition, some employers have problems with correct grammar or sentence construction. The language difference or inability to speak Cantonese intensifies the DHs' vulnerability to abuse, as they are sometimes made the butt of jokes as well as objects of insults and malicious talk without their knowledge.

The difference in the Chinese and Filipino idea of a domestic helper, especially a foreign domestic helper (hereinafter FDH), is also a cultural issue. A domestic worker is not a professional nanny or housekeeper as most of the predominantly educated DHs tend to think of themselves or want themselves to be treated.[7] For the Chinese employers, a domestic worker (especially an FDH) is more of a "muijai", an indentured unskilled, inferior servant or a young girl who can never be an equal and has minimal rights.[8] Muijai may actually mean "younger sister" or "girl." But as older mature women being called a "girl" is insulting for DHs since a "girl" is someone who is perpetually immature, inferior, and one who has to submit herself. Muijai is also an old Chinese term associated with the slavery of young girls who were usually sold with or without their parents' consent.

Differences in religious affiliation, reinforced by class differences, also spawn difficulties and tensions. DHs have to learn to adjust to the reality that they are in a predominantly non-Christian place, as

7 See, for example Pidgeon, 1996, p. 1.
8 See Jaschok, as cited in Constable, 1997, pp. 45-8.

compared to the Philippines, which is predominantly Christian. The employers' ignorance of Catholicism sometimes hinders DHs from practicing their faith, for example, going to Mass on Sundays.[9] Class issues also make the local Christian community dissociate from a Filipina DH church. This dissociation is affirmed by the following excerpt from the report on Hong Kong, presented at a symposium on Filipino migrant workers in Asia:

> As we appreciate the contribution of our Filipino brethren to the Church of Hong Kong, we also recognize the difficulties in establishing a Church that is both Filipino and Chinese. We are aware that we still need to inculcate among our Chinese people that the Church is universal and that two cultures can proclaim the same faith in the same Church, in different ways and languages. The Diocese of Hong Kong would like to see the Chinese and the Filipinos join one another at Mass and gatherings, as equals and as friends.[10]

Racial discrimination plagues the lives of the women workers. The best-known such discrimination occurred in the "Battle of Chater Road".[11] Resentful of the "invasion" by Filipinas of Chater Road and Statue Square during Sunday, shop owners proposed banning them from congregating in public places. There were proposals to re-open Chater Road to public traffic on Sundays, amidst the very public knowledge, that the road was a "haven" of Filipina DHs on Sundays. The DHs decried this as another manouevre to keep them "out of sight," just as existing rules forced them to use back entrances to buildings, and confined them to certain waiting areas in elite clubs.[12]

---

9 Pidgeon, 1999, p. 24.

10 As quoted in "Filipino Migrant Workers in Hong Kong", p. 7.

11 Commission for Filipinos Overseas, p. 3.

12 For a list of examples of instances in which DHs feel discriminated see Borlongan, 1996, p. 12.

Some residents, who came to the defense of the Filipinas, even labelled the suggestion as "ethnic cleansing". [13] The DHs fought against the proposal until the Executive Council mediated and allowed them to use the park and road again.

Hong Kong's policies in relation to FDHs, while one of the most expansive in Asia, also contributes to the DHs' marginalisation. The NCS (New Conditions of Stay), more popularly known as the Two-Weeks Rule, automatically reduces the DHs' visas to two weeks upon termination of their employment. This means they have to apply for a visitor visa if they want to stay beyond two weeks even though the NCS limits the granting of visitor visas to those who have ongoing disputes. Applying for a visa extension would mean that women have to shell out more money and, if the case drags on, they have to keep re-applying. On top of this, the application is still subject to the approval of the Immigration Department. Some FDHs, who have been victims of injustice, do not file charges but agree to accepting unfair out-of-court settlements, or just simply give up and go home. Thus, they end up doubly victimised. [14]

Other policies make life difficult for FDHs. Article 24 of the Basic Law, Hong Kong's de-facto mini-constitution, states that "persons not of Chinese nationality who have entered Hong Kong with valid travel documents, have ordinarily resided in Hong Kong for a continuous period of not less than seven years, and have taken Hong Kong as their place of permanent residence before or after the establishment of the Hong Kong Special Administrative Region" may become a Hong Kong Permanent Resident. A Hong Kong Immigration ordinance, however, stipulates that "a person shall not be treated as ordinarily resident in Hong Kong while employed as a

---

13 Constable, 1997, pp. 4-6.
14 See Boase, 1991, p. 88.

domestic helper who is from outside Hong Kong". Other foreigners, in the meantime, can apply to settle permanently after seven years. In early 2012 one DH won international attention when she challenged the policy and won in the lower court.[15] The ruling was then struck down by Hong Kong's High Court.[16]

Foreign domestic helpers in Hong Kong are also excluded from the Statutory Minimum Wage (SMW). For years the city has been keeping FDHs' wages artificially low with a two-tiered structure. As of September 2013, for example, the minimum wage a month for foreign domestic workers was HK$4010 (US$515) and between HK$5760 and HK$6240 a month for everyone else, based on a 48-hour working week. Moreover, the FDHs' Minimum Allowable Wage (MAW) is subject to an annual review. While this has advantages as it provides possibilities for wage increases, it also makes the FDHs' wage easy target in times of economic slowdown. For example, after failing to impose its proposed 20 per cent wage cut (the employers wanted 35 per cent) in 1998, the Hong Kong government reduced FDHs' minimum wage by five per cent during the economic crisis in 1999. Because of a growing budget deficit, the government implemented another deeper wage cut for contracts signed after 1 April 2003. Between 2003 and 2009 the FDHs' minimum wage increased. As a result of the global economic crisis, however, FDHs were again targeted for a wage freeze in August 2009.[17] Accommodation is also a serious problem for them. Since 2003, Hong Kong has required that foreign domestic workers live with their employers, a rule that exposes workers to unlimited working hours and gives them few avenues for

---

15 By the end of 2010, 117,000 DHs had been resident for seven years or more. "Filipino maid takes fight for permanent residency to Hong Kong's top court", *Guardian* UK web-site.

16 Ibid.

17 See Aning, "Pinoys, Asians protest low HK wage for maids," Inquirer.net web-site.

escape if their employers become abusive. Exacerbated by the housing problem, the majority of the DHs do not have their own room and are forced to share a room with the employer's children. Some sleep along the corridor, the ironing area or any available space. The United Filipinos in Hong Kong (UNIFIL) has also received complaints from DHs who report being made to sleep in cupboards, in the toilets or even on top of washing machines because of the small house of their employers. A survey by the Asia Pacific Mission for Migrants (APMM) reveals that as many as 70 per cent of maids put up with these living conditions.[18]

Frontiers of contestations

Life for the Filipina domestic workers in Hong Kong is not just about marginalisation. It is also about the strategies used to resist or negotiate and, consequently, define or re-define the boundaries of their marginalisation. In the past few decades there has been a consistent scholarly attention to everyday forms of resistance, especially in anthropological and sociological research.[19] In these studies resisters are portrayed not as helpless victims of domination but as conscious, intentional subjects who are skilled in managing and negotiating power relations in their daily lives, whether between colonised and coloniser, between workers and managers, or between women and men [and between women].[20] This theme of everyday resistance dominates feminist scholarship, challenging the stereotypical view of

---

18 Heyzer and Wee, 1994, p.75. Also see, for example, "No More Sleeping in the Bathroom", *TNT Hong Kong*, p. 28.

19 Originally theorised by Gramsci the concept of everyday resistance refers to the small, seemingly trivial daily acts through which subordinate individuals and groups undermine, rather than overthrow, oppressive relations of power. See Gramsci, as cited in Chang and Groves, 2002, p. 316.

20 Ibid., p. 317.

women as victims, and pointing to the many small, yet significant, ways in which women defy control.[21]

The most obvious form of resistance for the DHs is, of course, organised protest.[22] DHs also resort to building formal and informal networks, associations, clubs, unions, alliances or federations, many of which are identified according to ethnic or geographic boundaries such as the Abra Tinguian Ilocano Society (ATIS-H.K.). These associations also create organised mechanisms to help members. For example, the Abra-Tinguian Ilocano Society , a federation of 25 organisations from the Philippine province of Abra, gives shelter and para-legal counselling to its members as well as scholarships to indigent students from each of the municipalities in the province of Abra. It has also established an OFW Center in Abra, which serves as a linkage with the families of member DHs in case of urgent problems.[23] The United Filipinos in Hong Kong (UNIFIL-H.K.), in the meantime, is broadly affiliated. Made up of an alliance of more or less 25 Filipino migrant organizations in Hong Kong, UNIFIL is very active in advocacy and empowerment activities for the DHs on vital issues both in Hong Kong and the Philippines. Together with the Hong Kong and Philippine churches (especially Christian churches) and Filipino-run migrant NGOs like Mission for Filipino Migrant Workers (MFMW), Asia-Pacific Mission for Migrant Filipinos (APMMF), and Bethune House, UNIFIL has aided DHs extensively in helping themselves and their fellow DHs not only to survive but triumph over some of the anti-migrant and anti-(Filipina) DHs policies of Hong Kong. It is linked to the equally active and influential alliance of migrant domestic worker organisations in Hong Kong,

---

21 See Abu-Lughod; Ong, and Rollins, as cited in Ibid., p. 317.
22 Constable, 1997, p. 155.
23 Casia-Cabantac, 1999, pp. 26-7.

the Asian Migrant Coordinating Body (AMCB). The AMCB, which counts UNIFIL as a founding member, includes the Association of Sri Lankans, Far East Overseas Nepalese Association, Friends of Thai, and Association of Indonesian Migrant Workers. DHs are also key players in the other umbrella group – Coalition for Migrants' Rights (CMR) – which is the broadest coalition of grassroots migrant organizations in Hong Kong.

Socially and politically, the DHs' Sunday gatherings at Chater Road and Statue Square have become, literally and figuratively, symbolic of their resistance. Gillian Youngs considers this "successful and dramatic claim to high-profile public space," as one of those rare "sightings" of gender resistance, especially since it "represents a disruption of public/private divides".[24] Aside from fostering visibility, it is also an indirect assertion of autonomy.

Sisterhood and solidarity also provides sources and resources for resistance strategies for the DHs. Jocelyn Manuit experienced this five times. The first time was when she told another Filipina she had met that she was not given breakfast for three days, and the Filipina gave her some bread. Then when she was unceremoniously terminated and hurriedly brought to the airport on her fourth day of work she looked for Filipinas to ask for help so she could call her aunt. Sure enough she found one who gave her money so she could make the call. Her aunt came and rescued her. A friend of her aunt then took her under her wings for some time. Finally, Bethune House – a shelter run by Filipinas – took her in.[25] DHs also keep each other abreast of potentially oppressive employers and deter other Filipinas from working with such employers. In one case, in a residential building, the DHs' highly developed informal network prevented an employer,

---

24 Youngs, 2003, p. 51 and p. 54.
25 Mission for Filipino Migrant Workers, 2002, pp. 18-9.

whom they considered as a common enemy, from being able to hire a Filipina as a domestic worker.[26] Some of those who work in the same building create "safe meeting places", like the garbage area and the car park. These creative resistances illustrate strategies that anthropologist James Scott calls hidden transcripts or weapons of the weak.[27]

In *Domination and the Arts of Resistance*, Scott draws attention to a politics of disguise and anonymity among subordinate groups that is partly sanitised, ambiguous, and coded. He says this is often expressed in rumours, gossip, folktales, jokes, songs, rituals, codes, and euphemisms that usually come from folk culture.[28] The women use their religio-cultural identity to respond to marginalisation. Similarly, most DHs draw upon Filipino culture, particularly folk culture, to negotiate their marginalisation. Laughter or laughing is one of these. Their jokes about themselves even have a caricature in the person of "Maria the stupid DH," a caricature the DHs have created of/for themselves (especially those who are largely uninitiated to city life) for their jokes on their travails, adventures, and misadventures in Hong Kong.

Jokes are a common strategy for them to feel that the capitulation is not complete. First, these discursive and creative communicative strategies help them mitigate their oppressive interactions with their employers, especially those who are pervasively controlling. Second, jokes allow them to indirectly attack the local community, which

---

26 The "sanctioning" of the employer by the DHs occurred because her previous (Filipina) DH resigned allegedly due to overwork. See Ozeki, 1995, p. 45.

27 These in-between strategies, or strategies that neither simply resist the oppression nor accept it, are couched or veiled in non-threatening methods and arguably fall into what Leslie Salzinger refer to as "unaggressive aggressiveness," or what Pierrette Hondagneu-Sotelo designates as "negotiate." See Salzinger, 1991, pp. 139-60 and Hondagneu-Sotelo, 2001.

28 Scott, 1990, p. 19.

could be openly condescending towards the DHs' presence. Lastly, jokes make the DHs feel that they are smarter and that they have come a long way in learning to adjust to the difficulties arising from their situation. As such, jokes that make fun of themselves and their day-to-day problems also abound. One popular joke tells of Maria who has just arrived in Hong Kong and was asked to accompany her employer on the bus. They went up the upper deck. When the bus started moving, Maria stood up abruptly:

> Employer: What's the matter?
>
> Maria: Ma'am we have to go down.
>
> Employer: Why? (with astonishment)
>
> Maria: Ma'am there's no driver here![29]

While laughter can definitely be escapist, it is also validated in folk wisdom as a means of resistance. Filipina feminist Rina Jimenez-David, for example, points to it as a strategy of resistance. She says this obstinate cheerfulness serves as a personal bulwark against the vicissitudes of loneliness and alienation.[30]

Singing is also a typical Filipino practice that DHs use creatively. Singing is employed as a form of hidden transcript. On Sundays, for example, DHs serve as accomplices to their cash-strapped compatriots who sell "halo-halo" (a concoction of fruits, milk, sugar, and shaved ice) illegally, by providing the vendor a human camouflage every time the Urban Services Guard passes by.[31] If one is caught selling food by the patrol for illegal hawking, the cluster of Filipina customers suddenly sing "Happy Birthday", and instantly transform the activity into one of many birthday parties celebrated at the square. Clearly

---

29 Mariano, as quoted in Constable, 1997, pp. 175-6.
30 Jimenez-David, "Why Filipinos are happy", inq7.net web-site.
31 Federation of Asian Bishops' Conferences-Office of Human Development, 1994, p. 13.

the DHs are not simply passive victims or active resistors. They also negotiate their marginalisation in different, creative ways with the help of political-economic and religio-cultural sources that they deftly and subtly appropriate to their advantage, albeit not in a definitive and radical sense. While scholars like Constable maintain that some forms of resistance are merely attempts to reverse an inherently undignified power structure, rather than replace that negative power structure with something which has integrity, there are also concrete evidence of the success of these resistance strategies. [32] Three notable fruits of their efforts include: 1) winning an increase in DHs' minimum wage in 1993; 2) reduction of the wage cut from 20-35 per cent to just five per cent in January 1999; and 3) shelving of the proposals on the ban on driving duties, abolishment of maternity protection, and live-out arrangement in 2000.[33]

Marginality as heuristic lens

Undoubtedly, marginality in relation to identity is a critical analytical tool in making sense of the experience of the DHs. While their various identities bring problematic consequences they, at the same time, contest their marginalisation using these very identities. As their experience also shows, the DHs do not inhabit their identities in a static way but simultaneously and fluidly, or in an oscillating manner. To be sure, the DHs, like most unskilled migrant women workers from the global south, do not only negotiate multiple or hybrid identities, e.g. "Filipino," "women," "migrant," "DHs," and "banmui". They are also often forced to inhabit these marginal(ised) identities.

---

32 Constable specifically categorises such acts as accommodation.
33 For an elaboration on all these accomplishments, see Asian Migrant Coordinating Body, 2003, p. 11 and p. 15; UNIFIL-HK, 2003, pp. 4-16; and Mission for Filipino Migrant Workers, 2002, p. 3.

It is in view of these that I argue that Korean-American theologian Jung Young Lee's concept on marginality could serve as a tool for discursively framing the DHs' experience. Marginality is originally a sociological term normatively understood in relation to ethnic minorities or the personality orientation of those from different racial and cultural backgrounds. Lee adopted the term and re-interpreted it from a faith perspective. According to Lee, marginality has three dimensions. The first one is the "in-between" condition. For migrants, discrimination, often expressed through racism, contributes to their "in-between" condition, or the lot of being "poised in psychological uncertainty between two (or more) social worlds, reflecting in his soul the discords and harmonies, repulsions and attractions of these worlds."[34] The "in-between" boundaries in these worlds form a marginal condition, creating excessive self-consciousness and race consciousness, ambivalence, pessimism, sentimentalism and, consequently, self-alienation.[35] This is the classical understanding of marginalisation which, for Lee, is the central group's definition.

But marginality as experienced, especially by migrants today in multicultural societies, is more than being "in-between." Lee proposes a more contemporary self-affirming definition; "in-both," or being "part of two worlds without wholly belonging to either".[36] In the case of immigrants while "in-between" carries a negative connotation "in-both" has positive implications, as it "complements and balances in-between by bringing out the need to affirm not only one's 'roots' but also one's 'branches'".[37] The "in-beyond" marginal person, whom Lee considers as the new marginal person, is one who is able to

---

34 Stonequist, as quoted in Lee, 1995, p. 43.
35 Lee, 1995, pp. 45-7.
36 Ibid., p. 44.
37 Ibid., p. 49.

harmonise the experience of being "in-between" and "in-both". The marginal person, who creatively combines the knowledge and insight of the insider with the critical attitude of the outsider, embodies this dimension of marginality.

Lee's conception of marginality is related to what Rita Nakashima Brock speaks of as "interstitial integrity". For Brock, interstitial integrity provides the ground on which one is able to deal with, examine, and recognise differences; it is the spirit and the struggle in us to hold the many in the one; it is about seeking out the places where people are struggling for recognition, dignity, and respect.[38] By living in the interstice, which could be arguably construed as a 'third" or "in-beyond" space, people like the DHs not only become keenly aware of differences. They also find diverse resources, e.g. political, cultural, and religious to deal with or engage these differences. In this way interstitial integrity provides the ground on which people who live amidst marginalisation are able to create or negotiate some form of agency or subjectivity and be an "in-beyond" person as the interstice becomes a creative space.

Conclusion

Life for the DHs is obviously a constant negotiation and re-negotiation of their agency and subjectivity in their quest for full humanity and liberation. Their experience is that of struggle. It is marked by persistent and unremitting efforts to work out humane living conditions in the midst of oppressive situations. In the context of marginalisation, struggle requires not just immense and creative physical efforts. It also demands relentless courage, steadfast faith, and boundless hope expressed in persistent and creative resistance

---

38 Brock, 2007, p. 140.

strategies no matter how insignificant and possibly less effective these strategies may be. This is because struggles against oppressive conditions implies the pursuit of survival as human beings with dignity and integrity.

References

Abu-Lughod, L. (1986) *Veiled Sentiments.* Berkeley: University of California Press.

Abu-Lughod, L., Ong, A. and Rollins, J. (1985) *Between Women: Domestics and Their Employers.* Philadelphia: Temple University Press.

Aning, Jerome. "Pinoys, Asians protest low HK wage for maids". Inquirer.net.web-site.

Asian Migrant Coordinating Body. (2003) *Evaluation Report: Asian Migrants Coordinating Body.* Hong Kong: APMM.

Associated Press. "Filipino maid takes fight for permanent residency to Hong Kong's top court". *Guardian UK* web-site.

Boase, Melville. (1991) "The Two Weeks Rule in the Context of the Legal Position of Foreign Domestic Helpers (FDHs)". In Christian Conference of Asia. *Serving One Another: The Report of the Consultation on the Mission and Ministry to Filipino Migrant Workers in Hong Kong.* 28 April-1 May. Kowloon, Hong Kong: CCA Urban Rural Mission.

Borlongan, Remy. (1996) "Is Hong Kong a discriminatory society," *TNT Hong Kong.* 2(2) February: 12.

Brock, Rita Nakashima. (2007) "Cooking without recipes: Interstitial integrity". In Brock, Rita Nakashima. et al. (eds). *Off the Menu: Asian and Asian North American Women's Religion and Theology.* Louisville, KY: WJK Press: 125-43.

Casia-Cabantac, Vicky. (1999) "The Abra Tingguian Ilocano Society: A Family Away from Home". *TNT Hong Kong.* 5(7) July: 26-7.

Chang, Kimberly and McAllister Groves, Julian. (2002) "Romancing Resistance and Resisting Romance: Ethnography and the Construction of Power in the Filipina Domestic Worker Community in Hong Kong". In Aguilar, Filomeno V. (ed). *At Home in the World?: Filipinos in Global Migrations*. Quezon City: Philippine Migration Research Network: 316-43.

—————. (2000) "Neither 'Saints' nor 'Prostitutes': Sexual Discourse in the Filipina Domestic Worker Community in Hong Kong". *Women's Studies International Forum*. 23(1): 73-87.

Constable, Nicole. (1997) *Maid to Order in Hong Kong: Stories of Filipina Workers*. Ithaca, NY: Cornell University Press.

Episcopal Commission for Migrants and Itinerant People-Catholic Bishops Conference of the Philippines (ECMI-CBCP). (2002) *Character Formation Program on Migration*. Makati City, Philippines: St. Paul's.

Federation of Asian Bishops' Conferences-Office of Human Development. (1994) *Pilgrims of Progress? A Primer of Filipino Migrant Workers in Asia*. Manila: FABC-OHD.

"Filipino Migrant Workers in Hong Kong," (1994) *Asian Migrant*. 7 (1) January-March: 7.

French. Carolyn. (1986) *Filipina Domestic Workers in Hong Kong: A Preliminary Survey*. Hong Kong: The Chinese University of Hong Kong: 7-15.

Gramsci, Antonio. (1971) *Selections from the Prison Notebooks*, ed. and trans. Q. Hoare and G.N. Smith. New York: International Publishers.

Heyzer, Noeleen and Wee, Vivienne. (1994) "Domestic Workers in Transient Overseas Employment: Who Benefits, Who Profits". In Lycklama à Nijeholt, Geertje and Weerakom, Nedra. (eds). *The Trade in Domestic Workers: Causes, Mechanisms and Consequences of International Migration*. Kuala Lumpur: APDC: 31-101.

Hondagneu-Sotelo, Pierrette. (2001) *Doméstica: Immigrant Workers Cleaning and Caring in the Shadows of Affluence*. Los Angeles: University of California Press.

Jimenez-David, Rina. "Why Filipinos are happy". Inq7.net web-site.

Jaschok, Maria. (1988) *Concubines and Bondservants: The Social History of a Chinese Custom*. Hong Kong: Oxford University Press.

Lee, Jung Young. (1995) *Marginality: The Key to Multicultural Theology*. Minneapolis, MN: Fortress Press.

Mission for Filipino Migrant Workers. (2002) "Pagbaba ng Bayad sa Kontrata Ikinagalak ng mga OFWS sa Hong Kong". *New Migrant Focus*. 33 November: 3.

————. (2000) "Food for Thought (Or the lack of it…)". *Migrant Focus Magazine*. 1(20) October-December: 18-9.

"No More Sleeping in the Bathroom". (1996) *TNT Hong Kong*. 2(2) February: 28.

Mariano, Jocelyn,. (1992) "No Driver". In Layosa, Linda R. and Luminarias, Laura P. (eds). *Sapang Pagyuko Kawayan: A Collection of Jokes from Filipino Overseas Workers*. Hong Kong: Asia-Pacific: 23

Ong, A. (1987) *Spirit Resistance and Capitalist Discipline: Factory Women in Malaysia*. Albany, NY: State University of New York Press.

Ozeki, Erino. (1995) "At Arm's Length: The Filipina Domestic Helper-Chinese Employer Relationship in Hong Kong". *International Journal of Japanese Sociology*. 4: 37-55.

Pidgeon. F.J. (1996) "Knocking on Heaven's Door". *TNT Hong Kong*. 5(9) September: 24.

————. (1996) "Surrogate Parent?". *TNT Hong Kong*. 2(2) March: 1.

Stonequist, Everett. (1961) *The Marginal Man: A Study in Personality and Cultural Conflict*. New York: Russell and Russell.

Salzinger. Leslie. (1991) "'A Maid by Any Other Name': The Transformation of 'Dirty Work by Central American Immigrants".

In Burawoy, Michael. et al. (eds). *Ethnography Unbound: Power and Resistance in the Modern Metropolis*. Berkeley: University of California Press: 139-60.

Scott, James. (1990) *Domination and the Arts of Resistance: Hidden Transcripts*. New Haven, CT: Yale University Press.

Tulud Cruz, Gemma. (2009) "It Cuts Both Ways: Religion in the Life of the Filipina Domestic Workers in Hong Kong". In Tibe Bonifacio, Glenda and Angeles, Vivienne S.M. (eds). *Gender, Religion, and Migration: Pathways to Integration*. Lanham, MD: Lexington Books: 17-36.

UNIFIL-HK. (2003) *Seeking Strategies on how to Combat Racism and Discrimination among Migrant Workers in Hong Kong*. Hong Kong: UNIFIL-HK.

Ybanez, Riza Faith. (2000) "Labor Migration and HIV Vulnerability of Migrant Workers: The Filipina Domestic Workers in Hong Kong". In Ybanez, Riza Faith, Bugna, Sahlee and Sanga, Dyra. (eds). *Labor Migration and HIV AIDS: Vulnerability of Filipino Migrant Workers*. Kuala Lumpur: CARAM-Asia: 29-40.

Youngs, Gillian. (2003) "Breaking patriarchal bonds: Demythologizing the public/private". In Marchand, Marianne H. and Runyan, Anne Sisson. (eds). *Gender and Global Structuring: Sightings, Sites, and Resistances*. London: Routledge: 44-58.

5

Mike Dee

Urban public space and the marginalisation of children and young people

In the 21st century city, public space for a range of users, but especially children and young people, has come under threat. Watson proposed that "public space itself has come under attack from several directions – thematisation, enclosure into malls and other controlled spaces, and privatisation, or from urban planning and design interventions to erase its uniqueness".[1] Largely as a result of these trends, Scott observed that "young urbanites form a marginalised age class ... movement is restricted, out of fear and distrust, within aims to protect, monitored by city surveillance methods within the security-obsessed fabric".[2] The use of public space by children and young people is a contentious issue in a number of countries and a range of measures deployed to control public space curtail the rights of children and young people to claim the space for their use through curfews, oppressive camera surveillance and at times, the unwarranted attentions of police and private security personnel.[3]

Moreover, "positioned as aliens in the social and physical

---

1 Watson, 2006, p. 147.
2 Scott, 2002, p. 306.
3 Loader, 1996, p. 89, White and Wyn, 2004, p. 32.

architecture of our cities, young people in Australia are portrayed through media and police campaigns as deviant, barbaric and unclean – a threat to social order".[4] The discourse of "threat" is further exemplified in the separation of children from teenagers, where the treatment of younger children using public space is often dramatically different to that of older children and the most feared stage of all, "youth". For Harris the situation is thus:

> Young people are problematised within this discourse for taking up public space in inappropriate ways; and indeed, a mark of strong communities is their capacity to "deal with" young people in the urban environment by corralling them into suitable activities. Simultaneously, a few are selected for consultation, and law and order regimes delimit their use of public space through curfews or harsh penalties for graffiti, all under the imperative of keeping streets safe.[5]

Understanding the difficult, contested, nature of public space is important because it is both a contested reality and concept and a range of users have differing levels of access to and occupation of public space, depending on their power and societal status.[6]

Public space

Conceiving of public space as a "power landscape" riven with conflicts, residues of previous users of the land and contemporary developments, allows a critical view of the daily and perhaps taken-for-granted composition of the built environment. In this sense, public space is never still because it is "always in a process of becoming. It is

4 Malone, 2002, p. 87.
5 Harris, 2013, p. 92.
6 Kulynch, 2001, p. 127; Wilson, Rose and Colvin, 2010, p. 15; Sleight, 2013, p. 5.

always being made".[7] One political economy of the Australian urban landscape reveals the work of "gigantic hammers (of) applied power, the overwhelming drive of national self-interest, the single-minded pursuit of economic gain, colonisation and exploitation".[8]

Writing from a planning perspective, Iveson argues that four broad explanatory models of public space emerge from the literature across varying disciplines.[9] The "ceremonial" model depicts grand spaces for the celebration of major events in the life of "nation, state or city". This space heralds a significant investment by the local and nation state in the infrastructure of civic pride of place, but also marks a tension between the state and market, as many events have to realise a profit or gain commercial sponsorship, to survive. Recent examples of course are to be found in the reconstruction of the Adelaide Oval, relying on funding from the Australian Football League (AFL) or the new soccer/rugby stadium in Melbourne paid for by the state government of Victoria with naming rights for a corporation.

The "community" model suggests that the "publicness" of public space is determined not by state ownership, but, by the extent to which community is fostered through urban design and planning. Urban design (in this context) takes upon itself the mantle of social engineering in order to improve social lives and conditions. Critical questions remain as to the individuals and groups excluded in communities "created" around approved forms of activity, consumption, compliance and a unified view of what the local community is and wants.[10] The "liberal" model rests on the premise that public space is open to all users without regard to differences in

---

7 Massey, 1994, p. 283.

8 Ward, 1993, p. 11.

9 Iveson, 1998, p. 21.

10 Crane and Dee, 2001, p. 18; Harris, 2013, p. 92.

social class or status. Despite much vaunted claims to inclusivity, a great deal of public space is instead, predicated on various forms of exclusion of social groups, such as the homeless, the working class and young people, in favour of more "deserving" and potentially economically more active citizens.[11]

The "multi-public" model celebrates difference and diversity as public goods, rather than deficits to be expunged. Social relations are not configured on the inclusion of some and the exclusion of others. Instead, groups "overlap and intermingle" while maintaining a discrete identity and coherence.[12] The strength of this final model is the tolerance of some, if limited, difference, as opposed to a drive for homogeneity and also a recognition that a range of "publics" to make use of public space exist.

Iveson's typology is helpful in identifying different kinds of public space and the broad forms of uses and users that define these. It also provides for the possibility of "contested space". A possible flaw is the lack of recognition that public space is "conditioned by powerful interests" and those who may be excluded, such as young people, indigenous people and people from a range of cultural backgrounds, experience marginalisation repeatedly.[13] Another useful way of categorising public space with similarities and differences to Iveson's schema, is suggested by Tonkiss in "the square" indicating "collective belonging", "the café", "representing social exchange" and "the street", a place marked by "informal encounter".[14]

The square can be any public space "provided or protected by the state" and is formally open to all "as a simple expression of

---

11 Iveson, 1998, p. 25; Hollis, 2013, p. 129.
12 Ibid., Iveson p. 27.
13 Crane and Dee, 2001, p. 17; Harris, 2013, p. 130.
14 Tonkiss, 2005, p. 67.

citizenship". The second kind of space promotes contact between humans in a broad social setting that can be a public, private, commercial or hybrid space. The third form of space, the street, is seen as the "basic unit of public life", a routine if necessary conduit for "marginal encounters" based on the equal rights of all citizens to public space.[15]

The usual starting point for a discussion about citizenship rights is Marshall (1950).[16] He theorises citizenship as comprising three stages of broad historical evolution towards civil, political and social rights. Civil citizenship, from the 18th century onwards, is the right to personal freedom in the form of speech, movement and assembly. Political citizenship, emerging in the 19th century, is the right to vote and stand for public office. Social citizenship, a creation of the 20th century, includes economic security and access to health, education and employment opportunities.[17] Social citizenship rights are largely about quality of life issues and human dignity, guaranteed by the welfare state to ensure that individuals have the material wherewithal to take full part in society.[18] Civil, political and social citizenship rights are all relevant to children and young people as users of public space and link to a form of "spatial citizenship" in terms of liveability, social, spatial and emotional health and well-being and sustainability.[19] These are necessary elements of becoming satisfactory urban citizens in the broadest sense, as indicated by Jacobs:[20]

> The tolerance, the room for great difference among neighbours – differences that often go far deeper than

15 Ibid., 2005, p. 68.
16 Marshall, 1950.
17 Ibid., p. 34.
18 Standing 2011, p.67; Dean, 2013, p. 34.
19 Rowntree Foundation, 2011, p. 27.
20 Jacobs, 1948, p. 48.

differences in colour are possible and normal only when streets of great cities have built-in equipment allowing strangers to dwell in peace together on civilised but essentially dignified and reserved terms. Lowly and random as they may appear, sidewalk contacts are the small change from which a city's wealth of public life may grow.[21]

The societal position of young people may however, be described as one largely of constrained rights, where they frequently find themselves as the inferior party in respect of disputes within local communities over rights to use and occupy public space, which adults presume to exercise as a right of their citizenship.[22] The perception by young people that they are excluded from participation in community life and community decision-making is discussed by Measor and Squires in their study of children and young people "congregating" in public spaces in Brighton UK.[23] They point to concerns over a lack of consultation on community infrastructure and developments. The young people reported a demonstrable sense of marginalisation from community life as Measor and Squires comment: "All too often young people were talked about, typically they were talked about as a problem. Rather less often they were talked to, still less did they appear to be listened to".[24]

This point is supported by my own doctoral research undertaken with 1100 high school students in Brisbane and nearby Logan City, where a profound sense of wanting to be a valued part of their local communities was evident, but 40 per cent said they felt unwanted and

---

21 Ibid.
22 Loader, 1996, p. 71; Weller, 2007, p. 49.
23 Measor and Squires, 2000, p. 45.
24 Ibid.

even, disliked.[25] The importance of place, space and neighbourhood or "place-rootedness" to the physical and emotional maturity and well-being of children and young people and development of a "place-bound identity" is now strongly established.[26] However, the richness and complexity of their use of a range of public and semi-public spaces is often downplayed or dismissed by those for whom public space is more correctly understood as adult territory.[27]

Beyond being neglected in the design of public spaces it can be said that children and young people (to varying extents due to age, location and socio-economic factors) are propelled from "the street into their bedrooms".[28] Here, young people are no longer "free-range more battery-reared".[29] Not only is their marginalisation from public space exacerbated, but their marginalisation from citizenship, as mere "citizens-in-the-making" and their active role in making and re-making public space or the "micro-spaces of citizenship" also goes largely unregarded, but through camera and other electronic surveillance measures, not unwatched.[30]

Surveillance

The nature of surveillance in western democracies is now pervasive. Such surveillance can be understood in the broadest context of everyday human acts, including shopping in malls and streets, using shop loyalty cards, paying for goods with an "electronic funds transfer

---

25 Dee, 2008, p. 250.

26 Leonard, 2006, p. 234; Laughlin and Johnson, 2011, p. 440; Sibley, 1995, p. 14; Lynch, 1977, p. 67; Freeman, 2006, p. 45.

27 Valentine, 2004, p. 52; Harris, 2013, p. 107.

28 Summers, 1995, p. 9; Woolley, 2006, p. 55.

29 McNeish and Roberts, 1995, p. 3.

30 Weller, 2007, p. 11; Dee, 2008, p. 251.

at point of sale" (EFTPOS) card, using mobile phones and global positioning systems (GPS), paying utility bills, dealing with any level of government, logging on to computers, the internet, in fact through all the basic demands of everyday life.[31]

The extent of seemingly altruistic surveillance applications means that their negative aspects can frequently be minimised by advocates for even greater surveillance powers.[32] This phenomenon of routine mass surveillance largely coincides with the emergence of the "risk society". In Ulrich Beck's formulation, risk society emerges when the "social, political, ecological, and individual risks created by the momentum of innovation elude increasingly the control and protective institutions of industrial society".[33] Importantly, the surveillance gaze (in all its forms) does not fall evenly on all citizens as Norris and Armstrong established in relation to the urban CCTV (closed-circuit television) surveillance of poor, young people.[34]

Despite widespread reluctance to critically evaluate CCTV systems, the rush to install them continues apace, alongside the constant upgrading of system functionality, from loudspeakers to web-based storage of images, encouraged by a lucrative perhaps even rapacious, security industry.[35] In the UK the networking of a range of camera systems, from traffic, congestion charging, to open-street private and public surveillance, has been criticised for lurching unreflectively towards an integrated national surveillance network, a system with few transparent controls.[36] In several localities in Australia the

---

31 Lyon, 2001, p. 3.
32 Ibid., p. 4.
33 Beck, 1992, p. 27.
34 Norris and Armstrong, 1999, p. 279.
35 Baldry and Painter, 1998, p.43; Stedman, 2011, p. 46.
36 Geraghty, 2000, p.89; Stedman, 2011, p. 61.

proliferation of CCTV systems in the UK and Europe has become an aspirational benchmark. Suggestions have been made that in aid of counter-terrorism strategies, data from all CCTV cameras in Australia be linked into CrimTrac (operator of all police databases) so as to establish a national facial recognition database.[37]

Logan City Council (near Brisbane) recently purchased a Rapid Action Deployment Surveillance System or RDSS. For a substantial expenditure, Logan ratepayers get two mobile cameras that climb poles or street lights so as to survey public space, providing high quality, real-time images to a monitoring facility, as well as hand-held and in-vehicle devices.[38] Logan City has an estimated one camera for every one thousand residents.[39] Concerns expressed by the Queensland Council for Civil Liberties (QCCL) about the exponential growth in CCTV coverage in Logan and elsewhere throughout urban and rural centres in Queensland were officially rebuffed. Local police saw the issues clearly: "The benefits of this camera system will simply enhance community safety in the Logan area and will also greatly assist the police in providing our core business".[40] For the QCCL the number of cameras already operating in Logan seems excessive, posing a potential threat to privacy:

> The use of CCTV we consider to be a violation of privacy and another development of the sort of big brother state. So far as we're concerned CCTV cameras just provide a false sense of security because all they do is move crime to an area where the camera is no longer situated or there are no cameras.[41]

---

37 Parnell, 2011, p. 3.
38 Logan City Council, 2011.
39 Flack, 2011, p. 3.
40 Ibid.
41 Ibid., p. 3.

This intensification of surveillance marks a transition from older, mainly paper-based records to "new" data-based "scrutiny through the use of technical means to extract or create personal or group data, whether from individuals or contexts".[42] It could be extended to include DNA analysis, data profiling, matching and mining, CCTV with enhanced definition and predictive functionality and imaging and scanning capabilities. Regimes of new surveillance (unlike traditional surveillance) could presumably be undertaken at a distance (such as aerial drones equipped with CCTV, sound recording and public address capabilities) with "sponge-like absorbency and laser-like specificity" and might also require self-surveillance and the surveillance of others, for example in the workplace or the community.[43]

Questions of power, governance and democracy in relation to the development and deployment of surveillance measures remain unresolved.[44] While on one level, surveillance is "the collection and processing of personal data, whether identifiable or not, for the purposes of influencing or managing those whose data have been garnered" at another level, panoptic surveillance "tries to make visible the identities or behaviours of people of interest to the agency in question".[45] When Foucault wrote about the power of the panopticon he considered that this lay essentially in the "surveillance gaze" received, internalised and at least in part embraced, by the subject-object and was thus fundamental to the exercise by authorities of surveillant power.[46] Malone relates this concept to the discourse of threatening youth, where young people, uncertain if they are under

---

42 Marx, 2003, p. 2.

43 Ibid., p. 3.

44 Bauman and Lyon, 2013, p. 45.

45 Lyon, 2002, p. 2.

46 Foucault, 1977, p. 47.

surveillance, surveil themselves and the actions of other children and young people.[47] Familial surveillance is also a requirement for families with dependants subject to Anti-Social Behaviour Orders or ASBOs in the UK.[48]

While researchers argue that surveillance is not inherently designed to perpetuate inequality, it is apposite to note that in contemporary society, where everyone is subject to some forms of surveillance "not everyone is monitored in the same way or for the same purposes".[49] Surveillance is more than just watching, it is "a calculated practice for managing and manipulating human behaviour".[50] These practices tend more often than not, to "coagulate more heavily on the more disadvantaged members of society" such as young people.[51]

Children and young people are highly visible users of urban public space as they have limited resources to effectively shield their presence from public view. Denied access (initially, at least, by reason of age) from a whole host of cultural amenities, young people come to rely on local streets, public transport, city centres, shopping malls and the like as a means to build cultural identities away from the direct supervision of adult authority. Their social practices – both legal and illegal – are thus rendered public and visible.[52]

Public space presents them with the (often false) promise of inclusion and fulfilment through consumption.[53] It is a key issue for civic authorities increasingly concerned not just with what they do

47 Malone, 2002, p. 23.
48 Squires and Stephen, 2005, p. 89.
49 Gilliom, 2001, p.89; Henman, 2004, p. 145.
50 Henman, 2004, p. 176.
51 Henman and Marston, 2008, p. 201.
52 Loader, 1996, p. 69.
53 White, 1990, p. 8; Shields, 1992, p. 78; Miles and Miles, 2004, p. 12. On their "visible-ness" see Dwyer, 2010, p. 2.

or might do in public space, but with what they wear and how they look, including the now infamous "hoody" recently the subject of a proposed ban in the Brisbane suburb of Wynnum, and also at the Bluewater shopping centre in the UK.[54]

Similar findings are apparent in research conducted in Logan.[55] The research was carried out through a self-completion survey, designed by young people who were members of Logan City Youth Council. The methodology included a modified Grounded Theory approach to data collection, coding and sorting, to excavate key themes emerging from the data for further, exhaustive analysis.[56] Respondents were female (594) and male (528) aged 13-18 from six state high schools and one independent school. The survey instrument contained 17 questions. The relevant ones for this paper asked respondents about negative stereotyping, security cameras, facilities for young people, involvement and personal safety in their local community and schools, the meaning of the word citizenship and feelings of belonging.

Key findings from the data were as follows:

- Some communities are less concerned about young people, than others.
- Most schools are safe, but a number are not.
- Teachers contribute to student's feelings of safety at school.
- School should be about belonging and inclusiveness.
- The word citizenship carries important meanings for most young people around belonging, community and taking part in community and national life.

54 Flack, 2011; Flint 2006, p. 51.
55 Dee, p. 295.
56 Glaser, 2003, p. 90.

- Most young people feel negatively stereotyped by their community.

- Most local areas do not have enough youth facilities.

- Public spaces such as streets, parks and transport nodes should be clean, well maintained and well lit, should have more in the way of facilities, such as shaded areas and places and events for young people and need supervision by human agents – camera surveillance alone does not give confidence that personal safety is assured.

In the case of CCTV as one element in the arsenal of the surveillance state, three English CCTV systems were studied, with 148 cameras over 592 hours of observation in control rooms, finding that the young, the male and the black, were systematically targeted for surveillance, not because of their involvement in crime or disorder, but for "no obvious reason".[57] Forty per cent were targeted on the basis of "belonging to a particular or subcultural group" with black people more than twice as likely to be surveilled than others, and for longer time periods.[58] In my study the majority of the respondents said:

- CCTV did not make them feel safe when using public places.

- Conversely perhaps, roughly equal numbers of respondents said there should be more CCTV as were opposed to further installation of CCTV.

- Key issues for many respondents centred on the appropriate locations for CCTV, and its effectiveness in actually protecting them, rather than buildings or other pieces of infrastructure from harm in public space.[59]

---

57 Norris and Armstrong, 1999, p. 212.
58 Ibid., p. 150.
59 Dee, 2011, p. 298.

In addition to CCTV, there are recent innovations in the repertoire of public space controls such as the mosquito, a device emitting a high-pitched noise directly targeting children and young people under the age of 25 because their hearing is not yet fully developed.[60] Clearly, such a blunt instrument with blanket coverage over a 40-metre range fails to differentiate fairly between groups or individual children and young people and more importantly, brooks no discussion about rights to use and enjoy public space in the same way that other age groups do.[61] There is now a substantial body of critical material pointing to a social sorting and ordering of public space by civic authorities around the world that is almost entirely driven by support for "conspicuous consumption" and the exclusion, or at best, conditional inclusion, of "flawed consumers" or "vagabonds".[62] The increasing control and regulation of public space in Australia has been captured in the concept of the "Fortress City" comprising many of the features discussed by as the fortification and "destruction of public space" including shopping malls, transforming public space into "mass private property".[63] Suburban malls now act as de facto community centres and increasingly present themselves as town squares.[64] They may include modified seating to prevent sleeping, camera surveillance, a visible and daunting security presence, and may even resort to the playing of classical music which "could chase young people away" apparently making "such places safer".[65] As a result, Hubbard proposed that landscapes had become "Scanscapes"

---

60 Institute for Public Policy Research 2006, p. 7.
61 Dee, 2011, p. 3; Morrow, 2002, p. 78.
62 Zurawski and Czerwinski, 2008, p. 89; Baumann, 1998, p. 14.
63 Davis, 1995, p.24; White, 1996, p. 37 and p. 246.
64 Shields, 1992, p. 4; Copeland, 2004, p. 23; Flint, 2006, p. 54, with "paid for" seating in coffee shops. See Dee, op. cit., p. 250.
65 *Adelaide Advertiser* 15 May 1995, cited in White, 1996, p. 42.

wherein the electronic eyes of surveillance achieve a near totalising or "panoptic" gaze.[66]

Decisions about the installation and/or extension-upgrade of CCTV systems are barely concerned with questions of civil liberties and largely devoted to obtaining a technical resolution to irksome and persistent urban issues whose antecedence may lie in poverty and disadvantage but through reconstruction, become matters of governance and control on behalf of the responsible majority, as Clavell notes:

> CCTV has become an increasingly popular policy solution to security problems in urban environments: as part of a broader project to promote "civility" and eliminate "anti-social behaviour". The need to impose "proper behaviour" and sanction deviance is the discourse used to justify and legitimise the need to control what people do in open, public space through the electronic lens – as well as an increased police presence and powers.[67]

The installation of ever more sophisticated, extensive and costly CCTV systems is a form of "surveillance creep".[68] The process moved into "every village, parish and hamlet".[69] It is seemingly a badge of honour for civic authorities desperate to be seen as decisive and "doing something" about crime and so-called anti-social behaviour.[70]

In places like Logan (and other urban spaces worldwide) the role of CCTV surveillance is central to attempts to govern in ways that may eventually restrict those who are financially poor or simply

66 Hubbard, 2006, p. 249; Lyon, p. 10.
67 Clavell, 2011, p. 525.
68 Nelkin and Andrews, 2003, p. 17.
69 Walby, 2006, p. 40.
70 Garland, 2001, p. 98.

maladapted. These are the people who do not fit well within gentrified and "creative cities" – places fit for conspicuous consumption.[71] Creative cities strategies harnessing economic development with the encouragement of the creative classes and waves of urban renewal and refurbishment come with grand promises of enhanced community life and engagement, as well as substantial new employment opportunities.[72] The creative cities vision is both sweeping and total, travelling globally, seducing civic authorities with the lure of curing seemingly intractable urban issues of inequality, poverty or run-down, worn-out neighbourhoods and infrastructure. As Gibson and Klocker note, "the result is a representation of creativity and cultural industries as a panacea for urban economic development problems, a solution capable of overcoming inherited class and other socio-spatial relations to produce a more inclusive, democratically 'creative' society".[73]

In terms of public space and local community however, impacts in places such as Brisbane and Sydney have been less inclusive than handsomely presented strategy documents and brochures foretold. The gentrification of previously troubled neighbourhoods rather predictably demands moving on and out, a range of low-income residents and users, so that high-rise, high-priced apartment living can be facilitated and expanded.[74] Seemingly, the creative classes drawn to inner city locales by creative cities discourses, respond to assurances of safe yet vibrant, cosmopolitan liveability. Efforts to comfort these desired users of public space with pledges of safe family shopping, entertainment and lifestyle environments and precincts, are sustained at public expense to ensure private accumulation. They can easily run

---

71 Atkinson and Easthope, 2009, p. 71; Dee, 2011, p. 13.
72 Florida, 2004, p. 27.
73 Gibson and Klocker, 2004, p. 431.
74 Atkinson and Easthope, 2009, p. 75.

counter to civic advertising playing on the importance of celebrating diversity and the inclusion of all in the community including children and young people.[75]

The tolerance claimed by the creative classes in terms of race, sexual orientation and lifestyle behaviour as necessary for their participation in creative cities initiatives, may not be extended to the low income families and others residing in areas set for regeneration and under a glossy patina of inclusion, substantial marginalisation and resultant exclusion occurs, unless civic authorities are mindful and active in working for some semblance of meaningful social diversity and social justice. Now that would be truly creative.[76]

Issues of urban citizenship

Fundamental questions are raised in this chapter about the form, meaning and quality of urban citizenship and participation particularly by children and young people in the face of increasingly militaristic, hostile and technologically advanced (if democratically compromised) regulatory and exclusionary measures. Some of these measures include "smart" city initiatives, creative cities and safer cities programs, which aspire to harness artistic endeavours and activities with economic reform and development, usually in the form of extensive urban renewal. However, the highly publicised and promoted policy aim of inclusion can and does lead to forms of exclusion. Attempts to make urban places safe for approved activities and social actors may become self-defeating in the forcible exclusion of so many "dangerous others" that the public space remaining is bereft of any excitement, or real diversity and difference.[77]

---

75 Dee, 2008, p. 175.
76 Atkinson and Easthope, p. 75.
77 Watson, 2006, p. 65.

So called safe public space is predictable and patterned, largely as civic authorities and corporate entities require it to be, but lacking in the nurturing of engagement and social citizenship of encountering and understanding difference and practicing tolerance, essential elements of a confident and sophisticated urban population. Conversely, it can be said that places that work well for children and young people, that have a good level of amenity and provision, that are genuinely inclusive, go a long way to meeting the needs of *all* users of public space and consequently, require much less in the way of security and policing.[78]

Acknowledgements

The author would like to thank the Place and Displacement reviewers for their comments and suggestions on earlier drafts of this work.

References

Atkinson, R. and Easthope, H. (2009) "The consequences of the Creative Class: The Pursuit of Creativity Strategies in Australia's Cities". *International Journal of Urban and Regional Research*. 33(1) March: 64-79.

Baldrey, P., and Painter, K. (1988) "Watching Them Watching Us". *The Surveyor.*

Bauman, Z. (1988) *Work, consumerism and the new poor.* Buckingham: Open University Press.

Bauman, Z. and Lyon, D. (2013) *Liquid Surveillance.* Cambridge: Polity.

Beck, U. (1992) *Risk Society. Towards a New Modernity.* London: Sage.

Blagg, H., Wilkie, M. and Australian Youth Foundation. (1995) *Young people and police powers.* Sydney: The Australian Youth Foundation.

---

78 Jacobs, 1965, p. 50; Sennett, 1976, p. 89; Dee, 2008, p. 347; Freeman, 2006, p. 23.

Clancey, G. (2009) *Considerations for establishing a public space CCTV network*. Canberra: Australian Institute of Criminology.

Clavell, G. (2011) "The Political Economy of Surveillance in the (Wannabe) Global City". *Surveillance and Society*. 8(4): 523-6.

Copeland, A. (2004) "Public Space: A rights-based approach". *Youth Studies Australia*. 23(3): 40-5.

Crane, P. and Dee, M. (2011) "Young people, public space & New Urbanism". *Youth Studies Australia*. 20(1). 11-8.

Davis, Mike. (1995) "Fortress Los Angeles: The Militarization of Urban Space". In Kasinitz, P. (ed). *Metropolis Centre and Symbol of our Times*. London: Macmillan.

Dean, H. (2013) "The translation of needs into rights: Reconceptualising social citizenship as a global phenomenon". *International Journal of Social Welfare*. 22: 32-49.

Dee, Mike. (1995) "Caught on camera". *Young People Now*. 18-9.

————. (2000) "The use of CCTV to police public Spaces: A case of Big Brother or Big Friend?". Paper Presented at the 27th International Conference on Making Cities Liveable, Vienna Town Hall, Austria, July.

————. (2008) "Young People, Public Space and Citizenship". Unpublished Doctor of Philosophy Thesis. Queensland University of Technology. Brisbane. Australia.

————. (2011) "Governing the dangerous classes : welcome to E-Nose, CCTV and the Mosquito". In Threadgold, Steven, Kirby, Emma, and Germov, John. (eds). *Proceedings of the Australian Sociological Association (TASA) Local Lives/Global Networks*. The Australian Sociological Association (TASA); The University of Newcastle. NSW: 1-23.

Dwyer, A. (2009) *Visibly Invisible: Policing Queer Young People As A Research Gap*. ae.dwyer@qut.edu.au

Finer, C. and Nellis, M. (eds). (1998). *Crime and Social Exclusion*. Oxford: Blackwell.

Flack, M. (2011) "More eyes on Logan". *Albert and Logan News*. 21 July.

Flint, J. (2006) "Surveillance and exclusion practices in the governance of access to shopping centres on periphery estates in the UK". *Surveillance and Society*, 4(1/2): 52-68.

Florida, Richard. (2004) *Cities and the creative class*. New York: Routledge.

Fopp. R. (2002) "Increasing the Potential for Gaze, Surveillance and Normalisation: the transformation of an Australian policy for people who are homeless". *Surveillance and Society*. 1(1): 48-65.

Foucault, M. (1977) *Discipline and Punish: The Birth of the Prison*. London: Allan Lane.

Freeman, C. (2006) "Colliding worlds: planning with children and young people for better cities". In Gleeson, B and Snipe, N. (eds). *Creating Child Friendly Cities*. London: Routledge.

Garland, D. (2001) *The Culture of Control: Crime and Social Order in Contemporary Society*. Oxford: Oxford University Press.

Geraghty, T. (2000) *The Irish War*. London: Harper Collins. 2000.

Gibson, C. and Klocker, N. (2004) "Academic publishing as 'creative' industry, and recent discourses of 'creative economies': some critical reflections". *Area* 36(4): 423-34.

Gilliom, J. (2001) *Overseers of the Poor: Surveillance, Resistance, and the Limits of Privacy*. Chicago: University of Chicago Press.

Goold, B.J. (2006) " 'Open to all?' Regulating Open Street CCTV and the Case for "Symmetrical Surveillance". *Criminal Justice Ethics*. 25(1) Winter: 3-17.

Graham, S. and Marvin, S. (2001) *Splintering Urbanism*. London: Routledge.

Haggerty, K. and Ericson, R. (2006) *The New Politics of Surveillance and Visibility*. Toronto: University of Toronto Press.

Harris, A. (2013) *Young People and Everyday Multiculturalism*. London: Routledge. 2013.

Henman, P. (2004) "Population Segmentation, Electronic Surveillance and Governing the Unemployed in Australia". *International Sociology*. 19(2): 173-91.

Henman, P. and Marston, G. (2008) "The social division of welfare surveillance". *Journal of Social Policy*. 37(2): 187-206.

Hollis, L. (2013) *Cities are Good for You*. London: Bloomsbury.

Hubbard, P. (2006) *City*. London: Routledge.

Hussein, S. (1998) "More spy-cameras on the way". *Bradford Telegraph and Argus*. 1 December.

Institute for Public Policy Research web-site. *Cafe Politique: Big Brother policing: CCTV and Surveillance.*

Iveson, K. (1998) "Putting the Public back into Public Space". *Urban Policy and Research*. 16(1): 21-9.

Jacobs, J. (1965). *The Death and Life of Great American Cities*. New York: Random House.

Kearns, R. and Collins, D. (2006) "Children in the intensifying city: lessons from Auckland's walking school buses". In Gleeson, B. and Snipe, N. (eds). *Creating Child Friendly Cities*. London: Routledge.

Kulynych, J. (2001) "No playing in the public sphere: Democratic theory and the exclusion of children". *Social Theory and Practice*. 27(2): 231-64.

Laughlin, D. and Johnson, L. (2011) "Defining and exploring public space: perspectives of young people from Regent Park, Toronto". *Children's Geographies*. 9(2): 225-38.

Leonard, M. (2006) "Teens and territory in contested spaces: Negotiating sectarian interfaces in Northern Ireland". *Children's Geographies*. 4(2): 439-56.

Leslie, D and Catungal, J.P. (2012) "Social Justice and the Creative City: Class, Gender and Racial Inequalities". *Geography Compass*. 6(3): 111-22.

Loader, I. (1996) *Youth, Policing and Democracy*. London: Macmillan.

Logan City Council. (2011) *Logan captures an Australian safety first*. 15 July.

Lynch, K. (1977). *Growing Up in Cities*. Cambridge, MA: MIT Press.

Lyon, D. (2002) "Surveillance Studies: Understanding visibility, mobility and the phenetic fix". *Surveillance and Society*. 1(1): 1-7.

Lyon, D. (2001) *Surveillance Society*. Buckingham: Open University Press.

Malone, K. (2002) "Street life: youth, culture and competing uses of public space". *Environment and Urbanization*. 14(2) 157-68.

Malone, K. and Hasluck, L. (2008) "Geographies of Exclusion". *Family Matters*. (49) Autumn: 20-6.

Marshall, T. H., and Bottomore, T. (1950). *Citizenship and Social Class*. London: Pluto.

Marx, G.T. (2003) "A Tack in the Shoe: Neutralizing and Resisting the New Surveillance". *Journal of Social Issues*. 59(2): 369-90.

————. (2002) "What's New About the "New Surveillance"? Classifying for Change and Continuity". *Surveillance and Society*. 1(1): 9-29.

Measor, L. and Squires, P. (2000) *Young people and community safety: inclusion, risk, tolerance and disorder*. Aldershot: Ashgate.

Miles, S. and Miles, M. (2004) *Consuming Cities*. Basingstoke and New York: Palgrave.

Morrow, V. (2002) "Children's rights to public space: environment and curfews". In Franklin. B. (ed). (2002) *The New Handbook of Children's Rights*. London: Routledge.

Nelkin, D. and Andrews, L. (2003) "Surveillance creep in the genetic age". In Lyon, D. (ed). *Surveillance as Social Sorting*. London: Routledge.

Norris, C. and Armstrong, G. (1999). *The Maximum Surveillance Society: The rise of CCTV*. Oxford: Berg.

Parnell, S. (2011) "Agencies demand access to all CCTV". *The Australian*, 10 August.

Rowntree Foundation, the Joseph (2011). *The social value of public spaces.* York: Joseph Rowntree Foundation.

Scott, C. (2002). "Citizenship education: who pays the piper?". In Franklin, B. (ed). *The New Handbook of Children's Rights.* London: Routledge.

Sennett, R. (1976) *The Fall of Public Man.* New York: Knopf.

Shields, R. (1992) *Lifestyle Shopping: The Subject of Consumption.* London: Routledge.

Sibley, D. (1995). *Geographies of Exclusion: Society and Difference in the West.* London: Routledge.

Sleight, S. (2013) *Young People and the Shaping of Public Space in Melbourne, 1870-1914.* Surrey: Ashgate.

Spooner, P. (2001). "Moving in the wrong direction: An analysis of police move-on powers in Queensland". *Youth Studies Australia.* 20(1): 27-31.

Squires, P., and Stephen, D. (2005). "Rethinking ASBOs". *Critical Social Policy.* 25(4): 517-28.

Standing, G. (2011) *The Precariat: The New Dangerous Class.* London: Bloomsbury.

Stedman, A. (2011) "The camera never lies, or does it? The dangers of taking CCTV surveillance at face value". *Surveillance and Society.* 8(4): 527-34.

Tonkiss, F. (2005) *Space, the City and Social Theory.* Cambridge and New York: Polity Press.

Valentine, G. (2004) *Public Space and the Culture of Childhood.* Aldershot and New York: Ashgate.

Walby, K. (2006) "Little England? The rise of open-street Closed Circuit Television surveillance in Canada". *Surveillance and Society.* 4(1/2): 29-51.

Watson, S. (2006) *City Publics: The (dis)enchancements of urban encounters.* Oxford and New York: Routledge.

Weller, S. (2006) "Situating (young) teenagers in geographies of children and youth". *Children's Geographies.* 4(1): 97-198.

White, R., and Wyn, J. (2004) *Youth and Society, exploring the social dynamics of youth experience.* Melbourne: Oxford University Press.

White, R. (1990). *No Space of Their Own: Young People and Social Control in Australia.* Melbourne: Cambridge University Press.

White, R. (1992). Public Space. *Australian Youth Issues, 14*(2), 123-241.

White, R. (1996). 'No-go in the fortress city: Young people, inequality and space'. *Urban Policy and Research, 14*(1), 37-50.

White, R. (2001). Youth Participation in Designing Public Spaces. *Youth Studies Australia, 20*(1), 19-26.

Wilson, D., Rose, J. & Colvin, E. (2010) *Marginalised Young People, Surveillance & Public Space.* Youth Affairs Council of Victoria.

Woolley, H. (2006). Freedom of the city: contemporary issues and policy influences on children and young people's use of public open space in England. *Children's Geographies, 4*(1), 45-59.

Zurawski, N. & Czerwinski, S. (2008). Crime, Maps and Meaning: Views from a Survey on Safety and CCTV in Germany. *Surveillance and Society, 5*(1): 51-72.

6

Johannes Pieters

Recovering from bushfire related housing loss; lessons from Susan's journey to home

The 2009 bushfires in Victoria, like so many other bushfires in Australia, caused massive human, environmental and economic losses. A key strand within the debates which emerged following the fires and which has concerned building and planning researchers in particular, was the issue of where and under what conditions housing should be built in high bushfire prone areas.[1] The policy of "plan, stay and defend or leave early" now provides guidance to any householder caught in the kind of destructive forces unleashed in the Black Saturday fires in Victoria in 2009. The historian Tom Griffiths in commenting on this policy, questioned that a home could be defended under such circumstances:

> It [the policy] is libertarian; it recognises the reality that people prefer to stay in their own homes and defend them if they can; it seeks to minimise late evacuation which is so often fatal; it encourages sensible planning and preparation; and it has demonstrably saved lives and homes. It will continue to

1 Hughes and Mercer, 2009; Teague, McLeod et al., 2010; Groenhart, March et al., 2012.

guide people well in most areas of Australia. But I fear that
it has misled people in this distinctively deadly fire region to
believe that they could defend an ordinary home in the face
of an unimaginable force.[2]

Two discourses frame this discussion, firstly, that climate change
will lead to more frequent and intense fires and secondly, that such
intense fires are an inevitable and vital component of the Australian
landscape and its biodiversity.[3] The reconciliation between bushfire
and biodiversity with daily life and thus housing has led the Australian-
based architect Ian Weir to suggest that ecologically sustainable
habitation of bushfire-prone landscapes will emerge once we cease
fearing fire and embrace bushfires as catalysts for design innovation.[4]
Robinson and Tout argue that settler-colonial Australians remain
unsettled and disconnected, unable to belong, on the land on which
they live.[5] The challenge has been powerfully summarised by Collins
as "there is a real sense in which we will be judged by our attitude to
fire. If we learn to live with it, we will be truly at home in Australia.
Otherwise we will always remain transients here."[6]

Forest fuel management through controlled burns in National
Parks and private property was the subject of nearly five hundred
submissions (the largest category) to the 2009 Victorian Bushfires
Royal Commission.[7] Other key categories in descending order of
number of submissions were fire preparedness, warnings, planning
and local government, stay or go/evacuation/refuges, causes and
circumstances, building/rebuilding and recovery efforts. These

2 Griffiths, 2009.
3 Gill and Bradstock, 2003; IPPC, 2007.
4 Weir, 2012.
5 Tout and Robinson, 2012.
6 Collins, 2000, p. 349.
7 Teague, McLeod et al., 2010.

policy matters frame decision-making by victims of bushfire, whose capacity to focus on housing issues, is, to a greater or lesser extent, subject to their progression through the psycho-social processes typical of disaster/trauma recovery and to their ability to recover from any psychiatric implications of displacement.[8]

The role of gender in relation to risks in bushfire-prone areas has also been raised. Some have argued that there are gender differences regarding the awareness, preparedness and attitudes towards bushfires amongst landholders, going so far as to argue that bushfire should be conceptualised as an important means by which gender roles and power relations within rural landscapes are maintained.[9] Proudley concluded, based on research on recovery from bushfires in South Australia in 2005, that it is essential to recognise that family dynamics and women's role within the family influence behaviour during a crisis.[10]

To be "truly at home" in bushfire-prone areas now requires compliance with a range of regulatory measures. Where once the sense of home in these areas reflected expectations for healthy living, affordable housing, freedom to dwell in large open and natural spaces, privacy and autonomy from regulatory authorities, now the sense of home can perhaps only be recovered through prescriptions regarding defendable space, Bushfire Attack Level ratings and Flame Zones, fire-retardant building materials, secure underground bunkers, retreat and resettlement policies and the renewed call to "prepare, stay and defend or leave early".[11] These potential conditioners of and or constraints on the sense of home are examples of what

---

8 McFarlane, Clayer et al., 1997; Gordon, 2004; Fullilove, 1996.

9 Eriksen, Gill and Head, 2010.

10 Proudley, 2008.

11 Handmer and Tibbits, 2005.

Dovey referred to as processes, properties and conditions that have eroded the traditional sense of home. Dovey referred to these as the properties of homelessness, where homelessness is defined as the lack of the experiential phenomenon of home. For Dovey these processes, properties and conditions were rationalism and technology, commoditisation, bureaucracy, scale and speed, the erosion of communal space and professionalism. In relation to bureaucratic structure, Dovey argues that just as home establishes a certain order, bureaucratic structures and processes can impose a kind of order but this order and identity is diametrically opposed to those which assist becoming-at-home. In Dovey's words:

> ... whereas home is the kind of order that flows upward from the opportunities and problems of each unique place and context bureaucratic order flows downwards. Likewise bureaucratic organisation has its own identity that in the case of housing programs becomes stamped upon the landscape at the expense of the diverse identifications of the dwellers. Housing becomes symbolic of the organisation that produces it.[12]

If Dovey is correct then the extensive bureaucratic processes involved in disaster recovery and in particular housing reconstruction, may all operate to undermine the ability of households to feel at home. This chapter argues that the sense of home plays an important role in mediating recovery from bushfire-related housing loss. Firstly the chapter discusses how the sense of home and housing are linked. Secondly the chapter discusses the literature on the impact of and recovery from bushfire-related housing loss highlighting the importance of place. In section three the chapter outlines the qualitative research strategy used in assessing resettlement journeys

---

12 Dovey, 1985, p. 56.

of individuals whose houses were destroyed in the Black Saturday fires in Victoria in 2009. In the next section the lived experience of recovery following displacement is narrated by Susan (a pseudonym) whose house near Marysville, Victoria was destroyed in the Black Saturday fires. In the final section, the chapter briefly returns to the theoretical level to consider implications from this for understanding recovery from displacement and the sense of home.

The sense of home across the life course

How might we best conceptualise the relationship between home, the meaning of home, and place attachment?[13] Based on their life-course research on relocation and spatial experience, Watkins and Hosier argued that one's definition of home develops out of cumulative experience through life that is continually refined through the tension between the experienced and imagined home.[14]

Critical feminist geographers have argued that home should be understood as being simultaneously material and imaginative, as mediating power and identity and that home is multi-scalar.[15] Central to their analysis of home is the concept of home-making. According to Hayward meanings of home can be grouped under the following headings: home as physical structure; home as a territory; home as locus in space; home as self and self-identity; home as social and cultural unit.[16] As Dupuis and Thorns argue in relation to older homeowners in New Zealand, "the meanings of home are, therefore, not just about material possessions or identity but a complex interweaving of the quest for security and identity with the accumulation of assets and

13 Mallett, 2004.
14 Watkins and Hosier, 2005.
15 Blunt and Dowling, 2006.
16 Hayward, 1975.

other markers of achievement and the transfer of these to subsequent generations".[17]

Defining recovery from bushfire-related housing loss in the context of place

Recovery from bushfire disasters has received considerable attention sometimes extending to conceptualisations of home and place with a multi-disciplinary perspective emerging. The historian Peter Read has portrayed the minutiae of bushfire recovery though elegant, poignant ethnographic studies. He cites the story of Anne Boyd, whose home was destroyed by a fire in Ferntree Gully, Victoria in 1993:

> She began to a recover from depression at the moment the builders began constructing her new home. It was to be built to her own design. In the wreckage she had discovered a blue, terracotta and white ceramic plate which was bought in Assisi and which had hung in her home in London. She cleaned it, hung it in the restored bathroom and planned the new tile design around it. She told the author "there's a pattern, a continuity, a symmetry about that".[18]

Camilleri et al. surveyed 500 individuals who survived the 2003 Canberra bushfires over a three-year period. Just under half of those surveyed had lost dwellings, "homes not just houses" as some pointed out. Over 25 per cent experienced displacement and nearly 80 per cent loss of neighbourhood. Asked about improvements or deteriorations nearly half reported that neighbourhood relationships had improved compared to 28 per cent who claimed they had deteriorated.[19]

---

17 Dupuis and Thorns, 1996.
18 Read, 1996, p. 113.
19 Camilleri et al., 2012.

The importance of place for understanding recovery from trauma cannot be underestimated. Shamai understood the sense of place in Toronto as a continuum with seven levels: not having any sense of place, knowledge of being located in a place, belonging to a place, attachment to a place, identifying with the place goals, involvement with the place, and sacrifice for a place.[20] Cox and Holmes used phenomenological geography and ecological philosophy to identify the linkages between human beings and their dwelling places.[21] These authors use the concept of "at-homeness" defined by Seamon as "the power of home to organise the habitual, bodily stratum of the person's lived space".[22] Borrell explored recovery from bushfire destruction using concepts of rupture, loss, identity and place, seen through among other lenses, the relationship between ontological security and home.[23] Oliver proposed that recovery from displacement and environmental destruction should be seen through the lens of the concept of "solastalgia", a term coined by the Australian philosopher Glenn Albrecht in 2003 to describe psychic or existential distress caused by environmental change.[24] Similarly, Fullilove asserted that recovery from psychiatric implications of displacement involves a striving for a sense of belonging, establishment of a spatial identity and returning to routine.[25]

Methodology

Within the wider area burnt out on "Black Saturday" (7 February 2009), bushfires destroyed 141 out of the 217 occupied private

---

20 Shamai, 1991.
21 Cox and Holmes, 2000.
22 Seamon, 1979, p. 79.
23 Borrell, 2011.
24 Oliver, 2012.
25 Fullilove, 1996.

dwellings in Marysville, a small town of just over 500 people in the Great Dividing Range north-east of Melbourne. The fires killed 34 people.

The mixed methods research of this paper was conducted in Marysville, Victoria in November 2011, nearly three years after the fires of 9 February 2009. Preparation, involving contact with informants commenced in late 2009. In conducting this background work it became clear that among some human service providers there was a concern that some residents could not feel at home months after moving into their new house. Others faced more difficult adjustments. For example people who had been renting were eligible for less compensation; owners of holiday homes were not eligible for housing-based compensation. At the time of the interviews 161 houses had been rebuilt or reached lock-up stage and 16 retail businesses were functioning in Marysville. These interviews were with eight individuals and four couples regarding their recovery from bushfire-related housing loss. A semi-structured interview schedule guided the discussion and all interviews were recorded. Nine out of the total of sixteen participants were female. All participants were living either in the township or within eight kilometres of Marysville with an age range of 30 to 75 years. Interviews with residents comprised 25 questions designed to capture four key factors:

- Housing history and meaning of home prior to and after the fire.
- The impact of the fires.
- Key steps/decisions/feelings in the process of displacement and rebuilding.
- Definitions of recovery.

Some of the key questions, informed by the literature, included:

- Years of residence in Marysville prior to the fires.
- Plans regarding housing prior to the fire.
- Best and worst aspects of living in the town.
- What did home mean prior to and after fires.
- Sense of belonging in the town.
- The meaning/impact of the fires.
- Impact of temporary accommodation on sense of home.
- How did the question arise regarding whether to stay and rebuild or leave.
- Has complying with the building code regarding dwellings in high bushfire risk areas compromised and or enhanced your sense of security and or the meaning of home?
- Role of site clean-up, house design, rebuilding, moving in and homemaking.

Interviews were also conducted with Murrindindi Shire planning staff, non-government sector case management workers and a staff member of an agency contracted by the Victorian government to manage temporary housing in Marysville. Analysis involved an inductive process of coding and interpretation of the data with the aim of establishing to what extent the existing research findings and theory could help explain how a sense of home is maintained through and or informs or directs the personal recovery process, especially in relation to rebuilding of houses.

The key interview here was with one resident, pseudonym Susan, in her early thirties and who had moved from interstate to live in Marysville some 13 years earlier. She had married a long-time local man who worked in agriculture. They had two boys at primary school. The household was renting at the time of the fire and lived about eight kilometres out of town. Susan had occasional part-time work in

Marysville. At the time of the fires, the farm was about to be sold, so they would soon have had to move.

Susan's Story: Defining recovery from displacement

As we have seen, recovery from displacement requires striving for a sense of belonging, establishing a spatial identity and returning to routine. These themes, to a greater or lesser extent, can be identified in Susan's account of the impact of the bushfires. However they are not the whole of Susan's story, for it is also about family and housing tenure. Susan described plans prior to the fire to move to NSW where her husband would have guaranteed work. However the fire changed everything:

> So you know, we would have to not stress about getting a job or whatever and that was the plan. And then the fire came and neither of us wanted to leave Marysville. We didn't want to uproot the boys, we didn't want to; already, they'd been through so much, even though pre-fire we had planned on doing it they hadn't been through all that stress, so like it would have been just that one little upheaval for them but after having lost their friends, lost their babysitter, lost their possessions, lost their home we couldn't make them lose their town. So we – once we made up our mind, it was a lot of to-ing and fro-ing but pre-fire our plan was to bail. Post fire we couldn't, we couldn't do it so.[26]

Asked what the best things were about living in Marysville prior to the fire she assessed it in social, environmental and family terms.

---

26 Quotations from interview with Susan (pseudonym) in November 2011 as part of UniSA approved research "Rebuilding the imagined home – its role in the process of recovery following bushfire related housing loss"; permission to include quotations confirmed 14 April 2014.

Just the whole community. Everyone, as much as sometimes you don't like everyone knowing everything, but it's just all, everyone just helps out and on the farm it was just lovely, the views were spectacular that was just, we were only five minutes from town but it felt like we were out of town as well, you know, like it was quiet and on the farm the boys had motorbikes and stuff, you know it was just fish in the front paddock.

The only downsides to living in the area were the lack of socialising opportunities for her two children. Asked what home meant she assessed it in terms of family: "It just meant where we were. That was where our family was. That was, that was just somewhere where we would be a family". Asked if she felt whether the term "belonging" in Marysville would be too strong a description Susan was emphatic and referred to the embodied nature of the relationship with place and the need to return to 'normal' life:

No. Sometimes I wish I didn't, but yeah because especially after the fire we were thinking, right basically the house/the home, the house/home went, the job went because you know it was time for the job to finish up. My husband managed, the fellow that owned it had died eight years previous and so it had been run by a trust and whatever and then like with the fire it was, they were in the process of getting it all ready to sell anyway but the fire sped it up a bit, so you lost home, lost job and it's like right, do we just bail? But Marysville was imbedded in to us by that stage, sometimes like I said sometimes I wish we could have (relocated) because constantly, especially here because I work here in town every day there's fire questions or and you don't get the chance just to be normal again from like, from tourists and I understand that's their way of dealing with it too. But you've got it every

day, after you know two and a half years, you almost want to
say look – it happened!

They stayed in a small unit for a year after the fire. Asked if being
prevented from returning to the town for the six weeks or so that
was needed for forensic investigations to be undertaken had been
problematic she replied that it wasn't so much a problem for them
as they lived out of town however the ban had a major detrimental
impact on a friend:

> ... they were sort of locked out and it was, they needed to go
> there just to you know, to say to feel their connection with it
> but a part of all that and being locked out she contributed to
> the breakdown and part of the breakdown of her marriage
> as well like being locked out because they couldn't you know,
> deal with everything else. I mean there were other issues as
> well but . . .

The question of whether to stay or leave tested them although not
fundamentally and a key temptation was the desire to be away from an
environment which reinforced their status as victims:

> Absolutely. It was yeah and I like I said we thought about it
> but we just couldn't move away . . . well it would have been
> nice (just to get away) only to like, to like start again and not
> be victims, you know, after a little while you get sick of being
> a victim because we don't feel ourselves, I mean, I've got
> friends that lost family, you know, they're victims but we're
> not, we lost the house that was a home but we can rebuild
> a home and rebuild possessions but we can't rebuild family.

The process of the final decision about where to live may have
influenced the level of at-homeness she experienced in the new house:

> Yeah, so and then one night we were sitting down and it has

just got on the computer . . . why haven't we looked at this one in . . . and he goes, what one? And he come up and goes alright so he rang the real estate first thing that morning, they come up, met us up there, he walked through it with my brother-in-law who's a builder and he rang me up at work, he goes I'm going to put an offer in it. I'm like, no worries. He goes, do you want to look? I said no. [Really?] Yeah, I said you think that's where you want to live, no worries, I said we can live wherever you are as long as, you know. And he's like, alright and then they accepted the offer, that afternoon I went down and signed the contract, so like within a few hours we had done it and as I walked in, straight away, this is where, this is what you're going to like, I've walked in the front door and without feeling like I was walking into another person's house, it actually felt like I had come home [Really?], and it just washed totally over me like there was no, well, I just felt like I just walked in and it was yeah, so.

Susan also believed that she had an advantage over people who have rebuilt:

and that's where I'm a bit luckier, I guess, in a lot of ways that people that have lived in their own home and then rebuilt on the same land and even though they know it's their house, it still sometimes doesn't feel like their home yet, whereas me with this one it just, straight away it was, it was home.

The decision to stay and her willingness to respond to any perceived pressure to stay was also influenced by a commitment to a community and the social support they needed and were prepared to reciprocate, they also wanted to get back a key component of their sense of home, their neighbourhood.

Not so much that the town needs me but that we need

each other, all of our friends and everyone that lives here, we needed to stay to get Marysville back, so yes we did feel pressure to stay. But sometimes most of that pressure was put on by ourselves as well.

Asked if she felt the meaning of home had changed for her Susan described the features of the new house that reinforced the feeling of home and the change in housing tenure clearly influenced the perception of home:

> In the farmhouse, home was home and we loved it but there was never any, oh if we knock this wall out we could make this bigger or whatever because it wasn't "ours", but it was definitely without a doubt "home". But down here, in the new house, we've walked in and it's beautiful and it smelled like home and feels like home and it's somewhere where we can escape because in our back yard, the fellow that had it before, all the yard, he was a gardener and it's spectacular and the birds, so you don't see fire in our backyard, you see just a backyard with plants and then now if we want to knock a wall out, we can. That's probably the only real . . . because wherever we are we're alright.

Asked if she felt safe in the new house, in terms of living in a fire-prone area Susan was unequivocal in her response:

> No. Pre-fire, there was smoke on the hill and I'd go it's ok, it's only you know, it's going to travel slow down the hill. My neighbour used to ring up all the time, "there's a fire", I'm like no, no it's alright look there's a helicopter now, they're putting it out, just little spot fires or lightning fires. But now I see smoke and I freak out. Not, like you know, I'm more observant you know, paying attention. I won't relax if there's smoke now. I won't break down, but I won't, I'll be sort of like checking, do we need to get out, do we need to move.

Asked if she felt the term "recovering" was an apt description for what she had been doing since the fire Susan selected a different expression "Recovering is probably a good word but I think just getting on with it is another, unfortunately we can't take it back, we can't undo it, so we've just got to keep going".

Asked whether this was the same or a different Marysville, Susan felt there was some continuity regarding the people but that the town was different:

> Different. Same but different. We want it to be the same but it can't be the same. We've got the same community spirit but it is definitely different. It's still beautiful, it's still got great people in it and people that will rally around you no matter what, probably more so, but it's definitely different.

Asked about how she saw the future, Susan distinguished between place and family:

> I see it in Marysville. I see it, we'll be alright. We've come through this, we've come through really strong as a family. But I'm not sure what else is the future. That's about it, just that we'll be ok because and it will be yeah, and it will be in Marysville – well, (name of town removed to protect anonymity).

Discussion

Research on the individual and community processes of recovery from disasters, has led to the development of conceptual frameworks and models across psychology, psychiatry and social work that guide practitioners involved in supporting victims of natural disasters. This phenomenon is a challenge for land-use planners, architects, social planners and housing policy specialists. Policy, often informed by the findings of post-disaster reviews, must address issues such as development control, housing construction and design, housing-nature interface and forest fuel management. These policy decisions may influence residents regarding the most testing of issues; whether or not to stay and rebuild in the same town and risk another bushfire event. Can the town or place be home again? Knowing how to support victims requires better understanding of the ways in which rebuilding or relocating contribute to recovery, and how stages of recovery mediate relocation and rebuilding decisions. Recovery from displacement involves striving for a sense of belonging, establishing a sense of spatial identity and returning to routine. Bushfire-related housing loss involves a challenge to the process of resolving the tension between the "experienced" and "imagined" home. Susan's characterisation of the meaning of home and place attachment, were interpreted in relation to the theories discussed in the literature.

The recovery journey for Susan's household/family and its links to the sense of home are clear, home was very much about family and consequently recovery meant ensuring they were together and that they were emotionally safe. Home was also multi-scalar, it extended beyond the house to where her two children felt they belonged. Marysville had been "embedded" into their family, in terms of place attachment theory.[27] Susan, if not her whole family, had ticked three boxes: They belonged to a place, they were attached to a place and they had made a commitment to place. Because Susan's household was renting at the time of the fire they had avoided most of the bureaucratic processes involved in relocation and her sense of home did not appear to be diminished by the reconstruction regulations.

The household had plans to leave the area for interstate prior to

---

27 Shermi, 1991.

the bushfire, they would be closer to the "'imagined' home", however these plans could easily be put on hold in the interest of the children and their need for a secure base, a home to be "experienced" now. The concept of recovery for Susan was not about restoration to a former state or place, it was a focus on the needs of others and getting on with meeting daily needs, in terms of Watkins and Hosier's model the sense of home for Susan provided a platform for the challenges that lay ahead. Recovery was also about not being a victim. While Susan felt immediately at home in the new house, partly reflecting the new status as a home owner, she did not pretend she felt safe living in another high bushfire prone area. If as Camilleri et al. have argued, recovery comes about through the individual integrating the traumatic events into their memory and life story, then it would appear that Susan's recovery from displacement and trauma is still a work in progress. Her decision to stay in the area is, however, a very important step along that journey.

Acknowledgements

The idea for this research grew out of a discussion with Dr Clare Mouat currently Associate Professor at the University of Western Australia. I would like to thank the residents of Marysville who participated in the study and were prepared to share their journeys of recovery. Jim McKee, a friend for over 50 years and for many years a dedicated CFA worker based in Lilydale, drove me around the area following the bushfires and shared stories of community resilience and bravery. The research was funded by the Barbara Hardy Institute at the University of South Australia

References

Blunt, A. and Dowling, B. (2006). *Home*. Oxford: Routledge.

Borrell, J. (2011). "Rupture, loss, identity and place following the 2009 Victorian Bushfires: a theoretical exploration". *New Community Quarterly*. 9(2): 14-22.

Camilleri, P., C. Healy, C. et al. (2012). "Recovery from bushfires: The experience of the 2003 Canberra bushfires three years after". *Journal of Emergency Primary Health Care*. 8(1): 1-15.

Collins, P. (2000). *The Epic Story of Bushfire in Australia*. Sydney: Allen and Unwin.

Cox, H. and Holmes, C. (2000). "Loss, Healing, and the Power of Place". *Human Studies*. 23(1): 63-78.

Dovey, K. (1985). "Home and homelessness". Altman, I. and Werner, C. (eds) *Home Environments*. New York and London: Plenum Press.

Dupuis, A. and Thorns, D. (1996). "Meanings of home for older home owners". *Housing Studies*. 11: 484-501.

Eriksen, C., Gill, N. and Head, L. (2010) "The gendered dimensions of bushfire in changing rural landscapes in Australia", *Journal of Rural Studies*, 26(4): 332-42.

Fullilove, M. (1996). "Psychiatric Implications of Displacement; contributions from the psychology of place". *American Journal of Psychiatry*. 153(12): 1516-23.

Gammage, W. (2011). *The biggest estate on Earth: how Aborigines made Australia*. Sydney: Allen and Unwin.

Gill, M. and R. Bradstock (2003). "Fire regimes and biodiversity: a set of postulates". In Carey, G. and Lindenmeyer, D. (eds) *Australia Burning: fire ecology policy and management issues*. Collingwood, Vic.: CSIRO publishing.

Gordon, R. (2004). "The social system as a site of disaster impact and resource for recovery". *Australian Journal of Emergency Management.* 19(4): 1516-23.

Griffiths, T. (2009). "We have still not lived long enough". inside.org.au. web-site.

Groenhart, L. and March, A. et al. (2012). "Shifting Victoria's emphasis in land-use planning for bushfire: towards a place-based approach". *Australian Journal of Emergency Management.* 24(4): 33.

Handmer, J. and Tibbits. A. (2005). "Is staying at home the safest option during bushfires? Historical evidence for an Australian approach". *Environmental Hazards.* 6(2) Special Issue): 81-91.

Hayward, G. (1975). "Home as an environmental and psychological concept". *Landscape.* 20: 2-9.

Hughes, R. and Mercer, D. (2009). "Planning to Reduce Risk: The Wildfire Management Overlay in Victoria, Australia". *Geographical Research.* 47(2): 124-41.

IPPC (2007). *Report of the Intergovernmental Panel on Climate Change: Climate Change 2007: the physical science base; summary for policy makers.* Cambridge: IPPC.

Mallett, S. (2004). "Understanding Home: A Critical Review of the Literature". *The Sociological Review.* 52(1): 62-89.

McFarlane, A. C. et al. (1997). "Psychiatric morbidity following a natural disaster: An Australian bushfire". *Social Psychiatry and Psychiatric Epidemiology.* 32(5): 261-68.

Oliver, K. (2012). *Living in the fire flume.* Salvation Army, Pathways Bushfire Recovery Program.

Proudley, M. (2008). "Fire, Families and Decisions". *Australian Journal of Emergency Management.* 23(1): 37-43.

Read, P. (1996) *Returning to Nothing: The meaning of lost places.* Cambridge: Cambridge University Press.

Seamon, D. (1979). *A geography of the life world: movement, rest and encounter.* London: Croom-Helm.

Shamai, S. (1991). "Sense of place: an empirical measurement". *Geoforum.* 22(3): 347-58.

Teague, B. McLeod, R. et al. (2010). *2009 Victorian Bushfires Royal Commission final report.* Parliament of Victoria.

Tout, D. and A. Robinson (2012). "Unsettling conceptions of wilderness and nature". In Hinkson, J. James, P. and Veracini, L. (eds). *Stolen Lands, Broken Cultures: the Settler-Colonial Present.* North Carlton. Vic.: Arena

Watkins, J. and Hosier, A. (2005). "Conceptualising home and homelessness: a life course perspective". In Rowles, G. and Chaudhury, H. *Home and Identity in later life.* New York: Springer.

Weir, I. (2012). "Rethinking design in bushfire prone landscapes". *BPN. Architecture and Design* web-site.

PART TWO:

Images and symbols of place and belonging

7

Vivian Gerrand and Yusuf Sheikh Omar

The arts as cultural and identity resources for Somali youth in Australia: Nadia Faragaab's "Kronologies"

Young Somalis in Australia and in the diaspora in general are caught in between different cultures: the Somali culture on the one hand and the culture of the Australian "mainstream" on the other. They are – in between these cultures – making their own cultural identity and lifestyle which cannot be classified as a purely Somali or an Australian identity. Instead, it is a mixture of an old identity that is part of their existence whilst the new identity is becoming part of their existence; it is a multi-layered and "elusive identity".[1] There is, in other words what Collet describes as "a sense of fluidity within their identities" which is influenced by factors including their ethnicities, cultural backgrounds, individuals' past experiences, gender and age, the new context, faith, skin colour, and the kind of music and arts they perform.[2] Due to all these complex factors that mould and shape who they are, it is difficult to determine identity definitively; although, as time passes, identities are shaped by the culture of the

---

1 Ibrahim, 2008, p. 236.
2 Collet, 2007, p. 49.

host country as a consequence of their daily interactions with the wider Australian community. This can be accompanied by a gradual loss of their inherited culture. The process of cultural shift leads to cultural intermingling which can result in periods of confusion, self-doubt, contradicting manners and attitudes. This confusion and doubt may be exacerbated by dominant media frames that often fail to represent and make room for Somali migrants' complex identities and attachments in their new environments.

What might constitute a valid culture or form of display for such groups of Somalis? Where might they find appropriate expressions for their culture? What spaces do countries such as Australia provide for Somali identification and (re)imagining or imaging in the diaspora? What happens when Somalis find themselves in countries with which they have few obvious cultural links? In Australia, where a majority of Somalis are Australian citizens, this absence of cultural connection is only partly remedied within an official multicultural model, and they remain "one of the most marginal and disadvantaged groups" within the nation.[3] The key challenges facing Somalis living in Australia are language, culture shock and religion.[4]

The term "culture" may be understood as the way in which we organise life in order to create meaning via different forms of symbolic representation. It may be defined as a complex symbiosis of cognitions, traditions, technical procedures and behaviours, transmitted and employed systematically, characteristic of a social group, populace or of humanity at large.[5] Instead of viewing cultures or diasporas as fixed entities, representations of Somali culture and identity in Australia need to be understood in terms of a continual adaptation

3 Ange et al. 2002, p. 48.
4 Omar, 2005, p. 6.
5 Zingarelli, 2001.

to the circumstances of what Iain Chambers calls "migrancy" or "an endless journey between cultures, languages and complex configurations of meaning and power".[6]

The role of the media in framing Somali belonging in Australia

The media has been theorised as a "machine", or "machineries of meaning", through which nations are constituted.[7] The nation-state is as much a symbolic formation as it is a political one. Morley and Robins suggest "that the creation of a culture and identity in common would have been impossible without the contribution of print and subsequently broadcast media".[8] The nation is thus produced as an "imagined community" via what Hall terms a "system of representation".[9] Through an imaginary identification with its symbols, including mediatised images, citizens become "subjects".[10] Media production and representation, defined here as the communication of information via an encoding process that produces meaningful narratives, is thus central to the construction of identities and the popular narratives and national imaginaries that construct and frame these identities. Dominant ideologies are reflected in the way media messages accrue an a priori status through repetition. In this way, they become profoundly naturalised, and their codes may be accepted without question.[11]

The media, therefore, influences powerfully the ways in which group identity is constructed and framed. In their analysis of

6 Chambers, 1994, p. 12.
7 Morley and Robins, 1995, p. 196.
8 Ibid., p. 196.
9 Hall, 1999, p. 38.
10 Ibid., p. 38.
11 Hall, 1980. p. 130.

Australian print media, Foster et al. document the power of the media
'to "do" and "undo" the project of multiculturalism by representing it
as "conflicted, manipulated, fractured and value-laden".[12] In the case
of Somalis, stereotypes are complicated by an additional "clash of
civilisations" narrative of incompatibility and an intensive "othering"
campaign as part of the "war on terror" that has framed most
depictions of Islam in Western media post-9/11.[13] Moreover, the
racialised labelling of particular groups results in conflicts which, note
Poynting and Mason, produce "ongoing moral panics" and "shifts in
and limits to identification and belonging".[14] Within the context of a
multicultural model, Somalis are assigned an essentialist "community"
identity – in spite of their fragmentation.[15] Anti-African and anti-
Islamic stereotypes often combine with the "ethnic profiling" that
is a feature of this model to make some cultures appear to be more
compatible than others. An exclusive fixity, even culturalist racism,
has increasingly characterised debates over the past decade and has
had deleterious consequences for Australian Somalis' experiences of
belonging.

While culturally specific media in Australia, such as the Special
Broadcasting Service (SBS) and Channel 31, provide a range of
culturally and linguistically diverse programs, including Somali news
radio and television programs, scholars such as Andrew Jakubowicz
have argued that this has resulted in mainstream media making no
effort to cater for the needs and interests of cultural minorities.[16] The

---

12 Foster, et al. 2011, p. 621.
13 Ibid.; Kabir, 2011; Poynting and Mason, 2008.
14 Poynting and Mason, p. 366.
15 According to Alessandro Dal Lago, the "improper usage of terms such as 'community'" ascribed to migrants of the same nationality leads to the perception of migrants
as one kind of culture and an equivocation of "migrant cultures"; Dal Lago, 2006, p. 68.
16 Jakubowicz, et al., 1994.

public perception of Somalis as Australian is arguably less present than it is for migrants of other backgrounds. While Somalis can relatively readily become Australian citizens, their sense of cultural belonging remains elusive. The 2002 SBS Living Diversity Survey considered this paradox:

> On the one hand Australia is obviously a plural society with an increasingly diverse population, most of whom thrive well in their lives. On the other hand, Australian *culture* is still not as open and inclusive as it could be: it is still strongly dominated by a core, Anglo-Celtic culture from which people of other cultural backgrounds are marginalised. In essence, some of these people experience themselves as *in* Australia, but not *of* Australia. Their sense of belonging is incomplete.[17]

Somalis have been considered as among the most marginal and disadvantaged of migrant groups in Australia.[18] Formal spaces of citizenship and multiculturalism are arguably inadequate, or too thin to give Somalis a sense of being at home.[19] Cultural anthropologist Ghassan Hage writes of a "growing incompatibility between the state's formal acceptance of new citizens and the dominant community's everyday acceptance of such people".[20]

This incompatibility between formal and everyday acceptance of new citizens may be traced to an absence of "cultural citizenship" – a limitation of the Australian multicultural model.[21] Many scholars of

---

17 Ang, et al., 2002, p. 48. See also recent Mackay Ipsos Research on "The Mind and Mood of New Australians."

18 Ibid.

19 For definitions of "thick" and "thin" citizenship, see Bauböck, 1999.

20 Hage, 1998, p. 50.

21 For useful distinctions between cultural (thick) and official (thin) citizenship, see Behabib et al., 2007; Stevenson, 2003; Ommundsen et al., 2010.

the media and multiculturalism have reported a particular kind of hierarchy that is reproduced in accordance with Australia's version of multiculturalism. In the mid-1990s, Andrew Jakubowicz argued that racism in Australia was perpetuated by media stereotypes that partition different segments of society, often reinforcing a dominant hierarchy by failing to reflect the everyday lived realities of multiculturalism.[22] Hage and John Stratton similarly critiqued multiculturalism in Australia for reproducing a core Anglo-Celtic culture that remains fixed within a white Australian imaginary. Within this imaginary, migrant communities have figured as managed and marginal accessories, when they are not deemed culturally incompatible.[23]

In the contemporary context of substantial African migration to Australia, Joel Windle contends that "pre-existing institutional racism and racialising narrative frames" target new African arrivals in Australia.[24] Within this hierarchy, Somalis in Australia generally experience alienation on two fronts: on the one hand, they are not seen as white in a society that is still commonly imaged as white and, on the other, they are regarded with suspicion for being Muslim. Within the political economy of the media, most representations have reproduced this positioning of Somalis as an incompatible or "unmeltable" minority.[25]

Evelyn Leslie Hamdon writes of a global western tendency to view Muslims "as a homogenous identity group, without nuance, difference, or the ability to change over time and space".[26] Howard

---

22 Jakubowicz, et al., 1994, p. 3.
23 According to Hall, "Cultural belongingness" (redefined as an old, exclusive form of ethnicity) has replaced genetic purity and functions as a coded language for race and colour; Hall, 1999, p. 39.
24 Windle, 2008, p. 554.
25 Modood and Werbner, (eds), 1997.
26 Hamdon, 2010, p. 30.

Brasted sees popular conceptions of Islam and the negative stereotypes surrounding Muslims in Australia as emerging predominantly from journalistic coverage of events in the Muslim world as they unfold as news on a daily basis. This coverage tends to paint an "unflattering picture".[27] Thus:

> Mosques, bearded mullahs, menacing Muslim crowds, and *burqa*-clad women, which have collectively come to symbolize irrationality, fanaticism, intolerance, and discrimination on an almost medieval scale, are the most commonly projected images.[28]

During the Gulf War, the media played a part in engendering support for a UN intervention against Iraq via "images of the Orient well entrenched in Australian society", which reinforced a particularly reductive hermeneutics of complex histories that drew "on racist stereotypes dating back to the Crusades".[29]

The bestselling books by the Somali author, Ayaan Hirsi Ali, such as *The Caged Virgin* (2004)[30] and autobiography *Infidel* (2007) may be seen as contributing to this depiction as they received considerable public attention in Australia.[31] The writer, who became a polarising figure in the culture wars of contemporary Europe, received somewhat less media focus in Australia, but still reached a significant audience.[32] Her

27 Brasted, 2009, p. 58.

28 Ibid., p. 59.

29 Jakubowicz et al., 1994, p. 61.

30 *The Caged Virgin* is dedicated to the "the spirit of liberty" and appeals to indignation about the shortcomings of what the author terms an "Islamic Curtain." The book was praised by broadsheets such as the *Irish Times* and the *Observer* for its bravery and anger.

31 While Hirsi Ali was in Australia on a promotional tour of her book, *Nomad*, in 2010, the Australian Broadcasting Commission's *Lateline* featured extensive interviews with her. *Lateline*, ABC TV, 26 July 2010. *Late Night Live* with Phillip Adams, ABC Radio National's in-depth conversation program, has interviewed the author frequently.

32 Buruma, 2010, pp. 106-7.

controversial publications have fortified prejudices against Islam by upholding a worldview that is reminiscent of Samuel P. Huntington's prominent thesis in *The Clash of Civilizations* (1996).[33] The writings of Hirsi Ali both reflect and reinstate the narratives of incompatibility that are found in media reporting which work to fix identities into irreconcilable others rather than viewing them as dynamic and complex relations. Together with racialised stereotypes of African-ness, this homogenous image of Islam reproduces a desire to exclude Muslims from particular sectors of Australian society.

Drawing on content analysis of Australian media undertaken in recent years, Liza Hopkins writes that a "simplifying and 'othering' practice" has led to the construction of the "Muslim-Australian" categorical identity and reification of this as a "singular group". This has effectively muted "Australia's rich heritage of ethnic diversity".[34] Such othering has combined with the rise of extremely conservative Salafism which has led to many Muslims regarding images, music and particular cultural formations as *haram* or prohibited. The prohibitions prescribed by the Salafist interpretation of Islam have not traditionally applied to Somali culture and society and may be regarded as recent imports after decades of instability. The versions of Islam traditionally observed by Somalis are indeed highly particular to the Somali context.

An alternative to these media frames may be found in the artistic production and representation of Somalis in Australia. In the next section, we take into account the ways in which Somali cultural production may allow better understanding of the mechanics of contemporary belonging and the challenges faced by societies as they

---

33 Huntington has argued that the world's monotheistic religions are incompatible; Huntington, 1996.
34 Hopkins, 2011, p. 111.

attempt to "integrate" Somali migrants. We consider Nadia Faragaab's art exhibition, "Kronologies" – the first of its kind – as a critical cultural resource for its ability to present alternatives to exclusive nationalisms and conceptions of identity and belonging and offer new situated imaginings that respond to the trajectories of Somali migrants. Before proceeding to a critical analysis of Faragaab's artworks, we survey the quality and the availability of Somalis artistic resources for youth in Australia that can help strengthen sense of Somali-ness and their belonging to the Somali and Australian culture. The artistic resources discussed include examples of Somali films in the diaspora, Somali songs and music, drawing and painting, poetry, and storytelling.

An overview of Somali artistic production in the diaspora

Somali films made in the West – which are usually performed in Somali and English languages and sold in artistic Somali studios – play a critical role in the maintenance of Somali youth cultural identities in North America [and the UK], but a marginal role in Australia because there are no effective artistic Somali studios in Australia where the Somali films made in the West are distributed.[35] In addition to these diasporic Somali films, hundreds of Indian films translated into Somali are sold in the Somali community studios in North America and Europe and many young Somalis in the diaspora watch them, which may help improve their Somali language skills.[36] Although these films are translated into Somali, the cultural content they carry is very different from Somali culture. Most of these films can be bought from the community studios in North America and UK and some can be downloaded from the internet.

---

35 Oikonomidoy, 2005, p. 82.
36 Shepard, 2005, p. 172.

Somali songs and music entered into wide circulation after the civil war erupted in Somalia in 1991. Many Somali singers and actors resettled in Europe and North America rather than in Australia. Despite the challenges and critiques they face from literalist religious groups, these singers frequently perform songs, concerts, and other folkloric Somali cultural activities, mainly in Somali. These artistic activities attract a large number of young people and provide good cultural resources and a sense of Somali identity. Such powerful cultural resources are not available to Somali youth in Australia. However, occasionally, there are some singers who do come to Australia to perform Somali music and many young people attend their shows. The challenge is that these artistic activities are seen by many in the Melbourne Somali community – which tends to assume a greater religiosity than its counterparts in Europe and North America – as taboo and as a transgression of Islamic faith. Artistic music activities often take place in a social environment where boys and girls come together and some fear that this contact will encourage sexual promiscuity.[37] A study conducted about the social integration of Somali youth in Australia and USA found that many young Somalis note that they are not interested in attending music and dancing sessions at their respective schools; either because their parents do not allow it or they are in an Islamic school where music and dancing classes are not permitted. A young woman from Melbourne recounts: "In Islamic school, we had no dance or music classes. You don't get any of that stuff in Islamic school".[38] A young man from Minneapolis revealed that he would have loved to participate in music classes but his parents refused to enrol him because they felt if he attended music classes he might develop a bad character, since in Somali culture music

---

37 Farid and McMahan, 2004, p. 172.
38 Omar, 2011, p. 159.

and dancing are to some extent associated with negative behaviour.[39] Some Somali parents in the west become frustrated when they notice that their children attend music classes; therefore they take them to a school that does not teach music.[40]

In contrast to these negative Islamic interpretations associated with music, leading Islamic scholar Ramadan argues that despite the fact that entertainment and music are a necessary part of life, some literalist Islamic scholars want to impose:

> a kind of daily life devoid of entertainment ... without imagination, without music ... without even spiritual rest . . . this cannot be, and does not correspond to, Islam's teaching.[41]

Recently, studies have emphasised that music is an important tool for cultural transmission, language acquisition and educational performance. Usher stresses that there is scientific evidence to show that children who undertake music education improve in all other subjects and their general well-being.[42] Furthermore, the use of sound, rhythm and self-expression are integral parts of promoting harmony and cultural exchange.[43] To achieve recognition by the western mainstream, migrant identities must present the tangible parts of their cultures such as traditional music, food, dance, folklore and traditional dress code.[44]

Visual arts such as drawing and painting can be an important cultural and identity resource for young Somalis in diaspora; this

---

39 Ibid.
40 Farid and McMahan, 2004.
41 Ramadan, 2009, p. 196.
42 Usher, 2009, p. 3.
43 Kabir and Rickards, 2006, pp. 17-24.
44 Zevallos, 2002, pp. 41-9.

is because youth can express and portray their cultural identity and feeling in images and painting. However, drawing the image of a living creature is considered in some interpretations of Islam – particularly in the Salafist view which has been the dominating school of thought in Somalia since late 1980s – to be prohibited. Therefore, visual art curricula have been little developed in the Somali education system and "the carving of wooden masks or statues, clay modelling, and casting are rarely practiced in Somali schools".[45] The Salafist school of thought prevails within the Somali communities in the diaspora, particularly in Australia and the UK. As a result, the drawing, painting and visual arts have until recently constituted a very marginal role in the maintenance of Somali youth identity in Australia.

Nadia Faragaab's "Kronologies"

Despite the fact that Somali youth in Australia lack some of the artistic cultural resources of their US and UK counterparts, recently there has been a new artistic cultural resource initiated by Somali-Australian artist Nadia Faragaab. In search of resources for her identity and sense of belonging, Faragaab launched her exhibition in Melbourne reigniting "the debate and discussion surrounding the profound absence of Somali representation within the expanse of Australian culture".[46] Prior to the creation of the set of artworks that constitute "Kronologies", Faragaab had been asking herself "how ... Somalian Australians ... [can] have their Somali identity available to them on a visible and regular [basis] so it can form their sense of identity". The trigger and turning point was when she participated in an African festival in Senegal. Describing this experience at a talk about her exhibition, Nadia recounts:

---

45 Kahin, 1997, p. 73.
46 Facebook, 2011.

> For me it was a continuous search [of my identity and culture]
> you know in my everyday … I embrace my Australianness
> and … I [also] embrace my Somaliness to me what … drew
> me to the edge to install [this art exhibition] … was when I
> went to the world black arts festival in Senegal last year … it
> was arts of all kinds visual arts; performance arts; you know,
> sculpture; everything; there was books being launched; films;
> it was amazing! [I said aaaah!] But still I couldn't find anything
> Somali! The only thing Somali I saw was Somali flag among
> African flags … I said aah! This is beautiful but, you know?

Amongst the reasons for holding the exhibition was this admission:

> In the wider arts community there exists a void, within which
> exists a lack of support and encouragement for Somali
> artists and consequently, an absence of Somali imagery and
> symbolism in the arts and everyday life.

The two authors went to Faragaab's exhibition opening at the Blak
Dot gallery, East Brunswick, on the 3 November 2011.[47] An urn filled
with Shaah was positioned near the entrance to the gallery as was
a bar serving alcohol, suggesting the artist's desire to cater for and
interact with people within and outside of the "Somali" community
(who predominantly do not drink alcohol).

The title of the exhibition, "Kronologies", implies a series of
dimensions that are at play at different times. A chronology is a
location of historic events in time which may take the form of a
timeline. The spelling of the term may be read either as a deliberate
"misspelling" – confounding of the past, present and future which
lose their linearity and become ecstatic – or, alternatively in terms of

---

47 Open since 2011, the contemporary indigenous-run Melbourne based Blak Dot
Gallery's remit is to showcase the artwork of the world's indigenous cultures. www.blak-
dot.com.au/

the Greek term for time, "Kronos". The potential inherent in playing with time by combining and rearranging of fragments of history lends itself to hope as we imagine the time before and the time to come in Somalia, beyond the contemporary war-torn decades.

A heterotopic space, the exhibition featured installations that aligned artefacts from different historical periods. A pair of leather slippers typically worn in pre-modern Somalia were stationed at the foot of armchair on which one might sit in a contemporary diasporic Somali household. A clock and framed sepia-toned photographs of Medjeurtine relatives hung on the wall behind them, near a record album of Somali "Songs of the New Era".

Figure 2. "Somalia: Songs of the New Era"

Two canvases featured collages: "Kolajkayga" contained collections of images that represent a missing part of Australian culture: Faragaab's longing for "the media to reflect and project images of the true diversity of this country" is cited. "Google images – Somalia 2011" is a digital print on canvas that represents Somalia stereotypically, with the intention of displaying "a contrast between the contradictions within Somali identity", as its title suggests, by appropriating the images generated from a Google image "Somalia" search.

The installations dynamically drew together disparate Somali cultural, linguistic and historical artefacts that asked questions of the audience: "Qolka" wondered how Somali art and design might appear in "the absence of war, famine, drought and forced migration in 2011?" The Jalbaabka – a black garb with a similar appearance to the burqa worn by Somali women after the civil war – drew attention to the fact that Somali women have altered their style of clothing in response to the war.

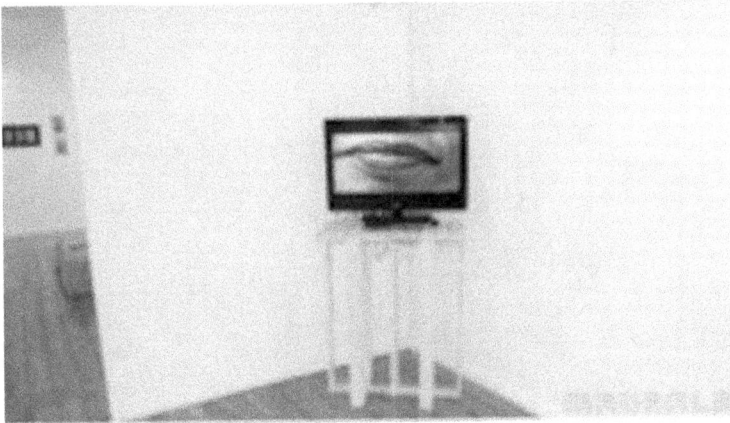

Figure 3. "Af" (mouth or language)

The installation "Af", a term meaning "mouth" and "language" in

Somali, included a talking mouth, children's posters of the Somali alphabet and numbers in addition to a collection of wooden toys with which children played. Finally, "Smoke Alarms" presented three columns of smoke alarms that were mounted on a wall directly above a series of incense burners.

Figure 4. "Smoke Alarms" (Idan/Dabqaad for Uunsi, a small object used for lighting Frankincense to perfume the house)

The sound of smoke alarms ringing in reaction to the burning of traditional incense, according to a description accompanying the work, is said to echo the deep feelings of displacement felt by the diaspora communities within Australia.

Audience responses to "Kronologies"

The majority of those in attendance at the exhibition, according to interviews and a circulated questionnaire were enthusiastic about the exhibition, evaluating it as a great achievement. Similarly, Nadia Faragaab was described by a young participant as a creative and artistic young woman who represents "[a] new generation that is really exploring the Somali identity". One participant viewed the stories told at the exhibition as important insofar as "understanding a situation of someone else is simple through stories".

When asked the reasons for attending the exhibition, participants gave diverse answers. Some were interested in Somali culture; wishing to support Faragaab's artwork and exhibition; to support Somali culture; and to visually witness the Somali arts. A young mother who attended the exhibition said:

> I got two children who are growing up this country; I want them to see . . . the Somali culture in visual ways . . . rather than hearing . . . I think it is an amazing thing and fantastic to bring my kids here to see what we used to cook, what we used to eat and how the Somali people dress.

Another young participant explained: "As Somalis we just have language; but now [in this exhibition] we can visualize it and actually touch it as tangible knowledge. So, that is great".

Figure 5. Participants awaiting artist's talk

Most participants felt that Somali identity was poorly resourced and under-represented in Australia. In fact, one participant argued that this exhibition was the first of its kind about Somali culture held in Australia. Another participant commented that the exhibition was "a good thing to do . . . because there [is] not much exhibition in Australia about Somali culture". This view was endorsed by a young participant who recounted a "non-existence [of Somali culture]; it is an interesting area that needs to be looked at more closely by the Somali community and outside the Somali community." Due to the poverty of cultural representation in Australia, argued another, "their [youth] identity is lost into wider Australians".

When questioned about how the exhibition made participants feel, the most common responses were: "enthusiastic", "happy", "excited", "connected", "curious", "optimistic" and "alive". One participant viewed the exhibition as a "new start" and held a sense of hope for the "future to come." Another said: "Would love to see more creative expression, representation and art from Somali Australians". Another participant identified a clear need for "more Somali arts and Somali identity. [Therefore] the young generation who are coming can see and say I am Somali; this is what Somalia is like". The exhibition whetted the appetites of some participants for more creative expression, representation and art from Somali-Australians. One participant felt it had given "insight into Somali culture" and "broadened my knowledge". The mood at the gallery was decidedly upbeat, and presented a significant fresh and alternative vision of Somalia to the one received in dominant media as positive aspects of Somalia were on display.

Figure 6. Nadia Faragaab. Source: Madaale web-site

Concluding remarks

Nadia Faragaab's "Kronologies" represents the artist's identity and, specifically, what it means to live in Australia with Somali heritage. Faragaab's "Kronologies" fruitfully articulates an interstitial belonging that resists categorisation, complicating pre-conceived notions of Australianness and Somali identity, and embodying the artist's multiple sites of identification. Faragaab's creative inhabitation of a space of "non-fixity" represents movement beyond the confines of reductive media representations. In addition to celebrating the ability to combine different cultural influences – fluency in moving between different ways of living – the representations reframe images of Somali migrants. There is an invitation to new forms of identification that are capable of redrawing the boundaries of belonging by envisaging identity as in a process of taking place. The enthusiastic responses of those present at the exhibition affirm the critical importance of the arts as cultural and identity resources of belonging for Somali youth in Australia.

References

Amir, Said, Ahmed and Dupre, Kelly. (2008) *The Travels of Igal Shidad.* Minneapolis: Minnesota Humanities Center.

Ang. Ien et al. (2002) *Living Diversity: Australia's Multicultural Future.* Artarmon NSW: Special Broadcasting Service Corporation.

Awad, Ibrahim. (2008) "The New Flaneur: Subaltern Cultural Studies, African Youth in Canada and the Semiology of in-Betweenness". *Cultural Studies.* 22: 234-53.

Bauböck, Rainer. (1999) *National Community, Citizenship and Cultural Diversity.* Institute for Advanced Studies, Vienna. Political Science Series No. 5. 1999.

Behabib, S. et al. (2007) *Identities, Affiliations and Allegiances.* Cambridge: Cambridge University Press.

Brasted. Howard (2009) "Contested Representations in Historical Perspective. Images of Islam and Australian Press, 1950-2000". In Fārūqī, N. (ed). *Muslims and Media Images: News versus Views.* New Delhi: Oxford University Press.

Buruma, Ian. (2010) *Taming the Gods: Religion and Democracy on Three Continents.* Princeton and Oxford: Princeton University Press.

Chambers, I. (1994) *Migrancy, Culture, Identity.* London and New York: Routledge.

Collet, Bruce. (2007) "Islam, National Identity and Public Secondary Education: Perspectives from the Somali Diaspora in Toronto, Canada". *Race Ethnicity and Education.* 10: 131-53.

Dal Lago, Alessandro. (2006) "Esistono davvero i conflitti fra le culture?". *Multiculturalismo: Ideologie e sfide.* Bologna: Il Mulino.

Facebook (2011). Kronologies: An exhibition by Nadia Faragaab. Available Online.

Farid, Mohamed and McMahan, Don. (2004) *Accommodating and Educating Somali Students in Minnesota Schools.* Saint Paul, MN: Hamline University Press.

Forman, Murray. (2001) "Straight Outta Mogadishu: Prescribed Identities and Performative Practices among Somali youth in North America High Schools". *Journal of Cultural Studies.* 5: 33–60.

Foster, Nena, Cook, Kay, Barter-Godfrey, Sarah and Furneaux, Samantha. (2011) "Fractured multiculturalism: Conflicting representations of Arab and Muslim Australians in Australian print media". *Media Culture and Society.* 33(4): 619-29.

Hage, G. (1998) *White Nation: Fantasies of White Supremacy in a Multicultural Society.* Sydney: Pluto Press.

Hall, Stuart. (1999) "Culture, Community, Nation." *Representing the Nation: A Reader.* London: Routledge.

Hall, Stuart. (ed). (1980) *Culture, Media, Language: working papers in cultural studies, 1972-79*. London: Hutchinson, University of Birmingham.

Hopkins, L. (2011) "A Contested Identity: Resisting the Category Muslim-Australian". *Immigrants & Minorities*. 29(1).

Hamdon. Evelyn L. (2010) *Islamophobia and the Question of Muslim Identity. The Politics of Difference and Solidarity*. Black Point, NS.: Fernwood.

Ibrahim, Awad. (2008) "The New Flaneur: Subaltern Cultural Studies, African Youth in Canada and the Semiology of in-Betweenness". *Cultural Studies*. 22: 234-53.

Huntington, Samuel P. (1996) *The Clash of Civilizations and the Remaking of World Order*. New York: Simon & Schuster.

Jakubowicz, Andrew. et al. (1994) *Racism, Ethnicity and the Media*. St Leonards: Allen & Unwin.

Kabir, Nahid Afrose. (2011) "A Study of Australian Muslim Youth Identity: The Melbourne Case". *Journal of Muslim Minority Affairs*. 31(2): 243-58.

Kabir, Nahid and Rickards, Tony. (2006) "Students at Risk, Can Connections Make a Difference?". *Youth Studies Australia*. 25: 17–24.

Kahin, Mohamed. (1997) *Educating Somali Children in Britain*. London: Trentham Books.

Madaale. (2011) First Somali exhibition in Melbourne by Nadia Faragaab. Madaale web-site.

Modood, Tariq and Werbner, Pnina. (eds). (1997) *The Politics of Multiculturalism in the New Europe*: Racism, Identity, and Community. London and New York: Zed Books.

Morley, David and Robins, Kevin. (1995) *Spaces of Identity: Global media, Electronic Landscapes, and Cultural Boundaries*. London, New York: Routledge.

Oikonomidoy, Eleni. (2005) "Constructing Academic Identity in Exile Among Somali Female High School Students". Doctor of Philosophy

Thesis. Department of Curriculum and Instruction. University of Washington.

Omar, Yusuf. (2011) "Integration from Youth Perspectives: A Comparative Study of Young Somali Men in Melbourne and Minneapolis". Doctor of Philosophy Thesis. School of Social Sciences. La Trobe University.

Ommundsen, W. et al. (2010) *Cultural Citizenship and the Challenges of Globalization.* Cresskill, NJ: Hampton Press,

Poynting, Scott and Mason, Victoria. (2008) "Muslim Communities post 9/11 – citizenship, security and social justice". *International Journal of Law, Crime and Justice.* 36(4): 230-46.

Poynting, Scott and Perry, Barbara. (2007) "Climates of Hate: Media and State Inspired Victimisation of Muslims in Canada and Australia since 9/11". *Current Issues in Criminal Justice.* 19(2): 15-71.

Ramadan, Tariq. (2009) *Radical Reform: Islamic Ethics and Liberation,* London: Oxford University Press.

Sharp, T. Director. (2009a) Home: "*An exploratory journey with young Somali-Australians*". *4US: young people with refugee backgrounds living in Australia.* Melbourne: DVD distributed by La Trobe University.

————. (2009b) See Through Me, "*Discrimination through the eyes of ten young Somali-Australians*". *4US: young people with refugee backgrounds living in Australia.* DVD distributed by La Trobe University.

Shepard, Raynel. (2005) "Acting Is Not Becoming: Cultural Adaptation Among Somali Refugee Youth". Doctor of Education Thesis. The Faculty of the Graduate School of Education. Harvard University.

Stevenson, Nick. (2003) *Cultural Citizenship: Cosmopolitan Questions.* Berkshire: Open University Press.

Usher, Robin. (2009) "Schools Music Bid Tunes Up." *The Age.* 2 September.

Windle. Joel. (2008) "The Racialisation of African Youth in Australia". *Social Identities: Journal for the Study of Race, Nation and Culture.* 14(5):553-66.

Young Achievers. (2008) *New Poets from the Block*. Minneapolis, MN: International Health Volunteers.

Zevallos, Zuleyka. (2002) "It is Like We're Their Culture: Second Generation Migrant Women Discuss Australian Culture". *People and Place*. 13: 41-9.

Zingarelli, Nicola. (2001) *Lo Zingarelli 2002: Vocabolario della Lingua Italiana*. Bologna: Zanichelli editore.

8

Christopher Sommer

A place apart? The representation of place identity and displacement in the special exhibition "The Mixing Room" at the Museum of New Zealand, Te Papa Tongarewa

To pack one's bags and venture out into the unknown is one of humanity's basic experiences. Whether arriving in New Zealand one hundred years ago or in the last decade, all immigrants experience displacement and the claiming of new spaces. In recent years museum scholars have taken an increased interest in migration processes and concepts of place and displacement.[1] This chapter outlines New Zealand's place identity, and concepts of displacement and belonging as represented in "The Mixing Room: stories from young refugees in New Zealand", an exhibition at the Museum of New Zealand Te Papa Tongarewa focusing on resettling young refugees.[2] No analysis of the actual exhibition exists although Gibson has explored the conceptual origins of the exhibit.[3] The Mixing Room's

---

1 This paper is based on research for a doctorate at the University of Auckland. I wish to acknowledge the support of my supervisors Professor Elizabeth Rankin and Professor James Bade.

2 This essay follows the broader UNESCO (2013a, 2013b) definitions of migrants and refugees, seeing the latter as a sub-category of migrants.

3 Te Papa, 2013a.

dual role in representing why people leave their home country and
the challenges they meet in a host country allow an analysis of "place
identity", displacement and belonging. New Zealand's involvement in
humanitarian programs needs to be analysed, as do physical aspects of
the representation and visitor perspectives as identified in qualitative
interviews.[4]

Unravelling museum exhibitions

A variety of disciplines have tried to grasp the different meanings of
the museum.[5] Exhibition staff try to disseminate information to their
audience by using objects and explanatory texts, video clips, media
stations, and so on. Any analysis must account for these intentions.
However, the objects themselves independently communicate, and
the visitor is not an empty shell.[6] The meaning of an exhibition is not
fixed but individually produced in the process of it being visited and
"read". In addition, visitor and museum staff are together members
of a specific society, a culture, and differentiated in characteristics such
as gender, ethnicity and socio-economic status. Recent commentary
tends towards elaborate models, as, for example, in analysis of spatial
arrangement drawing on Michel de Certeau or semiotic approaches
based on theories of Ferdinand de Saussure and Roland Barthes.[7]
This chapter will draw on these theories and methodologies to
enhance clarity, and follow the methodology of close reading applied
to a museum context.[8]

Bakewell's discussion of the term "displacement" as process,

---

4 Qualitative studies of visitor's motivation are still relatively small in number.
5 cf. Baur, 2010; Mieke Bal, 1996, p. 30 ff.
6 cf. Mastai, 2007; Noschka-Roos, 2003.
7 Buschmann, 2010; for semiotics derived from Ferdinand de Saussure and Roland
Barthes see Muttenthaler and Wonisch, 2006; Scholze, 2004.
8 cf. Geertz, 1993.

condition and category, provides a guide for the analysis, as it can be expected that all three will be addressed in an exhibition on the refugee experience. As a process, displacement can be understood as bringing about changes in people's physical location and accordingly their social, economic and cultural environment. However, this change is due to forced migration and not based on choice.[9] As a condition it is separated from physical movement, but is, rather, a self-imposed feeling of being displaced, being in exile or not belonging in a place, even though physical movement might have ceased. It furthermore relies on the perception of self and is not an objective state.[10] As a category, displacement becomes part of the official sphere, for instance as a policy category and is thus not self-imposed, but assigned by other actors.[11]

There is no harm in asking

To collect motivational as well as perceptual data, quantitative as well as qualitative research methods were employed over several days at Te Papa during two separate field trips.[12] It is assumed that motivations for visiting a museum are varied and together influence visitor perceptions.[13] No random and statistically representative sample can be achieved by this means. Instead, the design of the qualitative study relies on purposeful sampling, which attempts to select information-rich cases for in-depth study (n=28). As Patton puts it: "Studying information-rich cases yields insights and in-depth understanding rather than empirical generalizations".[14]

---

9 Bakewell, 2011, p. 19.
10 Ibid., p. 22.
11 Ibid., p. 24.
12 Responses in this paper do not account for all encountered perceptions, but shows instead the value of interviewing visitors.
13 Falk, 2009, 2011.
14 Patton, 2002, p. 230.

Each day during a set time-frame every visitor exiting the Mixing Room was approached.[15] Visitors were first asked to talk about their experience. No other instructions were given at this point, with the intention of prompting visitors to tell a personal story of their visit.[16] Only after visitors finished their narrative were follow-up questions asked. In addition three standardised photographs of object arrangements were presented. Data was analysed to develop a classification/coding scheme, subsequently used to find common themes and patterns.[17] Data acquired through qualitative interviews are not entirely unproblematic.[18] However, no other form of data acquisition could offer the same insight. The visitor experience allows inferences, to achieve a better cross-section of the communication potentialities of an exhibition. Every experience recorded can enable us to further unravel the meanings of museum exhibitions.

Refugees and New Zealand

New Zealand is one of the few countries to offer resettlement for refugees under a Quota Refugee Program. The program was established in 1987 by the New Zealand government and applicants must be recognised as refugees under the UNHCR's mandate. Since then, the annual resettlement quota of 750 places has not changed and in the period from 1999-2008, 7843 people were approved for residence in New Zealand through the programme.[19]

---

15 6 -9 November 2012 and 15 -8 May 2013 each day throughout opening hours.
16 This narrative approach is used by Philipp Schorch, 2010, p. 34 ff., in his study of Te Papa's response to "new museology".
17 Patton, 2002, p. 463 ff.
18 Alvesson, 2011.
19 For further details and extensive tables regarding composition of quota refugees see Department of Labour, New Zealand, 2006, 2009a, 2009b, p. 6.

A 2002 report on the program identified discrimination as a minor occurrence, although others argue that refugees are often seen as a "problem" and political campaigns aim to reduce the number of refugees.[20] Sobrun-Maharaj et al. suggest that most refugee youth do not feel settled or socially included. This process of exclusion, understood as social alienation or disaffiliation, is regarded by Chile as a major barrier for refugees in developing a feeling of citizenship.[21] It can also generate ongoing feelings of being "displaced".[22] How is this issue, of an ongoing feeling of displacement due to exclusion, addressed in the exhibition? Does the Mixing Room aim to educate visitors in order to reduce intolerance and to facilitate inclusion? To answer these questions we must look at the reasoning behind the exhibition.

The Mixing Room
Opened to the public in 2010, The Mixing Room joins the series of temporary exhibitions in Te Papa's Community Gallery.[23] While past exhibitions explored a specific migration ethnicity this new exhibition stresses community of interest:

> Bursting with creativity, over 70 young refugees to New Zealand tell their extraordinary stories – through art, film, poetry, performance and new digital media. They invite you to see the immense changes they have endured, and the hopeful new lives they are building on these shores.[24]

The main goal of the exhibition was to communicate specific

---

20 A very small number of visitor responses expressed disapproval at representing refugees in the form of an exhibition.

21 Chile, 2005.

22 Bakewell, 2011.

23 Fitzgerald, 2009.

24 "Te Papa, 2013b.

messages to mainstream audiences: visitors should consider what
it means to be a refugee; they should appreciate the strengths and
optimism of refugee-background youth as they settle into New
Zealand society and they should be challenged to consider their own
views on refugee resettlement and understand that the exhibition
contents were in part created by refugee-background youth with
support from Te Papa staff.[25] The interpretive strategy, as intended by
the development team, was based on the following principles:

1. The stories told should affect the visitor emotionally.

2. The exhibits were specifically produced during the
   workshops and entirely digital, so that dependency on and
   usage of material culture would be avoided.

3. The focus should lie on the current situation of refugees
   and future prospects rather than on historical models.

The exhibition is intended to give an overall positive impression
of refugee communities:

> Visitors will appreciate that refugees are individuals and
> New Zealanders – in this case young, energetic, ambitious,
> creative individuals. Contemporary in nature and movingly
> autobiographical in part, this is a process and a product
> that values the lively, the inventive, the surprising and the
> playful.[26]

An exhibition is also able to provide knowledge about refugees thus
enabling the public to reconsider their own beliefs and stereotypes
and challenge negative media images.[27] It is also noteworthy that the
participatory model employed had positive, even life-changing, effect

---

25 Gibson, 2013; Te Papa, 2011, p. 30.

26 Te Papa, 2010, p. 11.

27 Jones, 2004, p. xvii ff.

on participants.[28] The design process and final product explicitly aim to counteract exclusion and, accordingly, displacement as an ongoing condition.

Analysis of the exhibition

The Mixing Room is one room and rectangular in shape (see figures) There are two entrances/exits: while one entrance/exit (henceforth referred to as "main entrance" is marked by panels showing life-size photographs of participants in the exhibition. The second entrance/ exit (hereafter referred to as "secondary entrance"), is a small round-arched portal and leads to the neighbouring Passports exhibition.

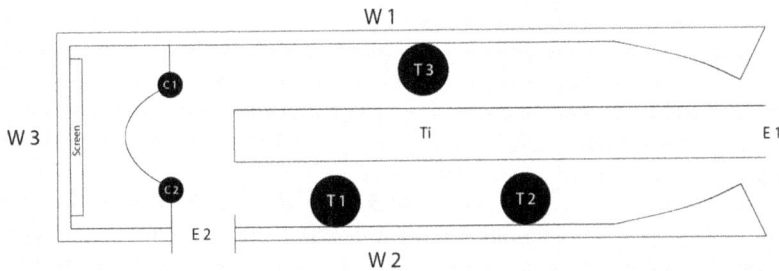

Figure 7. "The Mixing Room: stories from young refugees in New Zealand", Museum of New Zealand Te Papa Tongarewa. Layout. W: Walls with light-box. E 1: Main entrance. E 2: secondary entrance. T 1- T 3: Interactive tables covering three different overarching concepts: 1. 'Challenge', 2. 'Connection', 3. 'Freedom'. C1-2: Consoles providing further digital content. Ti: Timeline outlining pivotal points in New Zealand's involvement in refugee aid. Sketch: Author.

---

28 Gibson, 2013, provides some anecdotes illustrating the impact of the model employed. One participant expressed traumatic experience through the medium of poetry and is now a published author (Morris, 2013), while in general a cathartic and confidence-enhancing effect on participants was reported (Superville, 2013).

Visitor circulation is not predetermined by the exhibition's design. Visitors might enter through the main entrance, or through the secondary entrance, so influencing storyline elements.[29]

The walls on each of the longitudinal sides (W1; W2) have lightbox cavities, accommodating one or more photographs with quotes and captions. The centre of the room has a timeline of New Zealand's involvement in refugee aid. Three interactive tables occupy the space in front of the walls and have projection surfaces, with digital images projected from above. The surface is touch-sensitive. Finally the wall opposite to the entrance section (W 3) forms another projection area with a continually changing photomosaic. There are two consoles for further digital content (C1; C2).[30]

The refugee experience – the walls and floor

A gallery of backlit photographs confronts visitors with a conglomerate of different stages of the refugee's journey. This story commences in the home country, displays hardships of the flight and concludes with the arrival in New Zealand. Added to the photographs are quotes from the participants in the project, which match each photograph thematically. This section represents displacement as a process and also connects specific place identities with countries of origin and New Zealand.

Similarly to other visitors, one overseas visitor perceived New Zealand being represented as a welcoming country, which enables refugees to settle down: "The people all found a new home and were really accepted. This is also reflected in the quote, 'I like it here, I want

---

29 Te Papa's internal Summative Evaluation, 2011, pp. 11ff., also suggests that visitors spent significantly less time in the exhibition when entering through the secondary entrance, mainly due to confusion caused by the reversed order of "events".
30 Te Papa, 2010.

Figure 8. Main entrance of the exhibition marked by two panels to the right and left which show a group shot and a life-size full-length photographic portrait of participants of the exhibition project. Centre: Screen of 4 x 5 metres featuring a photomosaic constituting portraits of participants. Photo: Kate Whitley, Te Papa, MA_I.182891.

to stay here'. I like it that one is providing people with refuge" (Visitor 11, translation by the author).

The attempt to educate visitors about the positive impact of refugees on New Zealand society appears to have been successful. Displacement is apparently superseded by "belonging" through acceptance and aid in settling down. Accordingly displacement is represented as process, ending with the arrival in Wellington. To adhere to the mission statement and also respect the wishes of the participants, failure and ongoing displacement cannot be a focus of The Mixing Room leading to a particular if well-intended narration on the wall.

Figure 9. In the exhibition, "The Mixing Room: stories from young refugees in New Zealand", Museum of New Zealand Te Papa Tongarewa. The walls on each of the longitudinal sides of the room are appointed with lightbox cavities differing in size and shape, each accommodating one or more photographs with added quotes and captions. To the left and right interactive tables equipped with a touch sensitive surface are located. Photo: Author.

The first set of lightboxes focusing on the countries of origin provides good examples to support these findings further. Three photographs in the upper lightbox show a young Kurdish shepherd blinded by an Iranian mine.[31] Kurdish refugees returning to their demolished village

---

31 The photo was taken by Michael Coyne in the 1980s. The NGV online database offers a more detailed story about the events: "A Kurdish shepherd hugs his fourteen-year-old blind son who had stepped on an Iranian mine. The father, who sold most of his property to bring his son to Tehran, offered his eyes but the boy was too badly injured for a transplant", National Gallery of Victoria, 2011.

of Qala Diza are shown, as are Vietnamese soldiers and prisoners surveying a display of captured weaponry.[32] Associations like child soldiers, loss of home and collateral damage can be conjured up in these photographs. The meticulous scene arrangement, professional execution of the photographs, choice of perspective and lighting, together discourage association of the photographs with amateur photography. The depiction of scenes with great emotional effect, suggests an expression of art, and could potentially undermining the intended impact.

Figure 10. "The Mixing Room: stories from young refugees in New Zealand, Section "Fear and Persecution". Photo: Author.

---

32 All of the pictures in the Fear and Persecution sections were either made by National Geographic or UNHCR. Gibson explains the choice of those providers as representing a realistic approximation to the circumstances at the depicted places. Staff (Morris, 2013; Superville, 2013) did not perceive them as works of art, but rather as dependable sources.

Most visitors in the sample were drawn to the picture of the injured Kurdish shepherd and the children wielding weapons, one giving as a reason that: "It pushes the emotional buttons that's for sure and the fact that, well, probably anyone with guns or weapons is worlds and worlds away or apart from our daily lives here. That is what sticks out" (Visitor 10). Furthermore, the depicted violence was given as the main reason the image of the shepherd stood out for one visitor (Visitor 13), while in another case the contrast between innocent child and weapon was given as reason (Visitor 17). Visitors in the sample did not seem to acknowledge the photographs as expressions of art, but rather engaged with the depiction of shocking violence or contrasting life circumstances, when compared to daily life in a stable country.

One visitor projected her family history onto the template of an experience of "displacement" as represented by the photographs and text in this section:

> My father was a displaced person after World War II into Britain. He was Estonian and never ever saw any of his family again after the World War II so he arrived into England as a displaced person who was looked after and assimilated into the culture . . . this would be a similar story to my family story and at the moment my own family is divided in between myself here in New Zealand, my husband hasn't settled in New Zealand, so he is back in England. I have one daughter in Australia and one daughter in London so this sort of . . . understanding of how difficult it is to live all over the world, is I guess one that just makes it more emotional for me (Visitor 18).

In this particular example family history and exhibition contents become connected. One could argue that the specific content of the section is not of importance, but rather the focus on the concept of displacement, enabling the visitor to become emotionally invested. While war and fear of persecution made her father a displaced person, entailing a loss of home and a loss of family, her current situation entails a concept of displacement based on exceedingly mobile modern lifestyles. This displacement, driven by economic or lifestyle reasons is not the same as displacement represented in the exhibition section, which is caused by fear of persecution and violence. While an emotional connection is established, understanding of the situation can, for this visitor, only be approximated, based on personal experience, but never fully appreciated.

The quotes as well as the photographs, introduce the reason for having to leave, in all examples a state of war or civil unrest. Further, the passiveness with which refugees had to endure the events destroying the life they knew and the helplessness felt by individuals, is communicated. Displacement is thus represented as a loss of freedom, a loss of influencing one's own fate and being subject to often unimaginable circumstances. In the narration of the exhibition, man-made conflicts and not natural disasters are causing displacement.

The stage is now set for the next arrangement of photographs which encompass the flight and persecution of individuals. This journey, depicted by quotes and photographs as extremely unpleasant, perilous and demanding, ends in a refugee camp. The photographs in this section portray harsh camp conditions, dependence on inadequate food and water and finally the long process of resettlement application (See figure 11).

The overarching theme of losing one's freedom and the ability to influence the future stood out, especially for one visitor, who had a strong reaction to a photograph of a woman behind a camp fence: "She just looks like she wants to get out and she just can't. I have never felt that way myself. You know, you feel that way, but you are never trapped as a westerner really. There is always something you can do, but they obviously can't" (Visitor 16). The randomness of being selected in the program was also an aspect of the refugee experience visitors were able to engage with:

> The list that comes up, it is really interesting, isn't it. They don't really apply, they are on the list and then they just waited and waited. Where we just pay lots of money and hope for the best . . . I suppose they are going there every few days or weeks or so to see if their number or name comes up (Visitor 14).

Figure 11. "The Mixing Room". Section "Transition. Applying for Resettlement". Photo: Author.

In this case a connection is drawn between western attempts at solving problems with an infusion of money, and the fact that the success of such measures is uncertain. The wish to help and to become involved is also reflected in another response:

> I'm interested in the UN and stuff and how much can this poor person do? . . . I was just thinking this person must be over this, they have this problem and they have only one person, so what can they do? I want to work for the UN. I started studying international relations so was very interested in the human rights (Visitor 17).

Here a proactive rather than passive response emerges. While the exhibition did not prompt the career choice, it serves as an occasion to talk about future plans. Displacement as a process cannot be represented to visitors so that they can understand its full extent. Confronted with the incomprehensible, only one's own privilege can serve as a counterbalance, leading to an appreciation of how different is a refugee's lot, compared to the reality of life in New Zealand.

While the program is represented as the only way to leave the camps, the insufficient quota of refugees being admitted is problematised. No specific reasons are provided for the failings of the system and visitors might conclude that receiving countries are responsible, or, on the contrary, assume that these countries do their best and non-participating countries are to blame.[33] While refugees spend, in some cases, decades in the camps, these are never presented as "home" or as a replacement for the loss of home. They appear to be a continuation of displacement represented and perceived as lottery and limbo.

The final two sections focus on the arrival in New Zealand, the initial culture shock and subsequent acculturation. It could be expected that

---

33 This idea was expressed by one visitor in the sample (Visitor 26).

the transition from displacement to belonging is represented in this section. Scenes of families united at the airport or family members exchanging gestures of affection are accompanied by expressions of relief and a general positive outlook on the future. Unlike former sections, photographs here are mostly press photos. The press photos seem to portray real emotions of tangible individuals, as opposed to the preceding photographs showing general situations far away from visitor's personal experience. This reflects the opinion of one visitor regarding the photographs in this section: "I saw photos of them being reunited with their families and photos from Auckland Airport. You know I go there, but seeing it with the actual people makes it feel more real. I think if it was New Zealand [in the pictures] it had more impact" (Visitor 17).

The last element of the refugee experience is the process of settling down in a new country. Mangere Refugee Centre is depicted. In the course of six weeks individuals learn about the culture, language and mores of New Zealand and are then provided with a dwelling and initial help with settling. All visitors asked, perceived this section as cheerful, in stark contrast to the other sections. One overseas visitor even attributed traits he normally associated with New Zealanders, to the now resettled refugees: "I think especially that one, how he is carried on the sofa that looks funny. I would say, typically Kiwi, just laid back and easy-going. That is like: They arrived, that is a fact" (Visitor 11, translation by the author). In leaving the Mangere centre, refugees transform into settlers and displacement is superseded by belonging. If the narration ended this way, the exhibition would oversimplify complex resettlement processes, leaving visitors thinking that New Zealand easily integrates refugees.

Most visitors interviewed were not able to or did not want to use the interactive tables which were designed to enable deeper engagement.

The three tables cover three different overarching concepts: freedom, challenge and connection; with each divided in sub-categories. In this way a deeper and more nuanced understanding of the reality of life for youth with a refugee background is reserved for visitors, who take the time to engage with all elements.

Both ongoing displacement and belonging are represented through the creations of participants. Using the video poem "Questions" highlights the point:

> Born in a place I don't know, stranger in a place I call home.
> 13 years and still they stare. Where is my home? Where, where?

Figure 12. "The Mixing Room: stories from young refugees in New Zealand". Section "Mangere Refugee Resettlement Centre. Moving in a new Home". Photo: Author.

Many questions are also on my mind. If I was in Rwanda more friends I would find?

Different is something I'll always be. With no identity I am just me.

Where did you come from? Why are you here? Questions I laugh about with fear.

Go back! Go back! They say all the time.

I've been here since I was three. Is that such a crime?

In my heart I am more Kiwi than all of you. But to my Rwanda I stay true.

New Zealand is my home. It is what it is.

Coming here was through war, but it ends in true bliss.

Friendship and opportunities endless in count. In my heart there's happiness no doubt.

I am proud to be me. That's never going to change.

I'm Rwandese, I'm a Kiwi.

Better yet I'm just Ange (Te Papa, 2012).

Confronted with exclusion and discrimination the writer's identity is based on a mixing of cultural backgrounds. Self-identification as "Kiwi" is being questioned and connection to Rwanda is merely an early childhood memory, so that only an identity embedded in the individual as a person seems feasible. This is an identity governed by a feeling of ongoing displacement, a self-imposed condition, reinforced by exclusion. While the existence in New Zealand has advantages and is dominated by happiness, the feeling of being "displaced" and not belonging to either culture represents the other side of the medal of being a young person with a refugee background in New Zealand. This is not restricted to one contribution, but reflected in other poems and performances. While the positive aspects of the new life in New

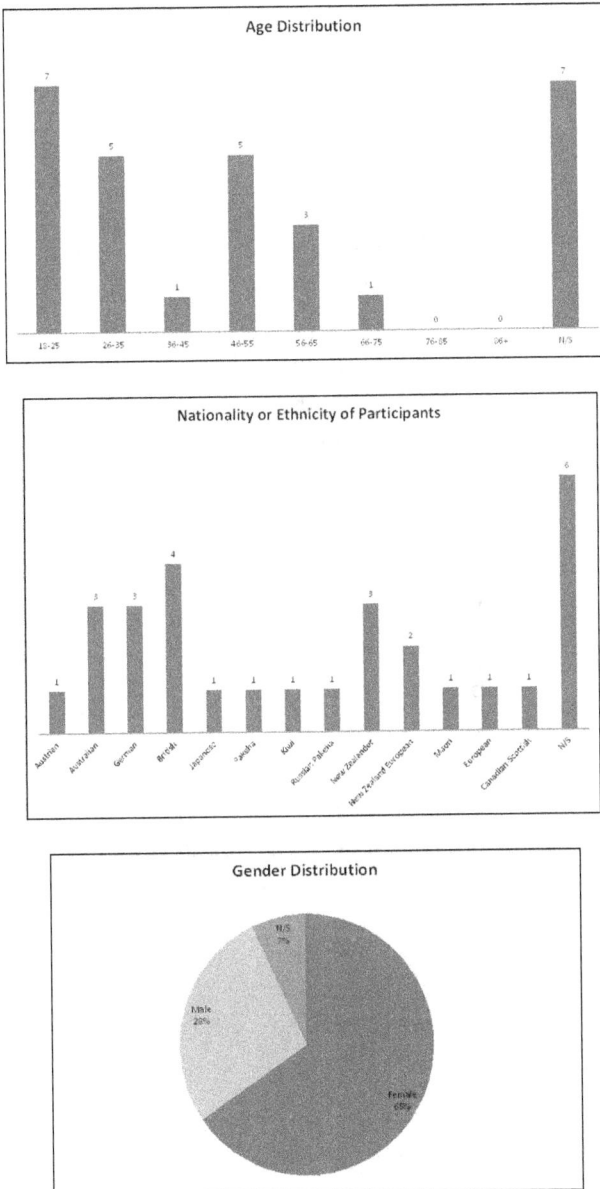

Figure 13. Visitor characteristics

Zealand still dominate, the struggles of the young people will become much more apparent to visitors through the interactive elements of the exhibition.

Conclusion

Overall, objectives formulated in the planning papers with regard to affecting visitors emotionally and making them aware of New Zealand's refugee quota program, as well as the traumatic experiences of refugees, were achieved in this exhibition.[34] New Zealand is presented as one of the few countries being actively involved in refugee aid, providing initial help and supervision, and as a country welcoming refugees. Shortcomings of the program are not omitted, however, reasons for these remain unclear and open to visitors' interpretation.

The Mixing Room focuses on topical cases of forced migration. While topics such as exclusion and discrimination are addressed through the contributions of the participants, an overall positive depiction remains. Any emphasis on failed integration combined with a harsh critique of the program's shortcomings might be detrimental to the exhibition's intentions. It is thus not surprising that New Zealand's place identity as represented in the Mixing Room is in line with other museums' depiction of contemporary New Zealand society: A welcoming place, were people can live free of persecution and threats to their lives.

It is feasible that displacement only appears as a process in the sections depicting the situation in the country of origin and the

---

34 This is also backed by the findings of the Summative Evaluation, which suggest that visitors were able to increase their knowledge about and modify their perception of refugees (Te Papa, 2011).

situation in the refugee camps, while ongoing displacement in New Zealand is not represented except through the interactive tables, ignored as indicated above, by most visitors.

Finally, taking into account visitor responses collected during this research project, the exhibition does seem to be able to inform visitors of the positive impact of refugee resettlement and, more importantly, the fate of individuals. Accordingly, prejudices and resulting exclusion could be decreased, with the Mixing Room making marginal impact on reducing ongoing displacement. It remains to be seen if the depiction of refugee resettlement and the representation of displacement and belonging will change when the current forced migration becomes merely historical and can be addressed in retrospective.

References:

Archival documents

Te Papa (2010) The Mixing Room. 90% Developed Design, File EP-EX-011-01-05#e01 (ref. 406338). Te Papa Archives. Wellington.

Allan, Lynne C. (2011) The Mixing Room – Stories from young Refugees in New Zealand Summative Evaluation. File VMAA-05-13-03#e01 (ref. 515479) Te Papa Archives. Wellington.

Te Papa (2012) "The Mixing Room". Wellington: Te Papa Tongarewa. Wellington.

Secondary literature

Alvesson, Mats. (2011) *Interpreting Interviews*. Thousand Oaks, CA; London; New Delhi; Singapore: Sage.

Bakewell, Oliver. (2011) "Conceptualising displacement and migration: Processes, conditions, and categories". In Koser, K. and Martin, S. (eds). *The Migration-Displacement Nexus: Patterns, Processes, and Policies*. Oxford: Berghahn Books.

Bal, Mieke. (1996) *Double Exposures: The Subject of Cultural Analysis*. New York: Routledge.

Baur, Joachim. (2010). Museumsanalyse: Zur Einführung". In Baur, J. (ed). *Museumsanalyse. Methoden und Konturen eines neuen Forschungsfeldes*. Bielefeld, Germany: Transcript.

Buschmann, Heike. (2010)"Geschichten im Raum. Erzähltheorie als Museumsanalyse". In Baur, J. (ed). *Museumsanalyse. Methoden und Konturen eines neuen Forschungsfeldes*. Bielefeld, Germany: Transcript.

Butcher, Andrew. Spoonley, Paul and Trlin, Andrew D. (2006). *Being Accepted: the Experience of Discrimination and Social Exclusion by Immigrants and Refugees in New Zealand*. Palmerston North, New Zealand: New Settlers Programme. Massey University.

Chile, Love. (2005). "Locating and belonging: transition from refugee to citizen". In Tasew, Y.T. (ed). *Diasporic Ghosts: a Discourse on Exile and Refugee Issues*. Wellington: 254-91.

Department of Labour, New Zealand (ed). (2009a) *Quota Refugees in New Zealand: Approvals and Movements (1999-2008)*. Wellington: Department of Labour

—————. (2009b) *Migration trends and Outlook 2007/2008*. Wellington: Department of Labour.

—————. (2006) *Migrant and Refugee Streams. A guide to understanding how migrants and refugees enter New Zealand*. Wellington: Department of Labour.

—————. (2002) *Refugee Resettlement Research Project: 'Refugee Voices'. Interim Report: A Journey Towards Resettlement*. Wellington: Department of Labour.

Falk, John H. (2009) *Identity and the Museum Visitor Experience*. Walnut Creek, CA. USA: Left Coast Press

—————. (2011) "Contextualizing Falk's Identity-Related Visitor Motivation Model". *Visitor Studies* 14(2): 141-57.

Fitzgerald, Michael. (2009) "Te Papa's Community Gallery. Presenting Migrant Stories at 'Our Place' ". *New Zealand Journal of History*. 43(2): 198-207.

Geertz, Clifford. (1993) *Dichte Beschreibung. Beiträge zum Verstehen kultureller Systeme*. Frankfurt am Main: Frankfurt am Main.

Gibson, Stephanie and Kindon, Sara. (2013) "The Mixing Room project at Te Papa: co-creating the museum with refugee background youth in Aotearoa/New Zealand". *Tuhinga*. 24: 65-83.

Jones, Sam. (2010) "Reframing Difference: Museums, Cross-cultural Communication and the Representation of Refugees". In Skartveit, H-L. and Goodnow, K. (eds). *Changes in Museum Practice. New Media, Refugees and Participation. New York:* Berghahn Books: xi-xxiv.

Noschka-Roos, Annette. (2003) *Besucherforschung in Museen. Instrumentarien zur Verbesserung der Ausstellungskommunikation*. München: Deutsches Museum.

Mastai, Judith. (2007) "'There Is No Such Thing as a Visitor'". In Pollock, G. and Zemans, J. (eds). *Museums after Modernism: Strategies of Engagement*. Malden: Blackwell: 173-7.

Muttenthaler, Roswitha and Wonisch, Regina. (2006) *Gesten des Zeigens. Zur Repräsentation von Gender und Race in Ausstellungen*. Bielefeld, Germany: Transcript.

Patton, Michael Quinn. (2002) *Qualitative Research & Evaluation Methods*. Edition Three. Thousand Oaks, CA; London; New Delhi: Sage.

Scholze, Jana. (2004) *Medium Ausstellung : Lektüren musealer Gestaltung in Oxford, Leipzig, Amsterdam und Berlin*. Bielefeld. Germany: Transcript.

Schorch, Philipp (2010) "Te Papa: a forum for the world? A narrative exploration of a global public sphere". Doctor of Philosophy Thesis. Victoria University of Wellington.

Sobrun-Maharaj, Amritha Tse, Samson, Hoque, Ekramul and Rossen, Fiona. (2008) *Migrant and Refugee Youth in New Zealand: a Study of Key Informants*. Wellington: Department of Labour.

Electronic sources

National Gallery of Victoria 2012. NGV Collection. Michael Coyne

Te Papa. (2013a) *The Museum of New Zealand. About Te Papa.*

————. (2013b) *The Museum of New Zealand. The Mixing Room. Stories from young refugees in New Zealand.*

UNESCO. (2013a) *Social and Human Sciences, International Migration, Glossary of Migration Related Terms, Migrant/Migration.*

————. (2013b) *Social and Human Sciences, International Migration, Glossary of Migration Related Terms, Refugee*

Interviews

Museum of New Zealand Te Papa Tongarewa staff.

Gibson, Stephanie. Curator History. *Museum of New Zealand Te Papa Tongarewa.* Interview by the Author.

Morris, Sarah. Exhibition Interpreter. *Museum of New Zealand Te Papa Tongarewa.* Interview by the Author.

Superville, Susan. Community Relations Manager, *Museum of New Zealand Te Papa Tongarewa.* Interview by the Author.

Participants visitor survey at Museum of New Zealand Te Papa Tongarewa.

Visitor 10 at the *Museum of New Zealand Te Papa Tongarewa. The Mixing Room.* Interview by the Author.

Visitor 11 at the *Museum of New Zealand Te Papa Tongarewa. The Mixing Room.* Interview by the Author.

Visitor 13 at the *Museum of New Zealand Te Papa Tongarewa. The Mixing Room.* Interview by the Author.

Visitor 14 at the *Museum of New Zealand Te Papa Tongarewa. The Mixing Room.* Interview by the Author.

Visitor 15 at the *Museum of New Zealand Te Papa Tongarewa. The Mixing Room.* Interview by the Author, .

Visitor 16 at the *Museum of New Zealand Te Papa Tongarewa*. The Mixing Room. Interview by the Author.

Visitor 17 at the *Museum of New Zealand Te Papa Tongarewa*. The Mixing Room. Interview by the Author.

Visitor 18 at the *Museum of New Zealand Te Papa Tongarewa*. The Mixing Room. Interview by the Author.

Visitor 26 at the *Museum of New Zealand Te Papa Tongarewa*. The Mixing Room. Interview by the Author.

Appendix 1:

Question Bank Visitor Interviews:

- Pre-visit Questions: Expectations, motivations and presuppositions

    1. Do you have any expectations with regard to your visit to *Name of Exhibition*?
    2. What is your main motivation for visiting *Name of Exhibition*?
    3. With whom are you here today?
    4. Would you be so kind to share with me what you already know about *Theme of Exhibition*?

- Post-Visit Questions: Design and content

    a) Design of the exhibition space and atmosphere:

    1. If you think back to your experience today in The Mixing Room, how did you feel about the exhibition's design?

1.1 What is your opinion about the choice of colours?

1.2 What is your opinion about the selection and presentation of text?

1.3 What is your opinion about the selection and presentation of photographs (if applicable)?

2. How would you describe the atmosphere of the exhibition to somebody who did not yet visit it?

3. Which design element stood out for you?

b) Content of exhibition:

1. Could you tell me, in your own words, about your experience today in the *Name of Exhibition*?

2. If you would have to tell somebody, who did not yet visit the exhibition, which story the exhibition tells, what would you tell him or her?

3. Was there anything in particular that made you feel very strongly about the subject – perhaps something that you saw, heard or talked about today?

4. What, if anything, did you experience that made you change your mind about something?

5. Which object or objects caught your attention and why?

6. What is the most important thing that you will remember about your experience here today?

• Visual associative element:

I will now show you photographs of objects you might have encountered in the exhibition. Could you tell me how you feel about them?

9

Marsha Berry and Catherine Gomes

Pinning poetry to place: making sense of place in the Pilbara

This chapter presents the findings of fieldwork undertaken by the two authors. It documents the process of writing undertaken when a community chooses sites for inclusion in the Pilbara Writers poetry map.[1] Here, the broader context is presented so as to situate the Pilbara ethnographic project. The authors received an invitation from the Pilbara Writers group to create poetry maps of sites in the Pilbara region of Western Australia, exploring perceptions of place for the online "Poetry 4 U" web-site. This invitation came about after the group had seen the web-site. The "Poetry 4 U" project brings poetry into geographical places while at the same time occupying the floating world of social media.[2] It embraces the rapid uptake on contemporary location-based social media services as suggested by the popular applications such as Foursquare, Gowalla and Facebook. This in turn, allows the re-imagining of places and identity and so reinvigorates our sense of place.[3]

---

1 For more detail see Berry and Goodwin, 2013.
2 Ibid.
3 Tuan, 1974; Augé, 1995.

The bigger picture: the poetry 4 U project

The proposition underpinning the research behind the wider and ongoing "Poetry 4 U" project is that to use technology is to "express a social vision" and furthermore it is to "engage ourselves in a form of life (as having) social and mythic dimensions".[4] Tacchi argues that "in order to explore the uses of new technologies, we need to see how they relate to those 'social visions' and 'forms of life' and understand the technology's 'social and mythic dimensions' ".[5]

"Poetry 4 U" is a participatory art project where crowd-sourced poetry is "pinned" using Google maps to specific geographic locations. It also provides a prism through which to view social and mythical dimensions of emerging media technologies.[6] The Pilbara poetry map is a step along the path towards understanding how social technology informs and contributes to symbolic understandings of places through poetic and narrative expressions. The web-site itself explores understandings of places as practices, drawing on postmodern geography where space, memory and spatiality are integral to ontological discussions about belonging; for as Edward Soja proposes, "we are first and always historical-social-spatial beings, actively participating individually and collectively in the construction/ production – the 'becoming' – of histories, geographies, societies".[7] Space then, like memory, is fluid and changes over time. Interpretations and responses to places are historically, socially and spatially bound and these change over time.[8] The cultural geographer, Cresswell

---

4 Pfaffenberger, 1998, p. 249.
5 Tacchi, 2004, p. 92.
6 See Berry and Goodwin, 2013.
7 Soja, 1996, p. 73.
8 Nora, 1989.

explores the fluidity of space by asking: "How do places (and actions in them) get the meanings they do . . . ?"[9]

Poetic expressions can reveal how people attribute meanings to places they encounter and/or inhabit. In this chapter, through an ethnographic study, we expose some of the spatialising processes of a creative writers' group. The chapter explores how they produce a space to explore their favourite landscapes through their craft, in order to better understand how they make sense of places, and how they make sense of themselves in various landscapes.

An ethnographic tour: choosing special places

The cultural geographer, Tuan asks: "What are our views on the physical environment, natural and man-made? How do we perceive, structure and evaluate it?"[10] He defines topophilia as the affective relation that exists between people and place. Tuan's question formed a cornerstone for the fieldwork in the Pilbara. In June 2012, the authors of this chapter undertook a field trip to Karratha, as guests of the Pilbara Writers group, in order to interview writers and document the process of choosing sites for their poetry map for the "Poetry 4 U" website.

The Pilbara Writers group put together an itinerary of places of significance to the group, places that they envisaged for inclusion on the poetry map. Members of the Pilbara Writers group took researchers to numerous sites in the second half of June 2012 to reveal "their" Pilbara. This somewhat packed itinerary included: Cossack, Burrup Rock Art, Burrup Industrial Area, Dampier Archipelago Cruise, Point Samson, Wickham, Cossack, Roebourne, Karratha, Millstream and Python Pool.

---

9 Cresswell, 1996, p. 17.
10 Tuan, 1974, p. 1.

An ethnographic approach allowed close proximity to the writers in the context of their lives so as to gain a better understanding of their social and cultural practices and how creative writing fitted within these practices.[11] Ethnography is a way of studying the meaning of the behaviour and interaction among members of a culture, for as Spradley states, "the essential core of ethnography is this concern with the meaning of actions and events to the people we seek to understand".[12] As a research methodology it is reflexive, exploratory, messy and inductive whereby the researchers immerse themselves in the context they wish to study. It enables what Geertz famously termed "thick descriptions".

The project's methodology following this ethnographic approach, including fieldwork, semi-structured interviews, round-table conversations and observations. Participants for interviews were sourced through the Pilbara Writers group. These were followed by field trips with volunteers to document the special places they wanted to include in the poetry map for the web-site.

A critical interest was in understanding how the writers constructed meaning, and how they imbued places in the Pilbara with significance. As researchers we felt we needed to be there physically with them to gain and to "invoke the complexities implied by an anthropological use of the phrase, 'a sense of place' ".[13] Furthermore, through being there, the research could highlight perceptions of place using all the senses.[14] Pink suggests walking with video is a way of experiencing place through the senses as well as emplacing the senses to comprehend place. Her technique involves recording walks through the landscape

---

11 Lewis, 1973.
12 Spradley, 1979, p. 5.
13 Pink, 2007, p. 240.
14 Feld and Basso, 1996.

directed by participants. This study required researchers to shoot photographs and videos of geographic sites with members of the Pilbara Writers group using Pink's walking with video technique.

The project also included poetry workshops, which conceptually explored connections to landscapes as a part of the research. The proposition underpinning these workshops was that settings are integral to creative writing whereby "we make places make meanings for us".[15] The workshops explored the manner in which places in the Pilbara were imagined by the writers, through conversations and the writing of short-form poems such as haiku.

The Pilbara region

The Pilbara region of Western Australia comprises 505,000 square kilometres. The official "Australia's North West" web-site states that it is the world's most ancient plateau dating back two billion years.[16] The Pilbara contains three distinct geographic formations; the immense coastal plain, the mountain ranges inland, and an arid desert stretching to the Northern Territory border. Its topography is characterised by spinifex grasslands and gabbro and granophyte boulder piles ranging in colour from deep orange to purple. There is a diversity of habitats including snappy gums and hakea, which support various fauna and flora.[17] The Pilbara is also key to Australia's mining boom and has developed a unique demography, since much of the population is transient rather than local. Karratha is the main town in the region. A Western Australian Government planning report in December 2010 states that:

15 Krauth, 2003.
16 Australia's North-West web-site.
17 Burbridge et al., 2006.

Compared to the rest of WA, Karratha has a high resident churn factor, recording a lower proportion of usual residents who resided at their current address one and five years ago. Approximately 56 and 24 per cent of Karratha residents lived at their current address one and five years ago respectively, compared to 75 per cent and 48 per cent for the State. Many Karratha residents had either moved to different addresses within the same statistical local area of had moved from other parts of WA. In terms of Karratha residents who previously resided in other states (5 years ago), the largest numbers were from Queensland (2.8 per cent), followed by Victoria (2.2 per cent).

The vast majority of these transients, unsurprisingly, work for high wages in the mining sector and its related industries. According to the Westjobs.com.au web-site, mining companies, for instance, pay skilled workers a minimum of $90,000 a year. However, the Pilbara does not only attract people drawn to the well-paid positions created in the mining boom. It also attracts workers who are employed outside the mining sector, and who similarly live and work, on a transient basis, in the Pilbara.

Research on transients often documents and theorises cross-national movements rather than movements within national boundaries. For instance work on transients in the Asia-Pacific region often looks at the circulation of foreign domestic workers in Asia.[18] Meanwhile, studies on transients in Australia frequently fall into historical studies on indentured workers or into improving the educational and social experiences of international students.[19] Furthermore, work on transients in the Pilbara often highlights

18 e.g. Yeoh, Huang and Gonzalez, 1999.
19 e.g. Banivanua-Mar's 2007 study of Fijian workers in Queensland; Gray, Chang and Kennedy, 2010; Sawir, 2008; and Kashima and Loh, 2006.

unionism by workers.[20] Our approach is significantly different from the studies we have cited above, in that we focused on people who travelled from other places in Australia to live and work in the Pilbara and interviewed them about their perceptions of the world's most ancient plateau, and how it impacts on their sense of belonging to the landscape they now inhabit.

Apart from local indigenous communities, most of the residents of the Pilbara are transient. These fall into two broad categories, those who live in the townships such as Karratha, and those who live in work camps. The latter are known as fly-in/fly-outs, and often come from within Western Australia, often from the capital city Perth, or from interstate. Usually, the fly-in/fly-outs spend two weeks in the Pilbara and then a week on leave where they fly back home or elsewhere for their rest and recreation as Rio Tinto's web-site notes.[21] Most of the time, the fly-in/fly-outs live in self-contained work camps which function as gated communities. The camps take care of the workers' basic needs and entertainment, since they house mess halls, grocery stores, mini-cinemas, game rooms, gyms and medical centres. Housing in these camps take the form of "dongas", which are portable, individual, small dwellings with kitchens and bathrooms. The continued media focus on transient mining workers ought not obscure other deep connections to place in the Pilbara. The sense of belonging amongst highly mobile mine workers seems, unsurprisingly, limited. This group as a result lay outside this study, and can be contrasted to members of the Pilbara Writers group residing in the Pilbara townships.

---

20 e.g. Ellem, 2003.
21 Rio Tinto web-site, fly-in/fly-out.

Figure 14. Karratha

In the following sections, two sites are presented: Cossack/Cossack Heritage Trail, and Millstream-Chichester National Park. They emerged as charged with multi-layered meanings for Pilbara writers. In what follows the Pilbara writers have been given pseudonyms to protect their identities. Then follows an account of the haiku workshop conducted with Yindjibarndi women affiliated with the Juluwarlu Aboriginal Corporation. For the Juluwarlu Aboriginal Corporation people, the Pilbara has always been their country. The poems are reproduced with the permission of the Juluwarlu Aboriginal Corporation.

Cossack and the Cossack Heritage Trail

A point on the journey to explore potential sites with Pilbara writers for their poetry map was a small township called Cossack, originally a port named Tien Tsin, after the boat that carried the first settlers to

Figure 15. Cossack

the region in 1863, and which had a devastating impact on indigenous communities. Relationships to places are coloured by cultural memories and projections of memories according to memory scholars such as Hirsch and Huyssen.[22] Places that were the sites of significant cultural or historical events will have symbolic qualities, which affect their meanings and processes according to Kuhn and McAllister.[23] In

22 Hirsch, 1996 and Huyssen, 2003.
23 Kuhn and McAllister, 2006.

1871, Governor Weld renamed the town after the warship "Cossack". It was the hub of the Japanese pearling industry in the region with a turtle factory and a leprosarium. The restored heritage buildings mark this historical phase and also serve as reminders of a very dark chapter of Australia's history, that of "blackbirding" which as it relates to Western Australian history, was the practice of kidnapping indigenous women to work in the pearling industry.[24] On show there too, are the manacles that were used on indigenous men who escaped from forced or indentured labour. These material artifacts displayed in the prison exhibition spoke of catastrophic events for the traditional owners of the land.

Cossack is a restored heritage town now, and is a focus for tourism in the region. It plays host to the famous Cossack Art Award. It remains in addition, a place that is often chosen for creative arts workshops by the local writers and photographers. Our guide showed us the heritage buildings including the prison. She spoke of her mixed feeling about the township briefly before telling us about a recent photography workshop she had undertaken and how the workshop had inspired her.

The next site visited was the Cossack Heritage Trail, which has been created for tourists to explore the region's history. It has walking trails laid out with snippets of information. Lee and Ingold argue, "the locomotive (or getting around) aspect of walking allows for an understanding of places being created by routes".[25] As she walked with the research team, a member of the Pilbara Writers group explained her understanding of the significance of Honeymoon Cove, a site on the Cossack Heritage trail.

---

24 Paterson, 2006.
25 Lee and Ingold, 2006, p. 68.

Figure 16. Walking with video to Honeymoon Cove

What follows is what she said as we walked along the path:

W: Honeymoon Cove (near Cossack) was a loading area once for ships, there is an arrow carved in at the end where the Afghan camel drivers used to drop off all their load for ships to collect – the beach has a natural amphitheater with the beautiful striated zebra rock a very ancient piece of country – they had a turtle soup factory at Cossack, this was a pearl diving area – their favourite workers were pregnant Aboriginal women because they had so much oxygen they could stay under water for the longest. On Jarman Island they used to run sheep until there were really harsh summers and they ran out of water.

Along the Cossack heritage trail there are great spots to whale watch, you can see the tankers queuing waiting to be loaded. Northwest bluebell plants are blooming everywhere. There are also kapok bushes brought by the Afghan camel traders.

You get the moon steps effect here when the tides are really low during the full moon. You also get it near Karratha and Dampier. (Monday, 18 June 2012)

The significance she drew from this landscape had historical and cultural aspects. The interpretation involved reading the landscape against settler historical discourses. This account also used a western epistemology including botanical taxonomies. Later she kept pointing out kapok and date palms growing by the sides of the roads to remind us of history the Afghan traders and their camels and how their plants had migrated and became a part of the contemporary Pilbara landscape. Plants were an integral part of the way she perceived, structured and evaluated the landscape.

Interviews with Liz and Corrine (of Pilbara Writers) explored their feelings about living in the Pilbara. Memory associations played a pivotal role in their feelings of "connecting to" the Pilbara. Both Liz and Corinne explained their love of the Pilbara landscape by referring to their childhood connections to landscapes that evoked a sense of freedom. The extract below is from the interview transcript:

C: I grew up in Sydney . . . it is about the vast . . . I grew up next to the ocean and the ocean has that vastness. That large sky . . . and that was always special to me, growing up. Umm . . .

L: I grew up on a farm. I guess that was when I was smaller . . . it was lovely to wander . . . as a child and when I got married. When I say it is open, it is free of infrastructure and fences. There was freedom because I did a lot of stuff on my own . . . we never went anywhere much.

They also explicitly referred to their profound spiritual and emotional connections to the desert:

> L: This is the oldest plateau in the world . . . it resonates to me the same way the Simpson desert was amazingly spiritual. It resonates with aboriginal people and it does here too. We are out in this vast beautiful land with these parallel sand dunes and now and then a powerful little waterhole or a rocky outcrop to climb up on . . . [At this point, Liz began to tear] . . . I am not very good talking about this because I am really emotional . . . um . . . ah . . . yeah . . . It is very powerful for me . . . very spiritual.
>
> C: It is very hard to put into words because it is very strong, very powerful . . . That is interesting because it reminded me why I became more and more interested in deserts because I had an epiphany in the Simpson Desert as well. And I was 21 or something and I had just finished uni. I used to be very anxious and scared. And even at uni I had to do a lot of bush work at night. I was absolutely petrified. Then I went to the Simpson Desert and I had this enormous experience where I had to record the Shit dunes . . . the Shit Dunes are a couple of parallel dunes to go to the toilet and I had to go out there on my own and I had never had the experience of walking on my own, in the dark and feeling completely and utterly safe. And it was deeply profound and spiritual experience. I became addicted to remote areas . . . it transforms things for me. People would often say to me . . . I had volunteers . . . a lot of students come and work on research projects and they would ask how come I am comfortable in the bush alone and I would tell them the story of the Simpson.

The sentiments expressed by both Liz and Corrine may be placed within the wider context of Australian cultural production.

Writers and artists in Australia have long represented the desert as having a rich symbolic meaning. It has been a rich site for poetic narratives and has been used as a trope for exile, self-discovery and alienation. Many writers have constructed it as a character in its own right. Haynes observes that European notions of the desert as an inhospitable, vast and monotonous place have coloured many attempts to understand it as a landscape.[26] She reminds us that in the 1930s and 1940s, through the images of the desert painted by Sidney Nolan and Russell Drysdale, it became "a powerful local metaphor for existential angst and a modernist perception of spiritual poverty in both the individual and the nation".[27] Clearly, deserts remain important in the cultural imaginary of Australia and this influences how writers and artists who reside in the Pilbara structure and evaluate local landscapes.

Both Liz and Corrine expressed a sense of belonging through their spiritual connections with the mythic arid and semi-arid landscapes of the Australian Outback. At a round-table discussion following a poetry workshop with Pilbara Writers, many of the writers discussed similar spiritual connections to the landscapes of the Pilbara and felt that these connections were what gave them a sense of belonging in this remote region of Australia and that this distinguished them from the fly-in/fly-out transient workers and the mining companies.

---

26 Haynes, 1998.
27 Ibid., p. 5.

Figure 17. Spinifex country

Millstream-Chichester National Park

On 21 June 2012, the project shifted focus from Karratha to the Millstream-Chichester National Park in Yindjibarndi Country. Here our guide shared her knowledge of the flora and fauna. Her affection for the life forms in the desert coloured her obvious love of the desert landscape. Walking along together, with the majestic Fortescue River carving its way through the gorge below, she gently drew attention to the things that mattered to her. Below is an extract of the conversation whilst walking through the landscape:

> Liz: Look at that bird of prey, [pointing to the sky] it's a called little eagle, there's that little plant – it's a weeping Mulla Mulla, just beautiful, very graceful, delicate desert plant

[pointing and stopping to watch the camera being focused on the plant]

MB: Good topic for a poem [smiling]

Liz: yes, just beautiful . . . so resilient . . .

The Mulla Mulla "Ptilotus" was a metaphor for resilience, symbolic of the fragile desert ecosystem. Through drawing attention to subtle nuances in the landscape, Liz was hoping others would see and experience what she saw and felt her Pilbara. Liz's knowledge and affection for the indigenous flora became apparent once more whilst walking with video on the way to the Millstream Pond:

W: See how crystal clear the water is . . . it all comes out of the aquifer . . . it's almost alpine . . . except for that long waving plant, sadly all the plants are introduced . . .

The track to Millstream Pond is built through a miniature delta with crystal clear streams and an abundance of vegetation:

Liz: Look at all the beautiful soft grass . . . there was rain last week or the week before . . . it's all lying down from the wind . . . I love the way these trees hang, their pendulous branches . . . they're paper barks, I love these paper barks, they're the biggest paper barks I have seen around here . . . and um, see those trees in the middle with the sort of feathery leaf?

MB: Yes

Liz: That's called a dragon tree and it has a very large leathery white flower that looks like a dragon [looks at M]

MB: Ah

Liz: And when they flower they fall into the river there and they're almost like lotus flowers but they're big and they're white . . .

MB: It's an idyllic place . . . [looks at Liz who nods smiling]

Walking with a guide enables outsiders to see place itself as a sensory

Figure 18. Millstream Pond

phenomenon and empathically sense what was important to local people.[28] Yet again the smallest details had the deepest resonance for our guide. At Millstream (Chinderwarriner) Pool she again pointed out the ephemera of life overlaying them with a simple story arc:

Liz: Look at the mudlark walking across the lily pads, they're opportunists those little mudlarks, I love them, look at those dragon flies, that one is red and you get blue ones too . . .

Look at it telling that fly to go away, it's saying this is my leaf.

Through her detailed knowledge of birds and plants, Liz creates an embodied awareness of the landscapes she is in for herself, so that even though she is in the Pilbara on a transient basis, she still feels

28 Feld and Basso, 1996, Pink, 2007.

strongly connected to places in the Pilbara. In the transcript excerpt
above, Liz employs a narrative structure to show her understanding of
the place as a complex ecology where each life form plays a vital role.

Talking about Haiku and Yindjibarndi Country around a table

The final section of this chapter deals with a workshop in Roebourne
at the Juluwarlu Aboriginal Corporation building. Initial discussions
were held with Elders about the Yindjibarndi country, encompassing
the Millstream-Chichester National Park. Their deep connection to
their "ngurra" (country) was obvious.

They showed books produced to bring together their narratives of
place – stories and songs. They also expressed a deep interest in using
the "Poetry 4 U" model to digitise their maps of Yindjibarndi country
and to create contemporary poetic bilingual narratives of place pinned
to their country whereby "the land is treated as a living, dynamic
entity".[29] They felt that digitised narrative maps would ignite their
children's pride in their culture and language because the youngsters
were more comfortable with iPads than printed books. There was an
agreement to work on grant applications for an interactive digital atlas
of Yindjibarndi country.

Three generations of Yindjibarndi women had come to learn about
haiku and other short poetry forms. The workshop commenced. The
nature of Japanese Zen aesthetics was outlined with special reference
to the techniques by which haiku writers sought to engage all of the
reader's senses so as to create an instance of "being there", connected
to the landscape. Renga (a Japanese form of collaborative poetry
using haiku type forms) was discussed with reference to medieval
Japanese courts in which people used to gather to write poetry chains

---

29 Juluwarlu Aboriginal Corporation, 2007, p. ii.

together. English translations of Bashō's haiku were read, to a positive response.

Amidst much laughter and blushing the group commenced writing a loose Renga together. The poetry created in the workshop is shared below with the permission of the people who participated:

> Why moon in the sky
> said my toddling curious child,
> where does it go in the day
> One of our owls are the
> Same as the moon
> Full moon you are so pretty
> light up the road to my country
> wish I can keep you
> isn't that a pity
> The full moon rises with pride
> and joy watching animals go
> while prey stalks prey

After sharing the Renga, the group wrote about feelings of place in short free verse. The poem below was written in the workshop to express feelings about being in country by the Yindjibarndi Elder, Tootsie. It is reproduced here with her permission.

> *Dedication Song*
> He stands and looks
> as far as the eyes
> can see!
> The soft breeze of his country
> welcomes his presence,

the soft gentle breeze
and the tree and birds
make joyful noise
of his welcoming visit to
the country.
Proudly he stands,
sings his song,
this is my country,
the place I belong!
(Tootsie 2012)

Afterword

The Pilbara takes on mythic proportions in the imaginations of writers who reside there. The week after this field trip, the local writers went on a walking meditation together to practice haiku, writing at sunset at the Karratha golf course. Some of the results are pinned to the Pilbara Writers map and may be accessed on the web-site. The mapping project for the Pilbara Writers has now passed its first phase. The first call for poetry resulted in numerous poems being pinned to a Google map of the Pilbara on the "Poetry 4 U" website.

It is clear that Pilbara writers do form a connection to the Pilbara through creative practice inspired by the landscape and also through belonging to communities involved in creative practice in the region. The key role, played by a personal and often, spiritual connection to the landscape, emerged strongly as a theme. Memory also played an important role. For the interviewees who turn to creative practice for personal expression, their connections to the landscape was much more significant and profound since they could trace their strong bonds to the positive memories and personal experiences they link with landscapes from their past memories. These memories and experiences stemmed from a sense of self-awareness, a reflexivity, which they feel has guided them not only to the Pilbara but also allowed them to feel a strong sense of belonging. However, what also became clear through fieldwork is that if participants expressed strong connection to the landscape, this was still not enough for them to envisage themselves as permanent residents in the region. The workshop with women from the Juluwarlu Aboriginal Corporation revealed a different picture where connections to the land were strong and permanent.

The multitude of culturally diverse narratives and perspectives connected to places may be represented visually in different ways, using digital technologies and social media, with respect to physical, human, cultural, chronological, economic and spiritual geographies. This project was short, sharp and intense and uncovered some of the complexities of the relationships residents of the Pilbara have with the landscapes they inhabit, through the lens of poetic expressions. Findings provide a slice in time of the Pilbara Writers group and like the findings of many ethnographic studies, they cannot be generalised. However, they do raise interesting questions about the role social Web 2.0 technologies can play in what many consider to be geographically remote regions, particularly for creative practice and creative practice communities. These technologies do afford a way share poetic expressions globally as well as nationally. They also provide indigenous communities with ways of communicating and sharing their stories of and connections to landscapes, so as to further understandings of the importance of place and to provide alternative ways of providing socio-historical contexts for constructing landscapes.

The implications of the determinations and digital representations of cultural and spiritual geographies created through community mappings can be explored critically and reflexively through projects such as the Pilbara Writers group poetry map, which utilises Web 2.0. Such digital technologies are now an ubiquitous part of Australian cultural capital, or habitus, whereby indigenous communities in northern Australia are increasingly using digital technologies to promote the interests of their traditional groupings, histories and places.[30] The nexus between emerging technologies and poetic expressions can yield new perspectives on how we perceive, structure and evaluate the places we inhabit.

References

Auge, Marc. (1995) *Non-places: An Introduction to an Anthropology of Super Modernity*. London: Verso.

Banivanua Mar, Tracey. (2007) *Violence and Colonial Dialogue: The Australia-Pacific Labor Trade*. Honolulu: University of Hawai'i Press.

Berry, Marsha and Goodwin, Omega. (2013) "Poetry 4 U: Pinning Poems under/over/through the Streets". *New Media and Society* 15(6): 909-29.

Bitsui, Sherwin. (2011) "Converging Wor[l]ds: Nizhoni Bridges and Southwest Native Communities". In Coles, Katharine (ed). *Blueprints: Bring Poetry into Communities*. Salt Lake City: University of Utah Press with Poetry Foundation.

Bourdieu, Pierre. (1984) *Distinction: a Social Critique of the Judgment of Taste*. Cambridge, MA: Harvard University Press.

Cresswell, Tim. (1996) *In Place/Out of Place, Geography, Ideology, and Transgression*. Minneapolis, London: University of Minnesota Press.

De Certeau, Michel. (1984) *The Practice of Everyday Life*. Berkeley: University of California Press.

Ellem, B. (2003) "New Unionism in the Old Economy: Community and Collectivism in the Pilbara's Mining Towns". *The Journal of Industrial Relations*. 45: 423-41.

---

30 Bourdieu, 1984; Verran and Christie, 2007.

Feld, Steven, and Basso, Keith, H. (eds). (1996) *Senses of place*, Santa Fe, New Mexico: School of American Research Press.

Haynes, Roslynn, D. (1998) *Seeking the Centre: The Australian Desert in Literature, Art and Film*. Cambridge: Cambridge University Press.

Gray, K., Chang, Shanton and Kennedy, G. (2010) "Use of social web technologies by international and domestic undergraduate students: implications for internationalising learning and teaching in Australian universities". *Technology, Pedagogy and Education*. 19(1): 31-46.

Juluwarlu Aboriginal Corporation. (2007) *Ngurra Warndurala Buluyugayi: Exploring Yindjibarndi Country*. Roebourne: Juluwarlu Aboriginal Corporation.

Kashima, E. S. and Loh, E. (2006) " International Students acculturation: Effects of international, conational, and local ties and need for closure". *International Journal of Intercultural Relations*. 30(4): 471-85.

Krauth, Nigel. (2003) "Four Writers and their Settings". *Text Journal*. 7(1). n.p. Lee, Jo and Ingold, Tim. (2006) "Fieldwork on Foot: Perceiving, routing, socializing". In Coleman, Simon and Collins, Peter. (eds). *Locating the Field. Space, Place and Context in Anthropology*. Oxford: Berg: 67-86.

Lyotard, Jean-François. (1989) *The Lyotard Reader*. Benjamin, Andrew (ed.). Oxford: Blackwell.

McDonald, Jo and Veth, Peter. (2009) "Dampier Archipelago petroglyphs: archaeology, scientific values and National Heritage Listing". *Archaeology Oceania*. Supplement. 44: 49. "Mining Jobs No Experience". The West Online Group. Westjobs web-site.

Morgan, Sally and Kwaymullina, Ambelin. (2007) "Solid Rock, Sacred Ground: Cultural Vandalism in the Pilbara". *Australian Feminist Law Journal*. 26: 9-16.

Nora, Pierre. (1989) "Between memory and history: Les lieux de memoire". *Representations*. 26: 7-24.

Paterson, Alistair. (2006) "Towards a historical archaeology of Western Australia's Northwest". *Australasian Historical Archaeology*. 24: 99-111

Pink, Sarah. "Walking with Video". (2007) *Visual Studies*. 22(3). December: 240-52

Pfaffenberger, Bryan. (1988) "Fetishised Objects and Humanised Nature: Towards an Anthropology of Technology". *Man*. 23: 236-52.

Reynolds, R. (1987) "The Indenoona Contact Site: A Preliminary Report of an Engraving Site in the Pilbara Region of Western Australia". *Australian Archaeology*. 25: 80-7.

Sawir, Edward. (2008) "Loneliness and IS: An Australian Study". *Journal of Studies in International Education*. 12(2): 148-80.

Soja, Edward. (1996) *Thirdspace: Journeys to Los Angeles and Other Real-and Imagined Places*. Massachusetts: Blackwell Publishers.

Spradley, James, P. (1979) *The ethnographic interview*. New York: Holt, Rinehart and Winston.

Tacchi, Jo. (2004) "Researching creative applications of new information and communication technologies". *International Journal of Cultural Studies*. 7(1): 91-103

Tuan, Yi-Fu. (1974) *Topophilia: A Study of Environmental Perception, Attitudes and Values*. New York: Columbia University Press.

Verran, Helen and Christie, Michael. (2007) "Using/Designing Digital technologies of Representation in Aboriginal Australian Knowledge Practices". *Human Technology*. 3(2): 214-27.

Western Australia Planning Commission and Department of Planning, Government of Australia. (2010) *Karratha: Regional Hot Spots Land Supply Update*. December. Web-site.

Yeoh, Brenda, S.A., Huang, Shirlena and Gonzalez, Joaquin. (1999) "Migrant Female Domestic Workers: Debating the Economic, Social and Political Impacts in Singapore". *International Migration Review*. 33(1): 114-36.

10

Brigitte Lewis

If I'm not using rationality to know, then who am I?

R eason; Rationality; Objectivity. These concepts, philosophically gathered together as rationalism, organise the places we inhabit and our own identities in the modernised west. Rationalism has given us a language in which to talk to one another regardless of our religion, gender, race or sexuality. It decrees that as long as you and I both see the world at a distance in an objectified way and agree to knowing the world this way, then we can both speak back to one another as individual minds. These individual minds share a collective, material reality. At the same time that using reason gives us so much, including the internet and cures for once incomprehensible illnesses, it also takes away particular practices of being, understanding, feeling, doing and speaking. Reason creates blind spots. As we use reason, we literally vacate the body as much as humanly possible. We situate ourselves in our heads so as to feel as little as possible, and be as unaffected by our emotions and the outside world as possible. We do this because we are following René Descartes' pronouncement "I think, therefore I am" which goes hand in hand with his belief that the senses are deceptive and can deceive, but the mind cannot and will not, as long as we are following his four precepts of logic or what has come to be called "The Method".[1] Essentially, this demands that one accepts nothing as true which one doesn't recognise to be so, breaking down phenomena and using the same kind of thinking one does when doing mathematics.[2] Descartes married this Method to Bacon's induction, which Bacon had claimed as the end of infinite error caused by the senses.[3] These two scholars would create the foundation for what has become known as the scientific method.

Following the scientific method makes us wonderful thinkers but at the same time, it stymies our ability to feel and experience the world through our bodies and our senses. We grow up to be adult rationalists, but often we leave our emotional and embodied selves behind as children, because we simply have not been trained or allowed to utilise these sites of knowing in the same way as we use reason. We become walking blind spots. In taking up the position of a phenomenologist, for example, one consequently takes nothing to be certain and nothing to be true. In phenomenological terms we "bracket off" the rationalist mind as Edmund Husserl advised and go one step further than Descartes, presupposing that all ideas can be "no more true than the illusions of my dreams", even the logic of mathematics.[4] Phenomenology then leads to an experience of three ways of knowing the marginalisation produced by rationality. These are the spiritual dimension, the emotive dimension and the body as a site of knowing. This chapter relates to a fieldwork experiment in relating these dimensions to a pre-existing personal rationality. To experience these three dimensions this paper explores

1 Descartes, 1996, p. 21.
2 Ibid., p. 13.
3 Bacon, 1960, p. 16.
4 Husserl, 1931, p. 107.

three case studies that intentionally challenge a rationalist worldview and a personal identity as a rationalist. The case studies point to a 'living out" of theories and schools of thought: Modernism, postmodernism and post-structuralism. As Laurel Richardson reminds us, "post-structuralism, then, permits – nay, invites – no, incites – us to reflect upon our method and explore new ways of knowing".[5]

Luce Irigaray says that "the issue is not one of elaborating a new theory of which woman would be the *subject* or the *object*, but of jamming the theoretical machinery itself".[6] In this research the rationalist subject is investigated to identify particular ways to "jam" the "stylised repetition of acts through time" that rationally situated one human being (the author).[7] This requires learning to interrupt the habitual pattern of being rational, of situating oneself in one's head and looking at the world from there. Because before gender, sexuality and spirituality, the performance of "self" as a rationalist, dictated how the author existed in and perceived the world.

At the time of this research, the book, *The Secret*, was sweeping across the collective imagination, promoting the idea of the power of positive thinking and what author Rhonda Byrne called "The Power of Attraction".[8] In other words, "think it and you will create it in your world, if you want it enough". The book became a global bestseller, available in 46 languages and is one of the top 20 best-selling books of the past 15 years.[9] Simultaneously, Eckhart Tolle was reclaiming the power of "being in the moment consciously".

---

5 Richardson, 2000, p. 929.
6 Irigaray, 1991, p. 126.
7 Butler, 1988, p. 519.
8 Byrne, 2006.
9 TS Production, 2012.

He too wrote a global bestseller.[10] Self-improvement became
a dominant mantra for the 21st century west – no longer do we
"dare to know" as Immanuel Kant proclaimed – instead we dare to
improve, to experience more than that which our objectifying minds
can offer.[11] In the western turn from rationality these self-improving
and experiential goals are prominent and are addressed by way of
the case studies that follow.

The spiritual dimension

The first case study discussed here involved living as a Tantric sadhaka
or as a spiritual aspirant in an ashram in the unsettled state of Bihar,
in north-eastern India. This required taking a Yogic Studies Course
at the only accredited yoga university in the world at the time. Here
aspirants could be expected to shave their heads, get up at 3:50 a.m.
to make it to the freezing or boiling water (weather dependent) bucket
shower and become skilled at the tasks of a glorified cleaner, the likes
of who could make a bed to rival the staff at luxury hotel chains.
Mary Douglas says, "ideas about separating, purifying, demarcating
and punishing transgressions have as their main function to impose
system on an inherently untidy experience".[12] This is especially true in
an ashram. The aspirant becomes detached from a physical experience
of the universe and emerges as a witness, an actor in the game.
Ironically, even though this was the aim of spirituality, to become
the witness, the same habitual ritual of doing, keeping busy, staying
occupied, served only to mimic the rational "I", that this research
had intended to shed. In other words, this is the experience that
Anthony Giddens called the "importance of the reflexive monitoring

---

10 Tolle, 2013.
11 Kant, 1990.
12 Douglas, 1995, p. 5.

of conduct".[13] This implies that being rational involves thinking and being in action, focused on a future goal to become better. Being spiritual in an ashram context involved keeping the body and the mind entirely occupied with assigned tasks and mantra chanting respectively, so as to bring about the future goal of becoming enlightened or self-realised. Both ways of being are about doing and remaining mind-focused while making sure the body is busy. Both look toward the transcendent for answers. The ashram looks toward the transcendent spiritual, and science looks towards the transcendent rational. Both practises prioritise looking outside oneself for answers and they thus negate and purposely constrain the immanent body. This research led to the conclusion that the "difference between real-life and ashrams is that ashrams keep you busy so as to switch off your rational mind and the 'real-world' keeps you busy to switch off your sacral mind".[14] The routine of spirituality can trap us as much as can rationality. There is no space for anything other than the pre-destined and pre-designed according to the ashram's frameworks. This simply means giving away authority to another paradigm, this time the tradition of Satyananda Yoga.

The emotional dimension
The second case study required a year-long psychotherapeutic acting course called "Character Creation" with the aim of using all of one's emotions and unravelling fundamental experiences that shaped the self. This case study led to an understanding of Carolyn Ellis and Arthur Bochner's assertion about writing that "there's the vulnerability of revealing yourself, not being able to take back what you've written

13 Giddens, 1979, p. 39.
14 Lewis, 2008.

or having control over how your readers interpret it".[15] This acting course was built on the two-fold premise that acting is not performing but rather being in the moment and that to perform is to be able to experience emotion from a place inside oneself. That is, to not create an emotion, but to use a memory of a time when that emotion was felt most deeply, and then, to perform from this place. This process is designed to jam the "theoretical machinery itself".[16] This serves to not only create a "different sort of repeating, in the breaking or subversive repetition of that style" but to challenge that repetition by calling up vulnerability.[17] Such vulnerability, by its very nature, cannot repeat a style, because it operates in the present, which is unknown and unknowable by the rational mind. This then bridges the lack of "mutuality" that Susan Stocker says is missing in Butler's theory.[18] The aim is to let ourselves be "outside-of-control" of the rationalist gaze and inside the limits of our feeling bodies.[19]

The emotions, say Nancy Scheper-Hughes and Margaret Lock are the "mediatrix" between the mind and body.[20] To go further than this it could be argued that it is the act of being vulnerable that jams self-repetition and creates a space to be a "sobject" (a term coined by the author to express being both a self in Butler's bodily sense, and a self with emotions). As Jung remarked:

> whoever looks into the mirror of the water will see first of all his own face . . . the mirror does not flatter, it faithfully shows whatever looks into it; namely, the face we never show

---

15 Ellis and Bochner, 2000, p. 738.
16 Irigaray, 1991.
17 Ibid., p. 126.
18 Stocker, 2001.
19 Lewis, 2006, p. 18.
20 Scheper-Hughes and Lock, 1987, p. 28.

to the world because we cover it with the persona, the mask of the actor.[21]

The face discovered in this experiment was not pretty. In suggesting we need to jam the theoretical machinery in order to intentionally mimic the "original subordination" of the feminine in order to create "many femininities", Irigaray is departing from Butler's notion of gender performance as subversive.[22] What is suggested in this chapter is that we need to jam our identities using vulnerability in order to operate from the present. Such action embodies/creates/allows a self to exist in the moment-to-moment of time, rather than in a repetition that prohibits one from accessing the full potentialities of the self. As Margaret Shildrick asks, "given the precarious psychic constitution of the subject, and the ontological insecurity of self performativity, can we reconfigure vulnerability not as a term of weakness, but as the very possibility of becoming?"[23]

Butler noted that "one does not always stay intact . . . one may want to, or manage to for a while, but despite one's best efforts, one is undone, in the face of the other, by the touch, by the scent, by the feel, by the prospect of touch, by the memory of the feel".[24] In the space of vulnerability as "subject", I am undone, not by the self of the other, but by the other that my emotions become, once they are situated according to a rationalist paradigm. In this space, emotions act on the individual, upon a stylised "I". They create a space for the vulnerable "I" that speaks through feeling and reconstitutes the self in the process. In the words of Glen A. Mazis "the fact that 'we' are not our emotions . . . means that many within the Cartesian paradigm

---

21 Jung, 1990, p. 20.
22 Irigaray, 1991, p. 101.
23 Shildrick, 2000, p. 215.
24 Butler, 2004, p. 24.

experience their emotions as alien forces which are very powerful and before which they are helpless".[25]

The catch-cry of the Character Creation acting course was to "challenge yourself to explore the full range of your expressive potential".[26] Primarily an acting course, it was also a course in the phenomenology of the self, intermingled with techniques of humanist existential psychotherapy, cognitive behavioural therapy and gestalt therapy. The techniques were utilised to both create and deconstruct character types and unravel dysfunctional habitual patterns that limited human expression. Dysfunction here refers to patterns of behaviour or ways of being in the world that do not allow the actor to be in "flow" in the terminology used in the course, in "adream". Flow/adream here refers to the ability of the actor to access any part of their being, whether it be emotional, psychological or physical in manifestation rather than the psychological term "flow" coined by Mihaly Csikszentmihalyi.[27] Simply put, according to the theory of the course, we all create particular character types to embody, usually in "re-action" rather than in response to life's circumstances. We become stuck in these identities. This does not mean that one remains permanently stuck in a particular character type, one's character type can change over the course of a lifetime, however this requires effort on the part of the person to want to actively change how they respond to life and as a result, their character type. Before starting the course I had no real idea of how locked into my identity I had become or why. I was a passionately "out and proud" lesbian who had adopted a stereotypical lesbian, masculinist self (closer to femme than butch) to the exclusion of a softer more feminine one. This had

---

25 Mazis, 1993, p. 56.
26 Chater, 2009.
27 Csikszentmihalyi and Csikszentmihalyi, 1988; Csikszentmihalyi, 1991.

unconsciously linked femininity with powerlessness. Relationships to my feelings were that they were too much to bear and getting on with life was preferable. This made for a very reasonable, very rational and always intellectually justified person for whom Descartes really was an intellectual father.

The initial exercises in this course required learning to breathe into the body instead of escaping into the head. This is not a theoretical explanation and can only really be understood in practise. This process of breathing into the body helped the body to feel emotion as opposed to repressing it. Rationalism offered a safe place from the external world and the vicissitudes of emotion wanting to take us over as human beings. Rationalism is, as Max Weber said, the "iron cage" of protection.[28] In Butler's words:

> What grief displays . . . is the thrall in which our relations with others hold us, in ways that we cannot always recount or explain, in ways that often interrupt the self-conscious account of ourselves we might try to provide, in ways that challenge the very notion of ourselves as autonomous and in control.[29]

The acting course helped locate personal "polar points". Both ends of the spectrum served to disconnect the person from feelings. Miller explains that:

> . . . people resort to all kinds of remedies to compel the body to function normally . . . drugs, alcohol, nicotine, pills, immersion in work. It is an attempt to avoid understanding the revolt of the body, to prevent ourselves from experiencing the fact that feelings will not kill us but, on the contrary, can free us.[30]

28 Weber, 1958.
29 Butler, 2004, p. 23.
30 Miller, 2006, p. 33.

The bodily dimension

One final case study was undertaken to fully explore the non-rational, exploring the body as a site of knowing, or as Tamara Kohn put it "the body as a field unto itself".[31] This case study was tantric bodywork. This required the author to lie completely naked against a massage table allowing a woman barely known to touch and see me at my most vulnerable. Naked, nipples to the ceiling, snot dripping, tears falling, screaming kind of vulnerable.[32] I am rising up and down like a crazed jack-in-box against the massage table, chest jutting, nipples hard and hips grinding into the hot Melbourne air. If this was in church it would be assumed that one was possessed by the devil or God himself. If this occurred at home the paramedics would be on the doorstep with syringes. But this was neither at home or in church but above a shop in the middle of hipster Fitzroy in a converted apartment space that screams (but not louder than the author) "New Age things happen here".[33]

Discussion

The scientific conventions of academic writing are not accidental. They are situated in a particular historical and social context that allows only certain people to speak in specific ways. They "create the illusion" of legitimacy as does the scientific paradigm itself.[34] Writing then, as a method of inquiry "offers an additional – or alternative – research practice" that has the potential to disrupt and highlight these claims of legitimacy by offering an alternative.[35] The alternative form

---

31 Kohn, 2011, p. 81.
32 Lewis, 2011, p. 204.
33 Ibid., p. 203.
34 Wall, 2006, p. 4.
35 Richardson, 2000, p. 923.

chosen here is poetry and performance because they give a form in which to express experience as an emotional being, one who is moved by life, either through ideas or through sensuous experience. This poetry is aligned with Ivan Brady's view of anthropological poetics in that "the aim in this poetry is not to exist only for its own sake or self, or merely to entertain, but to flag its language without losing its historical or ethnographic referentiality and authenticity".[36]

What was discovered at the end of the fieldwork was that that I had been taught like most people learn, to give myself away in the hope that a particular paradigm will speak for me, will offer the truth, the transcendent rational truth. However, despite our lofty aspirations both as minds and bodies who have minds to think with, we are limited, our theories are limited and blind spots are created every time we choose a point of focus. The challenge is to keep one foot firmly planted – the foot of self-knowing that knows the limits of the immanent self – while allowing the other foot to act as the feeler for all the other ways we can know, whether you believe in them or not. Knowing does not end with the use of reason, in fact, for us as modernists, this is where it begins.

---

36 Brady, 2000, p. 956.

Appendix 1

response-able

i[37] don't want to be a responsible citizen
don't wanna pledge my allegiance to my nation
i'd rather call my body my state
and order self-reflection

i want to be response-able
unhinged not a hinge-thinker
go off like a fire cracker
and quake a room if i want to

stake a place at my own self-built table
not the placemat of patriarchy
but the seat of humanity
that wild like the ocean
brighter than the moon

---

37 Please note that I use a lower case I in my poetry and when I refer to the 'vulnerable i', instead of an upper case I as convention dictates. This may seem like essentialist
reasoning that reinscribes the feminine as subordinate to the masculine by virtue of being signified by a lower case i but this is not my intention. My intent is to highlight that
the I is not representative of a humanity that has a voice but a particular sub-section of
humanity conceptualised as having no body to feel with, no feminine attributes to utilise
or emotions to experience. The upper case I is symbolic of a detached masculinist I given
privileged use to those who are biologically male, white, able-bodied and heterosexual. I
am not endorsing a simplistic male = masculine, female = feminine dichotomy but what
I am doing is referencing the history of this dichotomy and its usage in language that still
permeates and marks society today. What I am saying is that the masculinist position that
sees the mind as authority is the ideal strived for in both western men and women. I am
also referencing and utilising Audre Lorde's great proclamation that using "the master's
tools will never dismantle the master's house", Lorde, 2008, pp. 49-51.

crazier than a daredevil space
that only courage dares to venture to

i wanna rip off every last idea of sin
and replace it with a liberation is sexy
if you rock your hips right slogan
that brandishes love as its opium
not religion as e-man yes i said e-man-cipation
cos now we•ve got post-structural analysis we know universal means man
so we gotta re-label the verse and bring back the sacred from the
gender equation

take back my voice from my ego and its self hatred
and rewrite the songs of my past as odes to my future
cos this present is LOUD enough is **bold** enough is *soft* enough
to hold me and you in this sentence
trample all over the notion that we have only one legitimate way to
know
and that's
rational objectification
ladies and gents we gotta re-label the verse and bring back the sacred
from the science equation

re-construct the ivory tower and fit it out with meaning and the
feminine
give it a paint job of colours
and open up a verandah for the vulnerable
not repeat an identity based on alienation
not repeat an identity based on alienation

of us versus them
or me for my self
but us for each other
no matter our colour
cos personhood
is multi-faced
with a paris and a pub end
it just depends what day you walk in
as to whether the smiles are on
or the shadows have slid in

so brother
sister
Mary
jehovah
allah
professor
Oprah

i want you to imagine that you are change
now stop imagining and start being
take down your identity stop your projection
and start working on your own face
before you start placing blame on an other
cos we›re all a reflection
and ours
is a criminal history
a genocidal history

a history of sex slaves

man slaves

company slaves

and consumer slaves

when are we gonna shake off this slave

and start being sovereignty

cos i am sick of this sub-dom relationship

ibs been going on for far too long

so lebs cut the bullshit

cos we gotta re-label the verse

and bring back the sacred from the human equation

we gotta call up the vulnerable

and create a new kind of equation[38]

References

Bacon, Francis. (1960) *The New Organon and Related Writings*. New York: The Liberal Arts Press.

Brady, Ivan. (2000) "Anthropological Poetics". In Denzin, N. K. and Lincoln, Y. S. (eds). *Handbook of Qualitative Research*. Thousand Oaks: Sage.

Butler, Judith. (1988) "Performative Acts and Gender Constitution: An Essay in Phenomenology and Feminist Theory". *Theatre Journal*. 40(4): 519-31.

Butler, Judith. (2004) *Precarious Life: The Powers of Mourning and Violence*. London: Verso.

Byrne, Rhonda. (2006) *The Secret*. New York: Atria Books.

Chater, Penelope. (2009) *Character Creation*. Melbourne: Penelope Chater.

---

38 Lewis, 2001, p. 88.

Csikszentmihalyi, Mihaly and Csikszentmihalyi, Isabella Selega. (eds). (1988) *Optimal Experience: Psychological Studies of Flow in Consciousness*. New York: Cambridge Press.

Csikszentmihalyi, Mihaly. (1991) *Flow: The Psychology of Optimal Experience*. *USA*: Harper Perennial.

Descartes, Rene. (1996) "Discourse on the Method of Rightly Conducting the Reason and Seeking for Truth in the Sciences". In Weissman, D. (ed). *Discourse on the Method and Meditations on First Philosophy*. New Haven: Yale University. pp. 3-48

Douglas, Mary. (1996) *Purity and Danger: An Analysis of the Concept of Pollution and Taboo*. New York: Routledge.

Ellis, Carolyn and Arthur P. Bochner. (2000) "Autoethnography, Personal Narrative, Reflexivity: Researcher as Subject". In Denzin, N. K. and Lincoln, Y.S. (eds). *Handbook of Qualitative Research*. Thousand Oaks: Sage: 733-68

Giddens, Anthony. (1979) "Structuralism and the Theory of the Subject". In *Central Problems in Social Theory*. London: Macmillan Press: 9-48

Harrison, Paul. (2008) "Corporeal Remains: Vulnerability, Proximity, and Living on after the End of the World". *Environment and Planning* A. 40: 423-45.

Husserl, Edmund. (1931) *Ideas: General Introduction to Pure Phenomenology*. Translated by W. R. B. Gibson. London: Allen and Unwin.

—————. (1999) *Cartesian Meditations*. Translated by D. Cairns. Dordrecht: Kluwer Academic Publishers.

Irigaray, Luce. (1991) "The Power of Discourse and the Subordination of the Feminine". In Whitford, M. (ed). *The Irigaray Reader*. Oxford: Basil Blackwell.

Jung, C.G. (1990) *The Archetypes and the Collective Unconscious*. New York: Princeton University Press.

Kant, Immanuel. (1990) "What Is Enlightenment". In *Foundations of the*

Metaphysics of Morals and, What Is Enlightenment. New York: Macmillan: 83-90

Kohn, Tamara. (2011) "New Ways to Frame an Answer to 'Where Did You Do Your Fieldwork?' ". In Coleman, S. and Collins, P. (eds). *Dislocating Anthropology?: Bases of Longing and Belonging in the Analysis of Contemporary Societies.* Cambridge: Cambridge Scholars Press: 81-96.

Lewis, Brigitte. (2006) "Beyond the Reflexive Agent: Re-Thinking Agency and Flow". Bachelor of Arts (Hons.), School of Social and Political Sciences, University of Melbourne, Melbourne, Australia.

————. (2008) "Field Notes – Case Study 1) Yoga: Spirituality Yogic Style." Bihar Yoga Bharati.

————. (2011) "Epistemological Blind Spots and the Story of I: Returning the Vulnerable I to the Rational I". Doctor of Philosophy (Sociology) Thesis. The School of Social and Political Sciences. University of Melbourne, Melbourne.

Lorde, Audre. (2008) "The Master's Tools Will Never Dismantle the Master's House". In Bailey, A. and Cuomo, C. (eds). *The Feminist Philosophy Reader.* New York: McGraw-Hill: 49-51.

Mazis, Glen A. (1993) *Emotions and Embodiment.* New York: Peter Lang.

Miller, Alice. (2006) *Free from Lies.* New York: W.W. Norton and Company.

"News about Eckhart Tolle". *The New York Times.* New York Times web-site.

Richardson, Laurel. (2000) "Writing: A Method of Inquiry". In Denzin, N.K. and Lincoln, Y. S. (eds). *Handbook of Qualitative Research.* Thousand Oaks: Sage.

Scheper-Hughes, Nancy and Lock, Margaret. (1987) "The Mindful Body: A Prolegomenon to Future Work in Medical Anthropology ". *Medical Anthropology Quarterly.* 1(1): 6-41.

Shildrick, Margaret. (2000) "Becoming Vulnerable: Contagious Encounters and the Ethics of Risk". *Journal of Medical Humanities.* 21(4): 215-27.

Stocker, Susan S. (2001) "Problems of Embodiment and Problematic Embodiment." *Hypatia.* 16(3): 30-55.

Tolle, Eckhart. (1997) *The Power of Now.* Vancouver: Namaste Publishing.

TS Production, LLC. (2012) "Rhonda Byrne's Biography". *The Secret.* Creative Biography web-site.

Wall, Sarah. (2006) "An Autoethnography on Learning About Autoethnography". *International Journal of Qualitative Methods.* 5(2): 1-13.

Weber, Max. (1958) *The Protestant Ethic and the Spirit of Capitalism.* New York: Charles Scribner's Sons

11

Robert Pascoe and Michael Deery

Representations of culture: research structures for textual, graphic, aural and moving image sources

The high-speed transitions of digital networking make for an as yet unclear rerouting of our social being. In reflecting on these changes, some theorists of the digital world insist that place identities are now being erased. The digital world, we are told, makes location and locality irrelevant and a generation of digital natives/global citizens no longer see themselves as connected to place. However, the problem of the local and global is not necessarily one produced by digitisation. Connections between suburbia and identity, global events and local meaning, and migration and connection to place have all been in flux for much of the modern era. The great advantage which digitisation brings to scholars concerned with these issues is not so much to prove that localities no longer matter, but that the digital allows us to trace processes of belonging, identity and place in new ways. The methodology of digital historical research can be brought to bear on the transitions noted above, exploring new combinations of written text, moving image and sound. This paper reflects on research techniques pertinent to the changes brought by digitisation. It turns initially to local identities in the pre-digital age and the manner in which digitisation opens up new perspectives on these cultures across the 19th and 20th centuries. The paper secondly reflects on the global event whose one hundredth anniversary is now before us – the Great War of 1914-18. Again digital records allow a new perspective on this moment and its local meanings. The third area considered is that of migration in the digital era – the manner in which young Europeans move to and from Australia and how they identify with place in this new era. The critical aspect of digitisation explored here is the newfound ability of historians to take individual biographical records, digitise these and determine the way social connections, previously hidden, are exposed through reconstructed and linked biographies.

Collectors of materials relating to the history and culture of particular groups in society, including immigrants and other minorities, now have a far greater capacity to assemble textual, graphic, aural and moving image sources that relate to those groups. Textual material may be defined as written or printed words that relate to groups of interest. Textual material includes the dramatic spread of digitised newspapers such as those available on the National Library of Australia's Trove site, where anyone with an internet connection has access to literally dozens of newspapers across the years from 1804 to 1954.[1] On a smaller scale, the Vaccari Collection at Victoria University, accessible through the Library web-site, holds three dozen primary sources in Italian and in English translation.[2] The Vaccari Archive has begun to gather newer materials (eventually intended to reside within the University's research cloud) and will be a portal for Australian immigration research.

---

1 See National Library of Australia, Trove, Newspaper Collection web-site.
2 Victoria University Library Vaccari Collection. VU Library web-site.

Such digitisation of textual material relies upon three important developments: OCR (Optical Character Recognition) searchability; Boolean in place of hierarchical indexing; and Text correction through crowd-sourcing. Taken together, these three developments have seen more sophisticated digitisation projects, especially in the last decade. The sheer size of this textual avalanche is now irreversible.

Secondly, there exists now a vast store of graphical material, imagery relating to particular groups. An example from the graphical domain is the Lewis and Skinner project. This site is comprised of a large collection of business papers, photographs and associated miscellanea found abandoned in central Footscray, and digitised by Stefan Schutt of Victoria University.[3] With appropriate tags, each of the items in this collection can be readily accessed by researchers and lay people interested in the development of Melbourne in the post-war period. Thirdly, there are recorded sounds. Aural sources may perhaps be dated from 1978, with the establishment in Perth of the Oral History Association of Australia.[4] Excellent aural materials are held in the Victoria University Archive, including interviews held with past and present staff and students. The University plans celebratory activities for its one hundredth year as a tertiary institution in 2016. These aural sources will prove invaluable.[5] Finally, there are moving images. As bandwidth improves, more of these will become commonplace. YouTube (for example) already contains hundreds of clips of Victoria University staff and students talking about their educational experiences. What follows are three case studies in the digitisation of culture research projects being undertaken at Victoria University, followed by some philosophical speculations on the

---

3 Lewis and Skinner project Victoria University.
4 Robertson, 2008.
5 Archives of Victoria University Melbourne Australia web-site.

problems and possibilities lying ahead of us. These three case studies are: Sportsmen in colonial Victoria; Great War centennial community celebrations across Victoria; and Electronic media and the *globalisti*. Each will be considered in turn, and then general observations will be drawn.

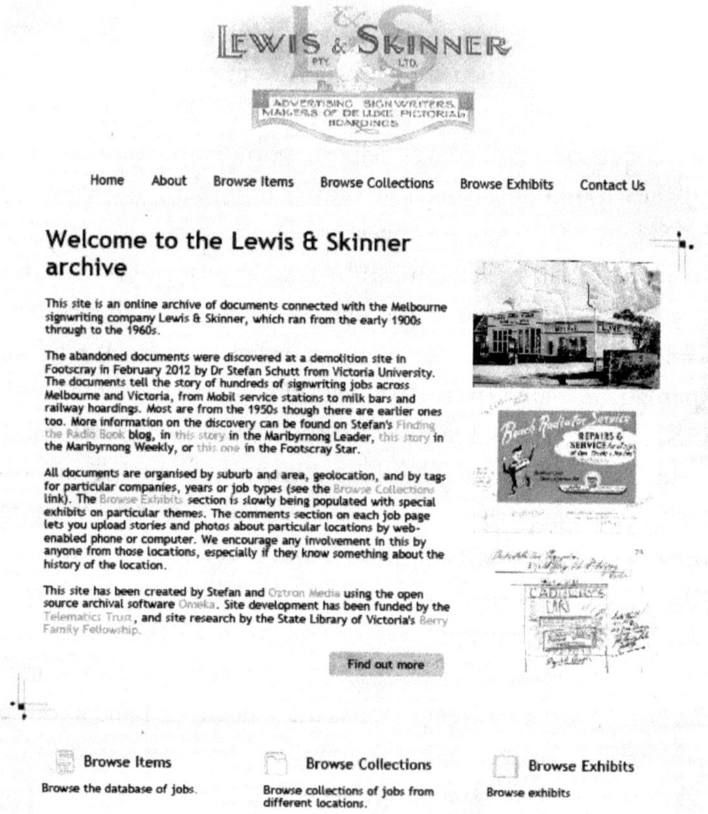

Figure 19. Opening screenshot of Lewis and Skinner site

Source: lewisandskinner.com [accessed 3 December 2012]

Sportsmen in colonial Victoria

In the period known as the Long Boom (1860-90) the new metropolis of Melbourne settled into its role as a leading Victorian-era city.[6] It epitomised what were seen as the virtues of Victorian Britain – it was politically democratic, it was loyal to the Empire, and it was, some exceptional locales notwithstanding, ethnically white. This Marvellous Melbourne has been studied from various standpoints, urban, architectural, literary, political, but what is proposed here is a new perspective, that of organised sport.[7] There is a rich, newly developed data set which can be mined to help understand how this metropolis came to be constructed, suburb by suburb. This data set is the list of the 7000 young men who played senior football in that era. Colonial Victoria is revealed as a complex mosaic of tribal, suburb-centred communities reflecting differences of class and creed.

The sporting character of the Colony of Victoria that set it apart from its older parent colony, New South Wales, was reflected in a football code that was open and fast, emphasising individual enterprise and a game with umpires, not referees.[8] Football clubs became repositories of social memory, institutions crucial to people's sense of belonging to particular communities. Taken together, these disparate communities (often as sporting rivals) were the warp and weft of colonial society in this rapidly growing outpost of the British Empire. Each tribe drew on an "imagining" of people's place in the larger social order.[9] This central role of the football club in people's

---

6 See generally, Davison, 1978.
7 Early findings using this technique appear in Pennings and Pascoe, 2012.
8 Pascoe, 1995, xi-xvii.
9 East, 2012.

sense of self helps explain the ferocity of support exhibited by the so-called "barrackers". Prior to digitisation sports enthusiasts and journalists transcribed newspaper reports to attempt to build up comprehensive lists of players for individual clubs. At least two authors have painstakingly constructed, through a series of editions, an encyclopaedia of players since the origin of the Victorian Football League (VFL).[10] For the pre-VFL era, club historians similarly tried to establish lists of players for individual clubs, especially the older organisations, Port Melbourne for example.[11] The enormous effort required prior to digital retrieval of newspaper files meant that even the most diligent researcher was bound to be frustrated by unknown people, names without stories and events with no context. Furthermore, the aim of these labours was not so much to build a picture of Melbourne as a series of localised social networks to which sport was critical, but to collate the fragmentary playing biographies of particular club stalwarts. Digitisation has made their task easier. At the same time, with football as a proxy, it opens up a more layered, nuanced and networked socio-cultural map of the city in the later-19th century.

10 Holmesby and Main, 2011.
11 See for one thorough example, Keenan, 1999.

Each player's name or surname in newspaper accounts of senior matches from 1858	Residence as revealed in the *Sands & McDougall's* directory 20 years later	Occupation and household members as indicated in Electoral Rolls	Newspaper articles, accessed via **nla.gov.au/ trove**, which refer to the player or his descendants
Full name as confirmed by **ancestry.com** using approximate date of birth	Known descendants of players	Professional and trade journals relevant to these occupations	Military, court and other records indicating social roles of players
Source and year of player's parents immigrating into Colony	Social and geographical mobility of players and their families	Revisions to existing AFL club histories and websites, including the NSM at MCG	Better understanding of historical role of AFL football
Ethnic origins of parents (English, Irish, Welsh, etc.)	New understandings of colonial and Edwardian society	Revisions to existing suburban and town histories	Questions for future research, especially in other AFL colonies (SA, WA, Tasmania)

Figure 20: Prosopographical methodology of sportsmen in colonial Victoria

Source: Pascoe, Pennings

The opening decades in Australian football are very well described by the prominent historian Geoffrey Blainey in his *A Game of Our Own*, first published in 1990.[12] This book features well-known players such as Tommy Wills and H.C.A. Harrison, but also a dozen or so others

---

12 Blainey, 1990 and 2003.

who are identified only by surname (and who therefore do not appear in the index to the book). Then, as now, individual players might be known simply by their surname (or even by their nickname) because in the individual communities of sports fans reading local newspapers, everyone assumed that everyone else knew the identity of the player in question. This project seeks to recover and analyse much of this forgotten knowledge. A biographical analysis of each of these men contributes to an understanding of the culture of the club (or clubs) that they represented in the senior competition across those seasons.

Two examples will suffice. "Goldsmith", described by Blainey merely as a Melbourne Football Club player, was in fact Benjamin J. Goldsmith, a journalist on the *Australasian* newspaper.[13] In 1908 he married Emily Firth, and they became Christian missionaries in China. "Sandilands", a St Kilda player who stood out by playing bare-footed was a Frederick Sandilands, one of the three sons of Benoni Nimmo Sandilands, a major South Melbourne landowner, who had himself played football when younger.[14] Frederick became an estate agent and land valuer active in the frenetic subdivision and house-building of Boomtime South Melbourne. So Goldsmith and Sandilands represent two of the important football clubs of this period – the patrician Melbourne club and the aspirant South Melbourne (eventually sent north to become the Sydney Swans).

Textual

Where are the sources for these 7000 players? One might expect the major organisation that today controls football, the Australian Football League (AFL), to hold colonial records. But the AFL has

---

13 Ibid., p. 90.
14 Ibid., p. 147.

only recently turned to a close examination of its long pre-history.[15] Mark Pennings has extracted these details from colonial newspapers and other publications for all the seasons from 1858 to 1896.[16] Pennings worked meticulously through primary texts and reels of microfilmed newspapers at the State Library of Queensland, the State Library of Victoria, and the Melbourne Cricket Club, (MCC) Library opening a new mine of historical data for quarrying. Across those four decades, a total of 25 clubs were accepted as senior in standing by the controlling authority, which became the Victorian Football Association (VFA). Three of these 25 clubs were located in Ballarat, two in Geelong, and the remainder across the suburbs of the Melbourne metropolis. Who exactly were these young male heroes of the football fields? What can we uncover about them and their life stories? We divide our questions into eight parts, as follows:

- The identity of each player: What was their surname? Was it correctly spelt by the newspapers of the day? And the forename: if the newspaper did not (as often) supply the forename of the player, can we ascertain it from other sources? The key source in following each player into adulthood is the *Sands & McDougall's Directory*, a house-by-house listing of household heads throughout Victoria.[17] Newspaper obituaries of the better-known players, or of those players who carved out successful careers off the field, also provide useful details (refer Figure 20).
- What was the individual player's football career?
- What do we know of each player's background? Who were their parents? What were their circumstances?

---

15 Pascoe, 1997.
16 Pennings, 2012, 2014.
17 *Sands & McDougall's Directories*, various years.

- Fourthly, from which club was each player recruited? This information usually provides a clue to his social milieu.

- For which other clubs did the player compete, after his service to the club in question?

- What was his career after playing senior football? Did he later become a leader in his local community? Different occupations or professions published magazines or other newsletters which provide information about the careers of particular players. Ex-University players feature in *Speculum*, a medical school magazine published three or four times a year.[18]

- Did the player undertake military service, especially in the Boer War?

- What do we know of his siblings and children? Footballing families have bloodlines rather like racehorses. In colonial football there was a high incidence of brothers playing for a club, famously the six Ireland brothers at Melbourne.

This data set is based on a group that has not been targeted before: healthy, young, mostly single, settled males. The data collected will be capable of revealing these men's life journeys in ways hitherto impossible. The total population of Melbourne in 1880 was 280,000; by 1890 it was 490,000. It was disproportionately comprised of young people, owing to the gold rushes of the 1850s and the subsequent generational effect in the 1880s. Even by 1901 only about five per cent of the population was aged over 65.[19]

---

18 *Speculum*, the Melbourne Medical School magazine, has now been digitised for the years 1884 to 1914, available University of Melbourne web-site.

19 Brown-May and Swain, 2005: 200-02 (Peter McDonald); 516-17 (Swain).

Graphic

Images of these players as individuals or in the course of a match are available in lithographs of the period, sometimes reproduced in newspapers or magazines, in personal photographic albums held by libraries or in private collections. Sources which have become common currency amongst fans rather than scholars are "football cards" traded at memorabilia fairs and over the internet.[20]

Aural

While there are no known recordings of these players and their supporters (barrackers), the calls of the barrackers are often recorded in newspaper and other contemporary accounts. Because colonial Australian English was still an unmixed combination of the three main sociolects from Britain that were still in the process of coalescing, transcripts of these barracking reveal Cockney London, Dublin or home-county traces.

Moving image

The earliest footage of Australian football dates to 1909, slightly outside the period in question, but close enough to give a strong visual sense of players and the style of play typical of the early years.

By linking these sources and building a sense of the biographies of players their localised connections come to the fore, in a manner impossible without a high level of reliance on digitised records.

Great War centennial community celebrations across Victoria

Between August 2014 and November 2018, communities throughout Victoria will be invited to commemorate the main battles of a hundred

---

20 *Australian Rules Football card Catalogue*, 2003.

years earlier. A Teachers Companion will be prepared by an appropriate military historian. It is intended to offer advice to teachers seeking to use the Great War centennial community celebrations in their local school context. It will show them how to locate sources of various kinds relating to the involvement of young men and women in their community in that war. It would then help them understand through these sources what the war did to their community in terms of its fearsome path of death and destruction. The variety of records that can be brought to bear on such a project are immense and impossible to manipulate without an ordering through digital technology.

In the era preceding the internet, historians tackled similar issues in attempting to write history "from below". The subsequent rise of "New Social History" in the later 1970s resulted in several detailed studies employing disaggregated data, often at a city-wide scale.[21] An absence of individual census files in Australian records meant that historians turned to the street directories mentioned above, rate books and other lists of names, occupations and addresses to construct statistical tables and so make those hidden from history, as the phrase went, visible once more. Several historians imaginatively applied social history techniques and archival records to analyse the composition of the First AIF.[22] This form of social reconstruction can now be vastly extended by linking records digitally rather than manually, so that in the commemorative events of 2015 a rich picture of those who went to war can be shared across localities. We might say that digitisation brings us closer to the Anzacs than at any time since the 1920s.

---

21 For one of the pioneering studies see Thernstrom, 1973.
22 For one of the first such projects see Robson, 1970.

Textual

Beginning with the web-site mapping, "ouranzacs.naa.gov.au", students will be encouraged to understand the imprint of this war on the life of their community. Let us take one community, Wangaratta, as an example. A total of 798 men enlisted in Wangaratta, of whom many (like Ainsworth in 7 Battalion, First AIF) took part in the 25 April 1915 landing at Gallipoli. So this landing, as described by men of 7 Battalion, would be taught to students in Wangaratta on the anniversary (25 April 2015) of the event. Military historians and some memorial organisers now conclude that Australians have placed far too much emphasis on Gallipoli at the expense of the Western Front battles. Battles like Fromelles deserve the attention of students, with an educational program timed to coincide with the centennial anniversary of the battle and emphasising those communities from which the combatants came.[23]

The *Sands & McDougall's* directories once again prove to be a valuable textual source for getting some understanding of the extent of the trauma of this war. The 1913 edition for each community can be studied for names of its inhabitants; this will enable a comparison to be made with an appropriate post-war year, for example 1923, when any surviving combatants would have returned.[24]

Graphic

One of the important graphical sources for this experience is the local war memorial, as these contain a set of important details, including the names of the veterans from the particular town or

---

23 The Shrine of Remembrance Education program is at http://www.shrine.org.au/Education

24 *Sands & McDougall's Directory of Victoria*, 1913, 1923

suburb in question, sometimes their battle honours, bas-reliefs or
other pictorial images, and sometimes plinths in the form of a soldier.
Curiously, these soldiers often depict Italian soldiers (*alpinisti*) as
their uniforms were close in appearance to the Great War Australian
soldiers.[25] Not all towns or suburbs contain public war memorials,
and this is in important in itself. Localities without such memorials
were often anti-conscription Irish-Australian localities like Koroit or
the Melbourne suburb of Richmond. The classic work on the subject
of Anzac memorials makes the claim that Richmond does contain a
war memorial. The bold claim is made by Inglis.[26] Using Trove it is
possible to discover that the newspaper reference is a political attack
on the Richmond MLA, E. J. Cotter by *The Argus*.[27] There is not, and
never has been, a memorial to the Great War in Richmond. Such was
the local hostility to this War, the mayor admitted that his Council was
forced 'to resort to subterfuge to obtain the money required…".[28]
The event described in *The Argus* is actually the laying of a stone for
a Memorial Hall at the corner of Church Street and Charlotte Street,
the home of the Richmond sub-branch of returned service personnel
league (RSL) that today has been replaced by a (less objectionable)
World War II plinth.[29] When Richmond along with other municipal
councils was asked to contribute to the cost of the national War
Memorial, the Council refused to contribute and Councillor Longfield
proposed that money might be better spent on finding work for
unemployed returned soldiers.[30]

---

25 Pascoe, 1987, p. 86.
26 Inglis, 1999, pp. 224-5.
27 *The Argus*, 13 March 1992, p. 6a.
28 Ibid., p. 6a.
29 A photograph of the plinth is on the Richmond RSL web-site.
30 *The Argus*, 11 February 1928, p. 30.

Aural

There is a plethora of interviews with Anzacs in several library collections throughout Australia. These give today's students the opportunity to hear wizened old veterans recalling episodes from their distant youth.

Moving image

Again, particularly through YouTube, the battles are surprisingly well documented. The first battle of Bullecourt, in the early hours of 11 April 1917, is well reconstructed in a You Tube clip dealing with the famous Albert Jacka VC.[31] Among the battalions in that engagement was his 14 Battalion, which also included Alf 'Lofty' Williamson, a professional Australian Rules footballer and manual arts teacher at Melbourne High School. In this example a student-led seminar on the anniversary date, 11 April 2017, would be an ideal occasion to bring together the diverse historical materials of that battle. The richness of digitised materials would result in an impressive commemoration of this important episode in the Great War.

Electronic media and the *globalisti*

Italian migration to Australia can be understood as comprising four waves, and the primary sources for understanding each of them differ markedly. The first two waves were the *esploratori* and the *pescatori*), followed by the third (post-war) wave, the *costruttori*, and the fourth (contemporary) wave, whom we have called the *globalisti* (the "globe-trotters"). To understand the third-wave immigrants requires the interrogation of traditional printed, hand-written and spoken sources, whereas fourth-wave Italians belong to an "imagined community"

31 v=MhtIDFMq56o on YouTube.

that is glued together by electronic media. While previous generations used hand-written letters, local newspapers, radio and the telephone, these *globalisti* are more comfortable with Facebook, blogs and other internet connectors. Previous immigrants built bricks-and-mortar halls in which to meet; these latest immigrants build web-sites together for the same purpose. How might historians begin to use these new sources to understand the imagined community of the *globalisti?*

Italian migration and imagined communities

In a chapter of the book celebrating its half-century of publication, we argued that the newspaper *Il Globo* played a crucial role in the "imagining" of an Italo-Australian community.[32] The newspaper began life in 1959, around the same time that some have presented as the moment when it is legitimate to speak of a community of Italians in Australia.[33] This juncture was important in so many ways. One is that a politics of a hybrid kind had formed. The Italo-Australian Left, once focused entirely on issues back home, especially its concerns about the Fascist regime during the 1930s and 1940s, now began to address the concerns of immigrant Italians, coming in such large numbers in the 1950s.

Now the crisis of youth unemployment across Southern Europe and Ireland has triggered a new wave of Italian emigration to Australia. These emigrants, the *globalisti*, are leaving Italy for much the same economic reasons as their grandparents, but they are arriving armed with tertiary qualifications, a more sophisticated understanding of politics, and the new technologies of electronic media. We use the term *globalisti* to underline their sense of "going global".

---

32 Cafarella and Pascoe, 2009.
33 Pascoe, 1992.

Some globalisti

Let us meet some of these *globalisti*. Cristina, 28 years old, comes from Bassano del Grappa, in the province of Vicenza. After high school she went to Paris for eight years. In March 2013 she decided to come to Australia to pursue a career in events management, and now works part-time in a Melbourne Docklands restaurant. Gerardo, aged 53, was born in Melbourne to parents who had emigrated from Scido, Reggio Calabria, and moved to Italy in his twenties to teach foreign languages at university. At the age of 37 he migrated to Australia for further study and to work in academia. Simone, a 28-year-old from Marostica, a province of Venezia, came to Australia in 2008 to undertake post-graduate study. He teaches Italian language in a primary school.[34]

Using snowball sampling we have identified and interviewed 30 *globalisti* in the Melbourne area.[35] A surprisingly large proportion of these Italians derive from Lombardia and Piemonte. Fewer come from the southern regions which were the sources of previous waves. These *globalisti* belong to the first generation of Italians coming to maturity in the internet age; most were born between 1970 and 1992. So the *globalisti* grew up with a greater familiarity with electronic media than their parents and grandparents had enjoyed with print media. In 1930s Fremantle, for example, those fishermen who were literate read the newspapers aloud to their confreres.[36] Only with the advent of newspapers such as *Il Globo*, after 1959, did many of the third wave begin to read more widely and to gain an appreciation of printed

---

34 Cafarella and Pascoe, 2013.
35 By snowballing we mean a research technique whereby each interviewee is invited to nominate other candidates for potential interview.
36 Macintyre, 1980.

newspapers. It gave journalists like Nino Randazzo great satisfaction that through the pages of his newspaper erstwhile peasant Italians could master concepts like a national budget. The Italian language employed in *Il Globo*, especially in the earlier decades, was very official, even at times officious, as its readership struggled to acquire mastery in what was for many a foreign, imposed language.[37]

It would be difficult to exaggerate the difference between this generation and the generation comprising the *globalisti*. With youth unemployment at historic levels, they have turned to the electronic media for help. On Facebook, the "Decrescita Felice Social Network" publicises a mix of shops using bartering systems, social supermarkets where people can work for their shopping, and activities for families to create their own playgrounds. A Swiss idea entitled "Te lo regalo se vieni a prenderlo" (I will give it to you if you come and collect it) has now spread throughout Italy, aiming to recycle everything that would be otherwise destined for landfill. From Bologna came the Facebook idea, Social Street, where people sharing the same street pool resources, pick up children from school, do shopping, share equipment, and generally consolidate their local friendship networks.[38]

The *globalisti*, then, come to Australia armed with skills and experience in the use of media that was unknown to their parents and grandparents. They use this electronic media throughout the process of researching Australia, travelling through the new country, and communicating with people back home. They are not tied to one linguistic convention, like the readers of *Il Globo*, but instead practise

---

37 Pascoe 1987, p. 96
38 Jane, 2014.

Texting	Non-texting Italian	English translation	Our comments
-	meno	less	The minus symbol in mathematics
:(	triste	sad	Corresponds to ☹ emoticon
:), =)	felice, allegro	happy	Corresponds to ☺ emoticon
:D	ghigno	grin	Seldom seen among English texters, suggesting the power of gesticulation in Italian communications
:p	linguaccia	tongue sticking out	No equivalent among English texters
;)	occhiolino	wink	
6	sei, sei?	you are / are you?	'Sei' has the two meanings in Italian, the number 'six' and the second person singular verb 'to be'
a dp	a dopo, ci vediamo dopo	see you later	
anke	anche	also	Sounding out the word 'anche' with a letter that is not formally part of the Italian alphabet
bb	bebè	baby	Amorous use of 'baby'
cad	cadauno	each	'Cadauno' is not a common term
ce ness1	c'è nessuno?	is anybody there?	'Uno' has the two meanings in Italian
cm va	come va?	what's up?	Literally, 'How is it going?'
cs dc?	cosa mi dici?	what's up?	Literally, 'What can you tell me?'
dim	dimmi	tell me	Or, 'Talk to me!'
dl	del, dello, della, degli, delle	of the	Texting has simplified what in Italian is a complex range of conjunctive pronouns

Figure 21: Texting in Italian. Source: Emanuele Occhipinti. (2010) *601 Italian Verbs*, Berlitz Publishing, New York, 680-3, with comments from the researchers (Cafarella, Pascoe).

a variety of communications that reflect their own regional and generational backgrounds.

It is time to begin collecting documentation on the *globalisti*, as they represent a new force in the Australian community. It would be impossible to understand these immigrants without recourse to the new social and digital media as a primary source. Whereas previous immigrants built bricks-and-mortar halls in which to meet; these latest immigrants build websites together for the same purpose. Like all such communities, the Italo-Australian one has been as much imagined as real.[39] Benedict Anderson's original formulation has come under fire in recent years as having underestimated the extent to which the imagined community is itself a product of globalisation.[40] Anderson was writing more about modern nationalism, of course, but immigrant groups within multicultural societies follow a similar path and can be understood to coalesce around similar symbolic constructions such as the ethnic newspaper. Anderson's thesis has already been used for gay communities and other sub-sets of national populations. Similarly, users of Twitter can be understood as a community, as much concrete as "virtual".[41] Now we propose a similar project for the *globalisti*. Their symbolic universe is electronic. Just as we found in the pages of *Il Globo* clues to the self-concept of the previous wave of Italian immigrants to Australia, how might a detailed study of texting, Tweeting, blogging and the like reveal for us the social identity of these *globalisti*?

We will not assume that Italians follow the same patterns as elsewhere. With newspapers, we argued that the original London

---

39 Anderson, 1991.
40 Robertson, 2011.
41 Gruzd, Wellman and Takhteyev, 2011.

prototype of the newspaper, although copied everywhere, was changed in observable ways in non-English contexts. Italian newspapers developed their own conventions, in matters like headlines and opening sentences that over time marked them off from the English original.[42] In electronic media we would expect to find similar differences between the American prototype and the Italian adaptation.

Sampling electronic media

We draw our samples from several areas of electronic media, listed in the order in which they became widespread: texting; websites; blogging; Facebook; YouTube; Twitter; and Instagram. We will deal with these one by one, and then attempt some general observations.

Texting (1993 on Nokia phones)

Texting or the use of SMS (Short Message Services) on the mobile phone is the oldest and one of the most ubiquitous uses of electronic media. In texting (Figure 21), the Italians have devised a wider range of abbreviations than is evident among English-language users of texting. Borrowings from English abound, such as the use of 'x' to mean a kiss, which was never part of traditional Italian usage. The ubiquitous "lol" makes its inevitable appearance, although in lower-case letters. These borrowings from English suggest the cross-over in friendship groups between Italians and English speakers. But some elements of Italian life persist. Italian texting assumes quite rigid distinctions between those who are loved because they are family, and those with whom one is romantically involved. Texting also enables its users to avoid complex constructions, such as the conjunctive

---

42 Cafarella and Pascoe, 2009.

pronouns, in favour of simpler formulations. Just as Italian is a highly regionalised language, spoken alongside traditional local languages (once called dialects, like Sicilian), texting conventions differ across regional (and perhaps generational) differences.

Web-sites (1993)

Web-sites have been constructed to help the *globalisti* find their way around the world. A Swiss journalist has created the multilingual site swissinfo.com, which serves as a conduit for news among the *ticinesi*, the Swiss-Italians, wherever they might live and work. Aldo Mencaraglia, based in Melbourne, in 2008 established www.Italiansinfuga.com, subsequently linked to Facebook.[43] The title of the site is in itself interesting, for these are Italians "in flight".

Blogging (1994)

Gone are the days when *Il Globo* needed to thunder on topics of interest to the previous immigrant community. Articles from the mainstream Italian press dealing with issues of youth unemployment, emigration and conditions in Australia now attract the immediate interest and comment of *globalisti*, both in individual comments and in blogs.[44] Now the lack of mediation is evident. Giovanni Tiso, a *globalisto* based in New Zealand, blogs about his experiences there as an immigrant, but also blogs in the Melbourne-based journal, *Overland*.[45] Blogging similarly respects the need to affirm the virtual community in which the bloggers find themselves or wish to be inserted.

---

43 www.Italiansinfuga.com
44 See, for example, NOMIT, Viaggio in Australia, La Maga di Oz, Internations, La Piazza in Oz, MELBOURNEPUNTOIT.com.
45 His site is bat-bean-beam.blogspot.com.au; see also, for example, Tiso, 2013.

Facebook (February 2004)

The appeal of Facebook is that it can be used to draw together like-minded *globalisti* who happen to be in the same Australian city, for whatever reason, social or political. Facebook operates at several levels. One is individual: users can constantly upgrade their status, as befits a form of social media that was originally designed in the mould of the American high-school yearbook. In this sense Facebook becomes a badge of identity, much as the newspaper was once carried ostentatiously in the Italian street as a marker of political identification. Memorials to deceased rock stars or close friends also appear, an electronic equivalent of the *manifesti*, the funerary notices that appear stuck to the walls of Italian towns to share the grim tidings of *paesani* who have just died. It is possible to construct groups with like interests. There is an image of Luigina Martelli published on Facebook taking a beachside holiday in Australia (Figure 22). The image of a woman wearing boots, not thongs, on the sand is a striking comment on cultural difference. Facebook is also used as a means of gathering like-minded Italians, because it can be an assemblage of people from a particular university or perhaps a shared hometown. For example, the page facebook.com/isolemagiche deals with the Eolian Islands as a place of great beauty.[46] Finally, Facebook can be used as a means of drawing together a crowd for a political or festive occasion, operating much like the Italian town's main piazza as a meeting place.

---

46 facebook.com/isolemagiche

Figure 22. Luigina Martella camping: Source: Facebook page of Roberto Giansella, YouTube (February 2005)

YouTube is as popular in Italy and in the Italian language as it is in English-language contexts. It carries Italian music videos, as well as Italo-Australian singers like Tina Arena and Gabriella Cilmi. YouTube also carries political content, such as "Il corpo delle donne" [women's bodies] by Lorella Zanardo (the 2009 exposé of the flagrant humiliation of scantily-clad women on mainstream Italian TV) and the sexual antics of Berlusconi. Italians are active consumers of YouTube. Entire Italian comedy movies (for example films with Lino Banfi or Diego Abatantuono) from the 1970s and 1980s appear on YouTube, suggesting that the *globalisti* carry their childhood memories in this electronic store. For example, Lino Banfi's Roman romp,

"Cornetti Alla Crema" (1981) was uploaded on 14 April 2012 and by 28 May 2014 already had 1,612,699 hits.[47]

Twitter (July 2006)

"Tweeting" short messages of up to 140 characters takes texting to larger audiences. Tweeting provides a two-sided view of both Italy and Australia. As people enjoy new experiences in their travels through Australia, they can record these moments directly, and their "followers" (and others) can know where their "scouts" have ventured. There is an old saying in Italian that perfectly captures this sentiment: "amici d'amici sono anche amici", or, "friends of friends are also friends". Any random sample of *globalisti* with twitter accounts can be used to determine the size and geographical spread of their followers.

Instagram (October 2010)

Taking and sending images by mobile phone via Instagram began only a few years ago but has already proved popular. What are the images of Italy that are communicated via social media? For example, Alessandra shows herself holidaying on Lipari via Instagram. There is an immediacy in the images embodied in Instagram that situates this new electronic medium in the overall suite of internet-based media.

Old and new sources

Earlier generations of immigrants defined themselves as members of a specific regional Italian culture by means of their letters and communications home. They sent letters, postcards, photographs and other correspondence to family and friends in the hometown.

---

47 Between March and May 2014 this film received more than 200,000 hits. Lino Banfi has acted in more than 100 films, mostly comedies, and many are available in whole or in part on YouTube.

These communications contained news of their adventures in the larger world and typically emphasised their successes rather than their setbacks.

But these emigrants also gradually found themselves redefined in the migration process as Italo-Australians. They found an affinity with other Italian immigrants whose lives they might barely have known or appreciated back in Italy. This new identity was hybrid, and it was this very fact of being singular and unique that strengthened their sense of having helped construct a new imagined community, one that saw itself reflected in multicultural radio (such as 3ZZZ in the 1970s), SBS television (another product of the 1970s, though expanded in the 1980s), and, of course, *Il Globo* itself. By the 1990s, the more successful clubs and societies had begun to build outer-suburban facilities that were variously regional (Melbourne's Veneto Club, the Foglar Furlan) but were becoming generically Italo-Australian.

The *globalisti* do not eschew these older forms of communication: some of our sample have attempted to join a traditional club. But typically they rely on the newer forms of electronic media to build networks in the new society. With the range of electronic media gradually broadening, the scope for developing an "imagined community" has also widened.

Conclusion

All cultural experience is available via the WWW to the scrutiny of people throughout the world. What might have been a local and very personal experience suddenly is open to the rest of humankind. Quite minute details also become available. These provide sometimes surprising insights into the phenomenon under study. A footballer also serves in the Boer War; an Anzac returns to Richmond, Victoria, to find his community opposed to the war; a *globalista* finds herself immortalised in a beach photo.

Trends toward "ubiquitous computing", in concert with open-linked data, suggest a transition of consciousness and human relations; a transition toward greater integration and connectedness. Previously stable categories, like footballer, Anzac and immigrant become radically relativised and points of connection with people whose lives we observe in such detail become more and more evident.

Archives are stores of collective memories; they are media records which extend human experience and alter our naive relation with time and space. The digitisation of archives further transforms collective memory media by communicating electronically, at "light speed". In the act of archiving, one can only suggest possible future applications, though one is constrained in the amount and style of archiving by physical capacity. As seen in previous record-keeping practice, some information is valued over others, consciously or not.

The traditional archive struggled to be free of the dominant political forces which had shaped it, particularly the public and governmental institutions (the sporting associations, the military, the immigration departments, etc.) which had created the files and records that made up the traditional archives. Footballers were ascribed to clubs, the Anzacs belonged to their battalions, and Italian travellers were defined by the border security personnel who stamped their passports.

The lives of these individuals were therefore understood through the pattern of their interactions with these institutions, not in the round. Now cultural life is digitised and other people's lives prove to be surprisingly open-ended, diverse and knowable. The nature of their connection to place, either the suburban place of the sports team, the memorial site and township of the World War 1 digger, or the places of Italy, Australia and the digital place of the globalised web are richer and more complex than can be understood through the traditional archive. In the dark days of the late 1930s, H.G. Wells dreamt of a "world brain", a storehouse of knowledge that make other cultures more knowable and thus less vulnerable to enemy aggression based on ignorance.[48] The World Wide Web might well have advanced that dream.

References

Anderson, Benjamin. (1991) *Imagined communities: reflections on the origin and spread of nationalism*, London: Verso.

Argus, newspaper (Melbourne). Various dates.

Blainey, Geoffrey. (2003) *A Game of Our Own. The origins of Australian football.* Second edition (First edition 1990). Melbourne: Black Inc.

Trading Card Heroes. (2003) *Australian Rules football card catalogue*, 2003, Wyndham Vale, Vic.: Trading Card heroes, 2003.

Brown-May, Andrew and Shurlee Swain. (eds). (2005) *The Encyclopedia of Melbourne*. Melbourne: Cambridge University Press, Melbourne.

Cafarella, Caterina and Pascoe, Robert. (2013) *"I globalisti:* The fourth wave of Italian migration to Australia". ACIS 7th Biennial Conference. "Re-Imagining Italian Studies". Adelaide. 5 December.

Davison, Graeme. (1978) *The Rise and Fall of Marvellous Melbourne*. Carlton: University of Melbourne Press.

East, B. with Parkin, D. (2012) *Australian football in a commercial era: catering for theatregoers and tribals*. Petersham, NSW: Walla Walla.

Gruzd, A. Wellman, B. and Takhteyev, Y. (2011) "Imagining twitter as an imagined community". *American Behavioural Scientist.* 55(10): 1294-318.

---

48 Wells, 1938.

Inglis, Kenneth. (2008) *Sacred Places: War memorials in the Australian Landscape*. First published 1998. Carlton: University of Melbourne Press.

Holmesby, Russell and Main, Jim. (2011) *The Encyclopedia of AFL Footballers: every AFL/VFL player since 1897*, Seaford: 9th ed., BAS Publishing.

Keenan, Terry. (1999) *A taste of Port; personal profiles, snapshots and statistical records drawn from the history of the Port Melbourne Football Club*, Albert Park, Vic.: Eucalyptus Press.

Macintyre, C.J. (1980) "The Ascent of Fascism in interwar Fremantle'. Murdoch University, unpublished, 1980.

Pascoe, Robert. (1987) *Buongiorno Australia: Our Italian Heritage*. Richmond, Vic.: Greenhouse Publications in association with Vaccari Italian Historical Trust

Pennings, Mark and Robert Pascoe. (2012) "The Corio Oval tribe: A Prosopographical perspective of the Geelong Football Club in the nineteenth century". *Sporting Traditions*. 29(1) May: 77-94.

Robertson, Beth M. (2008) "Long desperate hours at the typewriter: Establishing the Oral History Association of Australia". *Oral History Association of Australia Journal*. 30: 74-80.

Robson, L.L. (1970) *The first A.I.F. a study of its recruitment 1914-1918*. Carlton, Vic.: University of Melbourne Press.

Sands and McDougall's Melbourne and suburban Directory, 1863-1901. Melbourne: Sands and McDougall.

Speculum, the Melbourne Medical School magazine, digitised for 1884 -1914, available University of Melbourne web-site.

Tiso, Giovanni. (2013) "'The Net will save us'". *Overland*. 211 Winter: 55-60.

Thernstrom, Stephen. (1973) *The other Bostonians: poverty and progress in the American metropolis 1880-1970*. Cambridge Mass.: Harvard University Press.

Wells, H.G. (1938) *World Brain*. London: Methuen, London. available at ebooks.adelaide.edu.au.

12

Karen Berger

Finding Belonging in an Uncountry

In searching for belonging, a fundamental starting point is the earth to which we will all eventually return. The discussion that follows explores intersections between stories of cemeteries as told by Hélène Cixous, Margaret Somerville, Noongar writer, Kim Scott, and some of this author's own writing. Cemeteries as places and the ritual of funerary events leads to an investigation of "performed behaviour" that has occurred at such significant sites and the ritual gestures and monuments that remain. Is it possible to move from these explorations to a conception of an "uncountry" in which we are all allowed a level of belonging?

In 2012, I was the first member of my immediate family to visit Lithuania, the country of my ancestors. In the capital, Vilnius, I checked the web-site, "Holocaust Atlas of Lithuania", and found a map with blue Stars of David representing sites of mass graves.[1] I typed in the name of my father's hometown, Svėdasai, and read:

---

1 Jakulytė-Vasil, "Holocaust Atlas of Lithuania".

MASS MURDER OF THE JEWS FROM SVĖDASAI

ABOUT MASSACRE

In July 1941, according to some sources 245 people were murdered near Svėdasai, and according to others 386, most must have been Jews.

Address: Svėdasai administrative district, Bajorai village, Anyksciai district

Victim number: 245-386

Perpetrators

Unknown

HOW TO FIND?

From the centre of Svėdasai, near the church, turn onto Simoniu street. Then go straight ahead until you see the white chapel outside of town. Then turn left. After 200 meters you'll see a commemorative marker on the left side, by the road. Walk about 200 meters and you'll find the monument.

Latitude: 55.684833 Longitude: 25.348700

It took quite a while wandering around a young pine plantation before I found the monument.

Figures 23 and 24. Svėdasai with permission of photographer David Joseph

My grandfather, Faive Berger, had left Svėdasai in about 1914 as a young man. None of my immediate family have ever visited his hometown. I had asked my father if he wanted me to do anything for him there. He asked me to put stones on the grave.

Figure 25. Family photograph, Karen Berger's grandfather is the man in the centre; Karen's father is the boy on the right Figure 26. Placing stones on grave. Photo with permission David Joseph.

The practice of placing flowers on graves is ancient. Flowers are a good metaphor for life since they wither. But Jewish authorities have often objected to bringing flowers to the grave, seeing this as a pagan custom. Stones on a grave are intended to keep the soul from wandering around prematurely. They are a marker of a visit and a symbol of the permanence of our memory of the departed. According to Rabbi David Wolpe, "while other things fade, stones and souls endure".[2]

French academic and writer, Hélène Cixous, has lived most of her life in Paris, but was born in Algeria of a German refugee mother and a Mahgrebian father. Her memoir about growing up in Algeria, *Reveries of the Wild Woman*, begins, "The whole time I was living in Algeria I

2 Wolpe, "Putting Stones on Jewish Graves".

would dream of one day arriving in Algeria".[3] Cixous was deprived of French citizenship under the anti-semitic Vichy administration during World War II, and in 1998 she wrote that where she belongs is:

> Neither France, nor Germany, nor Algeria. No regrets. It is good fortune. Freedom, an inconvenient, intolerable freedom, a freedom that obliges one to let go, to rise above, to beat one's wings. To weave a flying carpet. *I felt perfectly at home, nowhere.*[4]

Four years previously, in her book, *Rootprints – Memory and Life Writing*, Cixous had written:

> When I speak today in terms of genealogy, it is no longer only Europe that I see, but, in an astral way, the totality of the universe – the families of my mother . . . had two fates: the concentration camps on the one hand; on the other, the scattering across the earth. This gives me a sort of world-wide resonance.[5]

An example of her family's "scattering across the earth" is the World War I grave of her German soldier grandfather in a Russian forest. In the book she reproduces photographs of his grave and writes:

> Why these tears? Because I am dead. I am so dead. Because I have become this raised wooden stone that repeats my name and my date of death to the air where I never lived. The wooden page informs the empty wood that henceforth it is here that I live, become foreign earth and wood.
>
> . . . I am planted in a forest where no one I know has ever come to see me . . . The shafts of the pine trees rise very

---

3 Cixous and Brahic, 2006, p. 9.

4 Cixous, 1998, p. 155.

5 Cixous and Calle-Gruber, 1997, p. 189.

straight among our crosses and our simple wooden stories.
God is an unknown pine forest.

. . . My life begins with graves. They go beyond the
individual, the singularity. I see a sort of genealogy of graves
. . . my father's grave is also a lost grave. It is in Algeria. No
one ever goes there any more or will ever go.[6]

But Cixous is brave both in her life and her writing, and she did
return to Algeria. In *So Close*, published in 2007, she recounts her visit
to her father's grave. First she visits the house where she grew up:

To go in spite of myself . . . to see the house that had no
longer existed for quite some time, whose total disappearance
and replacement by a tall building without opening I
discovered in 1970, thus to go and see the annihilation of all
remaining trace not a one anywhere in spite of myself I can't
prevent myself from doing it. It's not me, it's my body. I am
my body, I follow my body . . . it senses that we are going to
arrive in front of the Cemetery . . . We are coming close. In
the end, there will be no end.[7]

But in Algiers, the gate to the Jewish cemetery is closed. Cixous
imagines herself crawling through an underground hole, falling into
a narrow gorge, going back up a rock.[8] Finally inside the cemetery,
she cannot locate the tomb. She finds herself thunderstruck, as if
committing blasphemy by yelling her father's name "as if [he] were
dead", and as she "confesses" his date of death "blood streams
on [her] cheeks".[9] She walks towards the top of the hill, "shards

---

6 I think here of the young pine forest that shelters the mass grave in my grandfather's
village.
7 Cixous and Kamuf, 2009, pp. 106-7.
8 Ibid., p. 146.
9 Ibid., p. 149.

of gravestones" rolling beneath her soles, crossing the "edge of a crumbling wall":[10]

> I lay down upon you. I fastened myself with all my strength to the Tomb I felt how living it was, its hardness supple at my call . . . sin to wash your granite except with tears. Your red dust.[11]

In Algiers, at her father's grave, she has found "the immortal sadness" that will stay with her as she journeys on.[12] She returns to France but finds "I was in Paris, but I was not with Paris . . . I was with Algeria, I was not in Paris, I did not belong to Paris".[13]

We are back then with the sentiment, "I felt perfectly at home, nowhere".[14] Or, in a different formulation from *Three Steps on the Ladder of Writing*:

> Today we are in an era of nationalism . . . it is primarily a need for the proper, for a proper country, for a proper name, a need for separation and, at the same time, a rejection of the other . . . harsh trenchant desire not to be you . . . I want the word uncountry.[15]

A visit to a cemetery in Australia also figures in Margaret Somerville's *Body/landscape Journals*. Somerville recalls an afternoon crying about the loss of her home. In bed that night, Paul Carter's *Living in a New Country*, in which he analyses first contact meetings between settlers and indigenous people, gives

---

10 Ibid., p. 151.
11 Ibid., p. 154.
12 Ibid., p. 159.
13 Ibid., p. 161.
14 Cixous, 1998, p. 155.
15 Cixous, 1993, p. 131.

her comfort.[16] Somerville recognises that she sees her present day meetings with Aboriginal women in this light as "meanings are made on each occasion as if for the first time . . . it is a confirmation of new possibilities for re-visioning this land".[17]

The meeting considered here is that between Somerville and her Aboriginal friend, Emily O'Connor. O'Connor had requested that Somerville organise a trip to visit the grave of her ancestor, Queen Maryanne Sullivan, overlooking Bunawanjin Mountain in northern New South Wales. Queen Maryanne had been a powerful woman, possibly the daughter of King Billy of the Kamilaroi tribe. She won a land grant from the NSW government for the use of Aboriginal families and established a community there. Her status as "meengha" or mother of all mothers, meant that she wore a special kangaroo cloak and had three husbands. According to custom, when she was buried, sometime in the 1920s, her corpse was lain on top of their bodies.[18]

Somerville repeats Emily O'Connor's comparison of a visit to the Queen's grave with her mother, and that of forty years later, with Somerville herself:

> On our walk [in 1953], they took us up to the cemetery and it was all nice and clear then and you could see the graves. Our mother and the other elders showed us which grave it was and they told us that our queen was buried there. We did the graves up and we could see clearly where they were buried but when we went back the second time, just recently, we couldn't see a thing because of the long grass. That saddened

16 Somerville, 1999, p. 89.
17 Ibid., p. 93.
18 Ibid., pp. 96-7.

me, not being able to see where our Queen was buried, our Grandmother, Granny Maryanne Sullivan.[19]

O'Connor finds "fist-sized round stones outlining the elliptical shape of each grave" but is not able to identify which belongs to the Queen.[20] However for both O'Connor and Somerville the cemetery visit is still significant, providing them with the possibility of a performative enactment of their embeddedness in place.

Later, Somerville reflects on the fact that the cemetery is now on private property and the owners don't allow visitors. By then, O'Connor has died so they can "no longer sit and talk together".[21] Here, Somerville seems an exemplar of Miwon Kwon's "melancholic" artist and her writing "compensatory" behaviour for a "sense of loss and vacancy".[22] Somerville imagines herself and O'Connor at the cemetery:

> I am now sitting on top of the mountain; I become the mountain itself. I visit that space over and over and know there is a profound connection between Emily's performance on top of the mountain and my ability to perform myself at this point; to make sense of my bodily experience in space, to story it for myself and at the same time for you, my reader.[23]

I wonder if, in some sense, this is a good example of Cixous's "uncountry"? A woman visits a grave that is no longer recognisable as one, feels a connection with a dead woman of

---

19 Ibid., p. 106.
20 Ibid., p. 101.
21 Ibid., p. 29.
22 Kwon, 1997, p. 106.
23 Somerville, 1999, p. 29.

another culture, and shares that connection across multiple boundaries with her reader.

In 2011 Aboriginal writer Kim Scott's novel *That Deadman Dance* examined relationships between the Noongar people of south-western Australia and the first British settlers. In an interview Scott explained that he intended his novel to function by exploring empowering ways to connect an ancient heritage with contemporary life. Rather than laying to rest the "ghosts" of "identity, race and history", Scott advocates listening to these ghosts, "having courageous conversations and respectful dialogues".[24]

Two aspects of Scott's writing are particularly intriguing. Firstly there is metaphorical use of burial and secondly Scott contrasts performance (particularly dance) and writing as ways of communication between Noongar people and European settlers. Early in the story we meet the gregarious Wunyeran, who welcomes the newcomers, forming an especially close relationship with Dr Cross. When Wunyeran lies dying from the introduced disease that is decimating his people, Cross tends him closely.[25] Years later, Cross succumbs to the same disease and requests to be buried in Wunyeran's grave.[26]

To the novel's main protagonist, Bobby, Wunyeran and Cross's double grave becomes a sacred site, a place where their "spirits fus[e] in the earth".[27] But as the settlement grows, not everyone knows of these two founders and Bobby "worried for them because of all the digging for buildings and rubbish that went on".[28] The growth of the town results in pressure on diminishing resources. "Men of authority"

---

24 Whitmont, 2010, p. 39.
25 Scott, 2011, p. 136.
26 Ibid., p. 350.
27 Ibid.
28 Ibid.

decide that Dr Cross's coffined body must be removed to the new town cemetery where it is given a railing and engraved headstone.[29] But Wunyeran's skeleton, broken by the gravedigger employed to move Cross's coffin, is washed down to the sea in the next flood. As an old man, Bobby tells tourists that the town is shamed by not having a statue honouring Wunyeran because "he welcomed the first white people that sailed here, just like I welcome you now".[30]

The "deadman dance" of the title is an elaboration on the 1803 tale of explorer, Captain Matthew Flinders, ordering his marines to perform a military salute to honour the Noongar for their assistance. The dance so impressed the Noongar that they appropriated it, and a version (chests painted with white pipe clay with red crosses to mimic the "redcoats") could be found in their repertoire for at least fifty years afterwards.[31] Scott imagines an early performance of this dance:

> Laughing and loved, Bobby Wabalanginy never learned fear; not until he was pretty well a grown man did he ever even know it. Sure, he grew up doing the Dead Man Dance – those stiff movements, those jerking limbs . . . but with him it was a dance of life, a lively dance for people to do together.[32]

Scott uses the ambivalence inherent in the deadman dance as an important theme of the novel. The Noongar probably thought of the new arrivals as ghosts. At the same time the adoption of the dance "may have been the 'beginning of the end' of a way of life" for Bobby and his community.[33] In an interview, Scott stated that originally his intention was to finish the novel "on the upbeat", but then decided

29 Ibid., pp. 353-4.
30 Ibid., p. 78.
31 Veth, 2012, p. 150.
32 Scott, 2011, p. 67.
33 Whitmont, 2011, p. 39.

that he "wanted ambivalence", aiming for "a way of setting up all sorts of resonances to do with possibility and loss".[34]

In the final scene of the novel, Bobby sets out to convince a mainly white audience that the two peoples must live together:[35]

> One time, with Mr Cross, he share his food and his bed with us, because he say he our guest. But not now, so we gotta do it ourselves . . . They messing up the water, cutting the earth. . . . And we now strangers to our special places.[36]

But Bobby's real confidence lies in his skills as a dancer and singer and he soon abandons his English words (along with his English clothes) to perform his story. Initially his audience are enthralled but tragically the novel ends with their attention being drawn away by a violent attack on Bobby's relatives outside.[37]

Throughout the book there are references to Bobby's attempts to document his life in his journal. Scott has said he wishes for a literary tradition "with really strong Noongar roots".[38] He feels that in relaying Noongar information to interested non-indigenous people Bobby is playing a powerful role and that this situation "where it's indigenous people giving and sharing, and being valued for doing so" should be encouraged now.[39] Furthermore, once Noongars are in a position of power, there may be the possibility of non-indigenous people being accommodated by the local spirits of the ancestors and the place.[40]

---

34 Brewster, 2012, p. 231.
35 Scott, 2011, p. 390.
36 Ibid., pp. 391-2.
37 Ibid., p. 395.
38 Brewster, p. 231.
39 Ibid., p. 240.
40 Ibid., p. 242.

Though Scott's ending is not "upbeat", his ambivalence does allow for a way forward. He notes that:

> . . . the Noongars appropriated the dance and the fact that you can write a novel as a Noongar person, is in itself expressive of continuity, in that the resolution of that novel – the end, the last page – is not the end. There are possibilities still.[41]

During my travels in Lithuania, I also visited the home town of my mother's grandfather, Panevėžys. Before World War II, almost half the residents of this town were Jewish, and it was famous for its synagogues and religious schools.[42] Synagogues have now been converted into garages and private homes.

Figure 27. Former synagogue, Panevėžys. You can see where the two tablets of the ten commandments were, directly above the eight concreted little windows formerly used to house candles for the Channukah holiday. Photographer David Joseph.

There are three mass graves in the vicinity of the town, but the most significant site seemed to be the former Jewish cemetery. During World War II, it had been abandoned. Under Soviet rule, state-condoned

---

41 Ibid., p. 231.
42 Kofman, "Jewish Community of Panevėžys".

vandalism left the cemetery destroyed and in 1966 the council decided
to "liquidate the Jewish cemetery, and to replace it with a city park".[43]
Later that year granite gravestones were removed and used as building
materials. The several thousand gravestones are scattered across the
town. Some had their Hebrew inscriptions removed and were reused
as Christian gravestones, others found another use as street rubble.
Still others can be seen in a "decorative" outside wall of the municipal
theatre, the Hebrew fragments still showing quite clearly.[44]

Figure 28. Panevėžys. Figure 29. Hebrew Inscriptions. Panevėžys. Photograph
David Joseph.

Polish theatre director Tadeusz Kantor worked during and after
World War II He described his practice as "the theatre of death"
writing, "it is possible to express life in art only through the absence
of life, through an appeal to death".[45] Cemeteries and theatres are
both formalised places of transformation – from flesh to dust; the
performer transforms herself. Those who are believers recognise that
a cemetery is the repository of the physical remains of the deceased

43 Kofman, 2007.
44 Ibid.
45 Kantor and Kobialka, 1993, p. 112.

but believe that the spirit of the dead person has been released from the physical world. Theatre anthropologist, Richard Schechner asserts that our contemporary custom of clapping at the end of a performance is a remnant of the time when actors were considered to be possessed by another's spirit (often that of a dead person), that must be sent back to its own realm at the end of a performance – hence the need for the sound of vigorous applause.[46]

If countries are peopled by living humans, a place inhabited by the dead might be an example of Cixous' uncountry. What then of the possibility of some kind of universal "theatre country"? In his book *The Empty Space: A Book About the Theatre*, renowned director, Peter Brook articulates an opposition between everyday life and the theatre:

> Truth in theatre is always on the move . . . the slate is wiped clean all the time. In everyday life, "if" is a fiction, in the theatre "if" is an experiment. In everyday life, "if" is an evasion, in the theatre "if" is the truth.[47]

Is there a place where the theatre community shares this truth? One often hears people speak of their "theatre family", those people they have created theatre with over a period of time growing to feel like they are relatives. Contemporary director, Eugenio Barba emigrated from southern Italy to Norway at a time when you couldn't find spaghetti north of Switzerland. Nonetheless, he soon found himself firmly belonging to his renowned Odin Theatre.[48] In his preface, he writes that research for his book *The Paper Canoe* included "memories of and dialogues with my [theatre] 'ancestors' ".[49] And he continues:

> There is a land-less country, a country in transition, a country

---

46 Schechner, 2009.
47 Brook, 1990, p. 157.
48 Barba, 2010.
49 Barba, 2005, p. vii.

which consists of time not territory, and which is confluent with the theatrical profession. In this country, the artists who work in India or Bali, my Scandinavian companions, or those from Peru, Mexico or Canada, in spite of the distance between them, work elbow to elbow. I am able to understand them even if our languages separate us.[50]

The ephemeral space of theatre gives voice to (among others) the dead. And this is a political act. I'm inclined to think that cemeteries qualify as ephemeral in some ways, depositories of the non-living where we go to think about people who no longer exist, except as ephemera. I suggest that the theatre is also a manifestation of an uncountry, theatres all over the world providing a place for the same characters to meet with each other in the moving truth of an imaginary "if".

Neil Leach argues that identity associated with belonging to a particular place is created by ritualistic behaviour, communities "colonise" territories by performance, "mak[ing] material the belongings they purport to describe".[51] As he explained:

> The concept of "belonging" as a product of performativity enables us to go beyond the limitations of simple narrative. It privileges the idea not of reading the environment, as though its meaning were simply there and waiting to be deciphered, but rather of giving meaning to the environment by collective or individual behaviour. Belonging to place can therefore be understood as an aspect of territorialisation, and out of that belonging a sense of identity might be forged.[52]

---

50 Ibid.
51 Bell in Leach, 2002, p. 130.
52 Leach, 2002, p.22.

In this sense, a performance can have a political effect.[53]

To return to Lithuania. Ethnic Lithuanians have engaged in ongoing struggles against the outside forces of Poland, Germany and Soviet Union. Notable group performances of collective identity include the Hill of Crosses. The first crosses were probably placed here in the fourteenth century in protest against occupation by the Teutonic knights. During the Soviet era the hill was leveled three times, the crosses turned into scrap metal and the area covered with waste and sewerage. But each time, Lithuanians returned with more crosses. Since 1985 it has been left to grow.[54]

At Gediminas Castle in the Lithuanian capital Vilnius, an exhibition shows the "Baltic Way", a continuous linking of hands from Vilnius to Tallinn in Estonia via Riga, in Latvia, a crucial 1989 challenge to Soviet occupation. Less than 6 months later, Lithuanians won their independence.[55] These Lithuanian performances are both fascinating and moving because they are doing something quite mysterious and paradoxical in order to achieve a concrete political goal. They aim to take control of country by "uncountrying" it. A small hill, bulldozed and desecrated, is repeatedly remade as a holy memorial, to the death of a man from a far-away time and place, as a way of asserting independence. In the "Baltic Way" protest, three small nations demanded a border between themselves and the Soviet Union, by making a human chain that broke the borders between their own countries. They radically changed the way the surface of a highway was used by peopling it with stationary humans, whose linked hands in any other form of protest would symbolise a border between themselves and their opposition. Here the opposition is both outside

---

53 Ibid.
54 "Sacred Sites: Places of Peace and Power".
55 "The Baltic Way".

and inside – the Soviet Union was ruled from another country, Russia, but Lithuanians were also Soviet officials. It's a powerful reminder of the ability of a people to hold onto their identity through German, Polish and Russian occupations.

Since 1996, I have lived near the Merri Creek in Melbourne, very near the spot where many people believe John Batman, arguably Melbourne's founder, enacted a treaty with Wurundjeri elders on 6 June 1835.[56] Trees played an important part in this ceremony on the banks of the Merri Creek. As far as Batman and his legal counsel were concerned, the ritual being enacted was one of "feoffment", a feudal form of conveyancing already described in Batman's time as "after the ancient manner".[57] It required that the vendor first of all pass the vendee a twig, some grass, a lump of soil, or some other small part of the property regarded as symbolic of the whole. Secondly, the land needed to be perambulated, and physical objects on the boundaries described. Marked trees were used for this purpose, though the veracity of Batman's account of this is highly questionable, since it would have entailed walking further than is possible in one day. Finally, a deed needed to be "signed, sealed and delivered".[58]

Batman took pains in his diary to show that all these requirements had been fulfilled. On 6 June 1835 (from the State Library of Victoria transcription, which preserves the spelling and grammar mistakes intact) he wrote:

> . . . I found Eight Chiefs amongst them who possessed the whole of the Country near Port Phillip . . . and after a full explanation of what my object was, I purchased two large tracks of Land from them . . . the Parchment the Eight

---

56 Attwood and Doyle, 2009, p. 50.
57 Ibid., p. 44.
58 Ibid.

Chiefs signed this afternoon, delivering to me some of the soil Each of them, as giving me full possession of the tracks of Land, this took place along side of a beautiful stream of water, and from whence my Land commences – and when a tree is marked 4 way's to know the corner Boundary.[59]

The scarred tree is believed to be in Northcote and was still standing in 2007, when a local historian made an urgent plea for the tree to be saved, to no avail.[60] Today the monumental tree is remembered by a hole in the concrete.

Figure 30. Probable scarred tree site, Northcote

Tim Ingold observed that both trees and churches possess the attributes of what Mikhail Bakhtin terms a chronotype, in other words a place where temporality is palpable, "veritable monuments to the passage of time". As he observed, "the tree buries its roots in the ground, so also people's ancestors are buried in the graveyard beside the church, and both sets of roots may reach to approximately the same temporal depth".[61]

---

59 Batman, "Journal, 10 May-11 June 1835. [Manuscript] ", pp. 59-61.
60 "Batman Treaty Memorial Located"
61 Ingold, 1993, p.169.

Like the Lithuanian Hill of Crosses and Baltic Way, Batman's Treaty is an example of performed behaviour, grounded in a particular place, enacted primarily for its political effect and creating a version of "uncountrying". The original Aboriginal owners, the Wurundjeri, had a detailed and intimate connection to their land, bound to their ancestral ways of being in the world. Batman's grasping of half a million acres as his own would have been meaningless to them. The ensuing influx of foreigners literally uncountried the Wurundjeri from their homelands.

Nevertheless, this Treaty signing remained a significant historical marker to both indigenous and settler Melbournians. In 1937, 102 years after the event, the Batman story featured strongly in historical re-enactments, with the willing participation of the newly formed Australian Aborigines' League.[62] It seems that Aboriginal people in inter-war Melbourne were favourably disposed to Batman because of their own oral history, particularly the mythic stories passed on by William Barak, the traditional ngurungaeta (elder) of the Wurundjeri-willam clan.[63] Barak, born on the Merri Creek, was the son of Jerum Jerum, one of the chief signatories of Batman's Treaty and had been present at the Treaty signing as a young boy. In 1961 the treaty was again re-enacted in Oldis Gardens on the Merri Creek, just downstream from the signing site.

According to an observer, the re-enactment had a profound impact on the fifteen Aboriginal performers who "[felt] proud, they stood straighter".[64] Included in this re-enactment was the symbolic gesture reported in Batman's diary of the eight chiefs each presenting Batman

---

62 Atwood and Doyle, 2009, p. 243.
63 William Barak, "Articles on Barak, Last Chief of the Yarra Yarra Tribe., 1882-1931 [Manuscript]".
64 Attwood and Doyle, 2009, p. 255.

with soil. The significance of this gesture was recognised by Prime Minister, Gough Whitlam's consultant, H.C. (Nugget) Coombs in 1975, at the historic occasion of the Australian government returning some Gurindji land in the Northern Territory to its original owners. He recommended repeating the gesture in reverse. This Whitlam did, declaring, "I solemnly hand to you these deeds as proof in Australian law that these lands belong to the Gurindji people and I put into your hands this piece of the earth itself as a sign that we restore them to you and your children forever".[65]

When John Batman died of syphilis in 1839 at the age of 38, he was buried at the Old Cemetery, now the site of the Queen Victoria Market at the edge of Melbourne's city centre.[66] By 1880 a group of Melbourne intellectuals were decrying the fact that he had not been sufficiently recognised and organised a subscription fund to erect a memorial in his honour above his grave.[67] Its form is that of a classical obelisk, used by Egyptian pharaohs to proclaim victory over their enemies.[68] In this case the enemy claiming title to Victoria's foundation was Batman's detested rival John Pascoe Fawkner.

As the city expanded, and paralleling uncannily the process imagined by Kim Scott in early Western Australia, the first parts of the cemetery to go were the Aboriginal and Jewish sections.[69] In 1922 the Melbourne City Council decided to remove all the remaining bodies to a new northern cemetery, named after Batman's rival Fawkner.[70]

---

65 Ibid., 2009, p. 276.
66 Billot, 1979, p. 273.
67 Attwood and Doyle, 2009, pp. 135-8.
68 Ibid., pp. 143-4.
69 Melbourne City Council has recently approved plans to erect a memorial to the two men hanged in Melbourne's first execution, Tasmanian Aborigines, Tunnerminnerwait and Maulboyheenner. Webb, 2014.
70 Attwood and Doyle, 2009, p. 172.

After much controversy, it was decided that Batman's memorial would be relocated to a site on Batman Avenue, about five kilometres from the city centre. Later that same year, what were presumed to be Batman's remains were interred in a special Pioneers' section of the Fawkner cemetery and a replica of the memorial now on Batman Avenue was built above them.[71] Then in 1992, the Melbourne City Council celebrated its 150th anniversary and decided to return the Batman memorial to its original site, now a corner of the market's carpark. At the same time the council recognised an obligation to correct the original inscription which states that Batman had founded a settlement "on the site of Melbourne then unoccupied", strangely ignoring the reason for his Treaty.

Figure 31. John Batman Memorial original inscription

---

71 Ibid., p. 177.

The original inscription had certainly ignored indigenous possession, however as indicated above, it was specifically directed at Fawkner who had made rival claims to be the European founder of Melbourne. A corrective plaque was attached with the statement:

> When the monument was erected in 1881 the colony considered that the Aboriginal people did not occupy land . . . it is now clear that prior to colonisation of Victoria the land was inhabited and used by the Aboriginal people.

In 2004, after four years of consultation, including with the Council's Indigenous Arts Advisory Committee, the new plaque was removed and a newer one added regretting any offence caused by the earlier inscriptions. Since then, vandals have removed the plaque and a further plaque (with the same wording) was installed in 2012.[72]

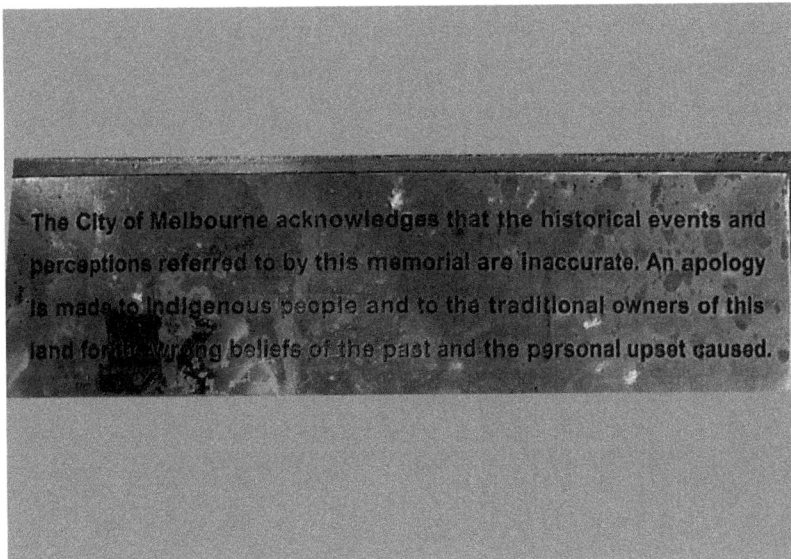

Figure 32. John Batman Memorial. Additional inscription

---

72 Hockey, 2012.

In the same Port Phillip newspapers that reported Batman's death in 1839 there appeared articles about the massive destruction that introduced disease was inflicting on the Aboriginal population. Aboriginal communities were so broken that people lay dead and dying around the town. A generation after Batman's arrival the Aboriginal population of Port Phillip had been reduced to about 2000 people.[73]

This chapter began with a visit to the mass grave at my father's father's village in Lithuania. I know that some of my ancestors are buried there, but not only are there no individual grave sites to identify, I don't know who those ancestors are.

Visiting Queen Victoria Market, I'm aware of those early graves under my feet and anywhere in Melbourne I often think of the many, many bodies interred in the land that Batman "bought". Thinking back to Cixous, I wonder if rather than embracing a nationalism associated with "a rejection of the other", we could share an "uncountry". [74] I have been sharing stories of people I admire, my own stories, the stories of my ancestors, and stories of the place where I live. I have looked at examples of performance and theatre as a means of telling stories. These are endeavours to make connections between people that have all eventually returned to the earth and those that will return to the earth. In the uncountry of our connection to the earth in death we are all inherently connected.

---

73 Attwood and Doyle, p. 99.
74 Cixous, 1993, p. 131.

References

Attwood, Bain, and Doyle, Helen. (2009) *Possession: Batman's Treaty and the Matter of History.* Second Series 115. Carlton, Vic: Miegunyah.

"The Baltic Way". Baltic Way web-site.

Barak, William. "Articles on Barak, Last Chief of the Yarra Yarra Tribe., 1882-1931". MS.15444. Manuscript collection. State Library of Victoria.

Barba, Eugenio. (2010) "Odin Week".

————. (2005) *The Paper Canoe.* U.K.: Taylor and Francis e-Library.

Batman, John. "The Batman Deed". H31718 and H36529. Manuscript collection. State Library of Victoria and library web-site.

————. "Journal, 10 May-11 June 1835". MS 13181 and MS 6945. Manuscript collection. State Library of Victoria.

"Batman Treaty Memorial Located", Vicnet. Pioneers web-site.

Billot, C.P. (1981) *The Story of John Batman and the Founding of Melbourne.* Melbourne: Hyland House.

Brewster, Anne. (2012) "Can You Anchor a Shimmering Nation State Via Regional Indigenous Roots?: Kim Scott Talks to Anne Brewster About 'That Deadman Dance'". *Cultural Studies Review.* 18(1): 228-46.

Brook, Peter. (1990) *The Empty Space.* London: Penguin.

Carter, Paul. (1992) *Living in a New Country: History, Travelling and Language.* London: Faber.

Cixous, Hélène. (1998) *Stigmata : Escaping Texts.* London and New York: Routledge.

————. (1993) *Three Steps on the Ladder of Writing.* The Wellek Library Lectures at the University of California, Irvine. New York: Columbia University Press.

Cixous, Hélène, and Beverley Bie Brahic. (2006) *Reveries of the Wild Woman: Primal Scenes.* Agm Collection. Evanston, Ill.: Northwestern University Press.

Cixous, Hélène, and Mireille Calle-Gruber. (1997) *Hélène Cixous, Rootprints*. Routledge.

Cixous, Hélène, and Peggy Kamuf. *So Close*. (2009) Cambridge and Malden, MA: Polity.

Hockey, Catherine. (2012) personal email, 22 November.

Ingold, Tim. (1993) "The Temporality of the landscape". *World Archaeology*. 25(2): 152-74.

Jakulytė-Vasil, Milda. "Holocaust Atlas of Lithuania". Vilna Gaon State Jewish Museum. Holocaust Atlas web-site.

Kantor, Tadeusz and Kobialka, Michal. (1993) *A Journey through Other Spaces : Essays and Manifestos, 1944-1990*. Berkeley: University of California Press.

Kofman, Gennady. (2013) personal communication. 23 August.

—————. (2007) "A City Park in a Jewish Cemetery". *Jerusalem of Lithuania*.

—————. "Jewish Community of Panevėžys". Regional-communities. Jewish community of Svencionys web-site.

Kwon, Miwon. (1997) "One Place after Another: Notes on site specificity". *October* 80. Spring: 85-110.

Leach, Neil. (2002) "Belonging: Towards a theory of identification with place". *Perspecta* 33: 126-33.

"Sacred Sites: Places of Peace and Power". Sacred Sites. Hill of Crosses web-site.

Schechner, Richard. (2009) "Rasa Boxes". Paper presented at The World as a Place of Truth, Wroclaw, Poland.

Scott, Kim. (2011) *That Deadman Dance*. Sydney: Pan Macmillan.

Somerville, Margaret. (1999) *Body/Landscape Journals*. North Melbourne, Vic.: Spinifex Press.

Veth, Peter. (2012) *Strangers on the Shore: Early Coastal Contact in Australia*. Canberra: National Museum of Australia.

Webb, Carolyn. (2008) "Aboriginal campaigner took up a faraway fight for the oppressed". *The Age*. 8 November.

Whitmont, Toni. "First Contact" [online]. *Bookseller & Publisher Magazine*. 90 (3). October 2010: 39.

Wolpe, Rabbi David. "Putting Stones on Jewish Graves". My Jewish learning.com web-site.

www.ingramcontent.com/pod-product-compliance
Lightning Source LLC
Chambersburg PA
CBHW071015280326
41935CB00011B/1357